THE
GARDEN DESIGNER

THE ROYAL HORTICULTURAL SOCIETY

THE GARDEN DESIGNER

Written and illustrated by

Robin Williams

FRANCES LINCOLN

CONTENTS

FRANCES LINCOLN LIMITED
4 Torriano Mews, Torriano Avenue
London NW5 2RZ

The Garden Designer
Copyright © Frances Lincoln Limited 1995
Text copyright © Robin Williams 1995
Artwork copyright © Frances Lincoln Limited 1995

British Library Cataloguing-in-Publication Data
A catalogue record for this book is available from the British Library

ISBN 0-7112-0812-3

Typeset in Berthold Baskerville

Printed and bound in Italy

First Frances Lincoln Edition
10 9 8 7 6 5 4 3 2 1

For my son Robin and daughter Victoria and their families.

INTRODUCTION

Good garden design is the art of making beautiful gardens so that every part fits harmoniously into the whole. The skill is to be able to transform ideas into plans and to choose each individual element in the garden composition with care. It requires getting to know the site well and developing a sense of how the different components you introduce will affect one another and influence the space and atmosphere of your garden.

There is a wealth of possibilities open to today's gardeners. Every conceivable kind of garden feature and building block, from arbours and fountains to fence panels and flagstones, is available in all possible materials and in an unprecedented range of styles. It is important to make informed decisions, both aesthetic and practical, about what you want. A professional designer embarking on a new project has an enormous store of knowledge and experience to draw on. He or she considers hundreds of possibilities, rejecting many and adapting others, before settling on a workable design. **The Garden Designer** gives you, the reader, access to this knowledge and experience. It works as a design and style sourcebook, illuminating and discussing the different options.

In this book I want to show how professionals achieve successful designs. I also want to make the process accessible to readers by explaining the advantages and disadvantages involved in each design choice. The first chapter, *The Basics of Garden Design*, demonstrates how a designer approaches a new site, from making a survey and sketching in the outline ideas to drawing up detailed plans and clearing the ground for action. Behind these practicalities are complex design principles. I have tried to explain these ideas – for example, concepts such as simplicity, harmony and rhythm – so that readers see what they mean in a garden setting. I want to show how you can create both a sense of movement or, alternatively, repose in a garden by sketching shapes on a ground plan that ultimately are realised in three dimensions.

The following chapters take you through the range of possible materials, styles and treatments for the garden components. In practice, of course, all these elements interact in a garden setting, but it is simpler for the purposes of comparing the different choices to treat them separately. Each is explained and illustrated in detail, helping you to make informed choices. *Horizontal Surfaces* looks at everything that covers the ground, from gravel and flagstones to expanses of concrete and grass. *Vertical Elements* examines the many types of walls, fences, decorative items such as pergolas and summerhouses, and planting, which give the garden its structure in three dimensions. *Furnishing the Garden* presents all the elements, from pots and statues to furniture and swimming pools, that contribute atmosphere, excitement and the ability to relax or to enjoy activities in the garden.

The final chapter, *Garden Plans*, presents a number of sample designs for situations as varied as water gardens, dry gardens, city gardens and seaside gardens. This produces a range of proposals and solutions attuned to the needs of different owners or the constraints of some special sites. However, each plan is full of individual ideas that you can adapt to your own circumstances. So, by the end, **The Garden Designer** draws together all the elements of successful garden-making to help you achieve your own beautiful garden.

RIGHT *Every detail in this garden composition combines to create a harmonious picture. A combination of evergreen and flowering shrubs provides a cosy feeling of enclosure and shelter around the semicircular seating area. The brick pattern radiates out into the surrounding lawn. The well-designed, weathered wooden seat with its curving arms and sloping back nestles among the foliage. At its feet on either side, collections of simple terracotta pots make an impact when placed together as a group.*

THE BASICS OF GARDEN DESIGN

HOW TO PLAN AND MAKE
A GARDEN

OPPOSITE *The basic design of this well-made garden is an underlying structure of straight lines softened with imaginative massed planting. Elegant features such as the sparkling fountain and the matching planted pots flanking the slatted wooden bridge add visual interest.*

A garden designer quickly appreciates that every garden and its owners are unique. One couple may want a safe play area for their children, another may want raised beds to avoid back-breaking work in their old age. One garden may have a sunny open view backing onto green fields, another may be only a small, shady town courtyard surrounded by old soil-depleting trees.

While each garden design presents a new challenge, they all have one thing in common. In every case the designer has to transform a real plot with all its constraints into the owner's vision, and adapt that vision into a garden that works.

When you are faced with either an established garden that simply does not meet your needs or a new garden left by the builders looking like a freshly ploughed field, the prospect of transforming your vision into reality may seem daunting. It can be less daunting though if you follow the same clearly defined steps that a professional garden designer uses.

Of course, any professional designer has the advantage of having a trained eye so that, when it comes to the design itself, he or she can quickly envisage what will appear pleasing and harmonious. So this chapter sets out to show you – the owner/designer – something of the basic principles of garden design so that you, too, will be able to judge if your design will look good, work well and be a pleasure for years to come.

With this general information, you will be ready to deal with any site. On pages 22-27, a hypothetical, roughly rectangular, established garden plot shows how easy it is for you to follow the steps used by a professional designer. Beginning with making a survey and ending with shaping and contouring the site, you will see how each step builds on the one before to create a garden that imaginatively and aesthetically blends the requirements of its owners with the constraints of the site.

The first thing the designer needs to know is what the clients want from the garden and in what order of priority. In the case of the imaginary plot, the owners have very definite ideas about what they want from their garden. In real life, the clients may not have such clearly defined views, but may be open to suggestion. As the planning stages progress, either designer or owner may suggest new proposals for consideration. Since you are both owner and designer, be aware that at each stage of the planning new ideas may arise to consider, evaluate and act upon.

The first practical step is to assess the plot itself in order to get a full picture of its possibilities and limitations. First impressions are important, but more important still is to do a thorough *survey* and *analysis* as outlined on pages 21 to 24. At this stage you should pace every corner of your site, viewing it from all angles and directions, both away from and towards the house, and take a lot of photographs. You may think you know your own garden, but you will be amazed at how much more you can learn about it.

The next stage is to draw up a *zoning plan* that roughly divides your site into the areas you envisage. At this stage you can see all the various elements you want to include in your garden in context – how the beds and borders fit with the lawn space you require or whether the seating area has enough surrounding shelter, for

example. Gradually the jigsaw begins to fit together, and you are ready to draw the *finished design*, showing the final positions and sizes of every element in the garden.

The finished design forms the basis for the *working plan*. This shows the features that must be measured and physically marked out on the ground before construction work begins. Especially where there is to be a lot of excavation, draw up a work schedule so that tasks are carried out in the most logical order. It would be foolish, say, to buy soil to build up a raised bed, only to discover that you could have used the soil from an excavated garden pool.

Finally, you are ready to make your garden dream a reality. Now you can clear the ground, improve the drainage and irrigation if necessary, mark out your layout and start reshaping your garden.

LEFT *A flower bed placed in the middle of a lawn can often look lost unless it makes a strong design statement. Here, the topiary spirals of box and the central sundial are eye-catching all year round. They also make a dramatic frame for the pastel tones of foxgloves, forget-me-nots and later-flowering lavender.*

OPPOSITE *It is important to provide the right setting for a seating area. This one is particularly pleasant to sit in because the surrounding trees and shrubs provide shelter while still allowing views of the garden beyond.*

ELEMENTS OF DESIGN

A garden designer plans a garden as an entire composition. The different areas of the garden require different shapes, but these must link together harmoniously. The garden must also blend with the house and with the surrounding landscape. For you to achieve the same result as a professional garden designer, you have to know something about the basic design principles of unity, balance, interest and rhythm and movement.

PRINCIPLES

A sense of unity can be achieved in a number of ways. You could have a planting theme such as roses or grasses, or you could stick to a strict palette of colours to make a cool white garden or a hot red one. You could use materials for the hard landscaping such as the paths and patio surfacing that repeat patterns in the garden walls or the walls of the house.

Or you can simply make sure that materials and plant colours do not clash by working in a single style. An Italianate garden with formally clipped green hedges, a geometric layout and classical marble and stone ornaments will always produce a pleasing effect. But such a disciplined approach does not suit everyone and will mean that certain elements you may want have to be discarded. The Italianate garden, for example, will not lend itself easily to incorporating a children's play area.

A freer approach is to use design to link and unify the different parts of the garden, making the transition between one area and the next graceful and seamless. So a circular lawn in a formal part of the garden can echo the shape of a circular pool elsewhere.

Balance brings a sense of order to a design. At one extreme balance can be achieved through formality and symmetry (see pages 14-15), by placing a pair of identically planted pots on either side of a decorative seat or four clipped standard roses at the corners of a square patio.

But you can also achieve a sense of balance through asymmetry, by planting an informal group of tall shrubs or small trees half-way up one side of the garden visually to 'balance' a tall solid evergreen on the other side. Balance also requires a sense of scale and proportion: narrow beds bordering a large expanse of grass will look unbalanced; a large weeping willow or too many large man-made structures in a small garden will look out of proportion and unbalanced; an expanse of small-scale, low planting has to be balanced by taller plants or climbers.

MOVEMENT IN THE GARDEN

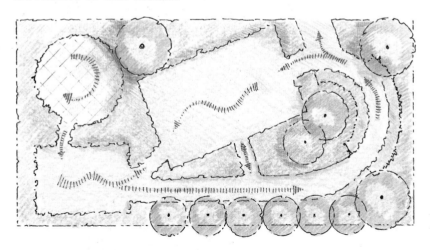

Movement in the garden can be manipulated by a design that divides the plot into different areas. This is displayed in the rough plan of an imaginary garden shown here. In the upper left corner, a restful circular area – perhaps a paved seating area – has a narrow opening providing a glimpse of another section of the garden beyond. This is followed by a broad rectangular area – possibly a lawn surrounded by flower beds – that encourages leisurely movement through it. From here, a choice of openings leads either to an even more spacious rectangular recreational area or to a narrow walkway that hurries on to a circular path. Remember that horizontal shapes on the ground plan must be visualized in three dimensions. That is, the shapes will be partly determined by the surrounding planting of trees and shrubs, and by vertical structures such as fences, walls and trellises.

A garden must also always have interest – something to attract the eye. Focal points such as urns, decorative seats, statues, striking plant combinations, or plants displayed in containers or grown as specimens, provide interest and contribute to the structure of the garden. There should only be one focal point to any view but, in one garden, a series of focal points can deliberately lead the onlooker around the plot, imparting a sense of movement, which is important in all but the tiniest garden.

Rhythm and movement are also determined by differently shaped areas – round, elliptical, square and rectangular. These in turn are defined partly by the ground plan and partly by the vertical elements – hedges, fences, walls, planting – that divide or enclose them. Square or round areas are static, giving a sense of rest or pausing. These are good shapes for seating areas. A broad rectangle or an ellipse suggests a meander or slow progression. These are good shapes for a herbaceous border or for other interesting plant effects that should be appreciated at leisure. A long narrow area suggests urgency and strong movement, an impression that can be heightened as its vertical sides get taller. A balanced combination of differently shaped areas makes for a good garden composition and you can ensure further interest in the garden if some areas are half-hidden with the promise of still more attractions to come.

STYLE

Later, as you work on your survey and plot analysis, the unique aspects of the site may suggest a style for your garden. Sometimes the architecture of the house provides guidelines, or even dictates the style of garden. A house in a vernacular style might suggest a cottage garden. A modern house might suit a minimalist composition that uses plants with strong architectural features. A house with a courtyard might cry out for a patio crammed with geraniums and wrought-ironwork or for a formal design based on classical Roman influences. The building material of the house can set the tone,

RIGHT *Hedges and a pergola planted with climbers are the vertical elements that divide this garden into separate 'rooms'. A wide spacious area in front of the pergola has been given a sense of movement by placing massed planting on either side of the grass path. The path and archway lead the eye towards the next 'room' beyond the hedge screen, providing a tantalizing glimpse of still more garden to explore.*

suggesting the use of particular bricks or stone in the garden to link the house with the outdoor space.

Basically though, there are two stylistic extremes – the formal and the informal. Many gardens will combine elements of the two, but it is important for you to understand how each style works on its own so that, if you wish, you can successfully combine them. If the entrance to your garden is centrally placed, a formal garden design emphasizes this balance. An off-centre access means that part of the garden may be hidden from view as you enter it. An

informal garden design can underline this sense of mystery by using a shrub here or a trellis there to add more screening.

THE FORMAL GARDEN

A formal style is usually based on mathematically arranged geometric shapes such as circles, squares and ellipses. These form the horizontal elements – the areas of lawn, paving or flower beds. There should be a flat surface for these to work best, or at least a wide, level terrace. Ideally, a formal, symmetrical garden will face due north or due south because it is easier to achieve matched planting this way. Added vertical elements will typically be regularly spaced cones, spheres and pyramids made either of stone or closely clipped foliage such as box or yew. The symmetry of the formal design may well be emphasized by the use of these vertical elements in pairs.

In a garden with an east-west orientation, one side of the garden will be permanently shady and this will affect what can be grown. In this situation an asymmetrically formal design might be better.

Formal designs are easily adaptable to sites of different sizes. Happily, formality can be achieved on a small scale, which is why designers often choose to make a formal garden in a tiny city plot bounded by high straight walls. It is also successful for individual features within a large garden. For example, you can make a focal point out of a pond, statue or seat set within a geometric 'frame' of hedging or fencing.

A formal area also often works well in the immediate vicinity of the house where it can echo the straight lines and flat surfaces of the building itself. A panel of lawn or a rectangular terrace may act as a complement to the mass of the house.

A formal garden demands a tidy, well-manicured look. The upkeep this involves may seem daunting but, with the clever use of low-maintenance plants and power tools such as hedge trimmers and leaf blowers, it can be achieved relatively easily.

LEFT *A geometric layout, long vistas, clipped hedges and symmetrically matched planting make this a perfect example of a formal garden. Yet, although the ground plan is precise, the rigid effect is softened by the soothing green of the lawn, hedges and trees and the touch of colour from the roses.*

SYMMETRICALLY FORMAL

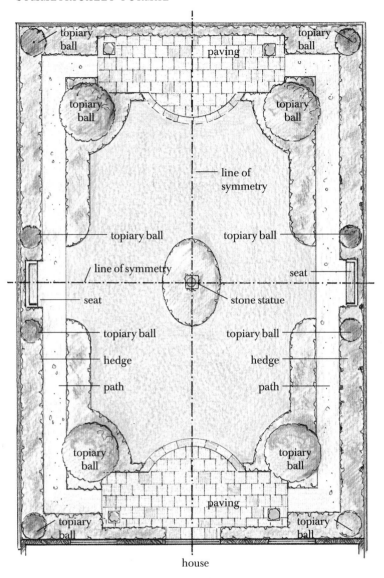

ASYMMETRICALLY FORMAL

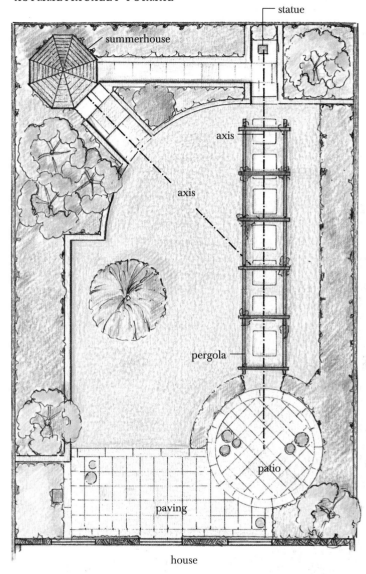

The symmetrically formal *garden has two main axis lines that intersect at the midpoint of the garden, dividing it into quarters that match symmetrically. Each quarter exactly reflects the one opposite and the hard and soft landscaping elements are those you would expect in a formal garden: regular paving patterns, evergreen hedging, topiary balls and stone statuary. A sense of peace and order prevails here.*

The asymmetrically formal *garden is still geometrical but, instead of being divided symmetrically, it has two axes, one from the centre of the circular patio following the line of the pergola to the statue at the end and the other from the summerhouse to the pergola. Geometric shapes are present in the design, but the effect is softened by the planting and by the fact that they are not repeated in a regular pattern.*

THE INFORMAL GARDEN

Some people feel that a formal garden looks out of place in the heart of the countryside or in a woodland setting. Others feel uncomfortable with the mathematical rigidity of a strictly formal garden design. What they prefer in these circumstances is a 'landscape' garden that flows seamlessly into the nearby countryside, or a 'wild' garden where nature is apparently in control. They are looking to create an informal ground plan.

The informal garden really calls for an absence of obviously man-made structures and materials. If such structures are needed then build them of natural wood or local stone so they blend unobtrusively with the surroundings.

An informal design suits plots with irregular shapes and uneven slopes. It may be used in a square or rectangular urban or suburban plot, but here the boundaries must be well disguised by profuse planting to draw the eye away from the fact that there is no rural landscape for the garden to flow into.

Don't be persuaded though by the myth that informal gardening equals low-maintenance gardening. Any plants that are vigorous enough to clothe boundaries and colonize areas within a season or two will not be happy stopping there. To maintain the balance of your original composition, training, pruning and weeding are needed. Knowledge and skill will help you choose the correct plants that will grow just when and where you want them.

THE COMBINATION GARDEN

Most gardens combine features of both the formal and the informal garden, so they can really be called combination gardens. Many plots are more or less regular in shape, though not symmetrical, and most have at least some man-made boundaries such as walls or fences to define them.

It is possible to design a garden that enhances both the formal and the informal aspects of the plot. You might decide on an area that is relatively formal next to the house, blending into a looser, more informal atmosphere in the distant corners. You can combine good-looking man-made paving with natural plant shapes. You can strike a balance between a layout that is neither tightly geometrical nor amorphously natural.

LEFT *Informality in a garden can provide a secluded haven even at the edge of a city, as here. The flowing organic shapes of the lawn and surrounding planting provide a soft relaxed atmosphere where, seated in the far corner surrounded by roses and foxgloves, you can forget about the city and all its cares.*

INFORMAL

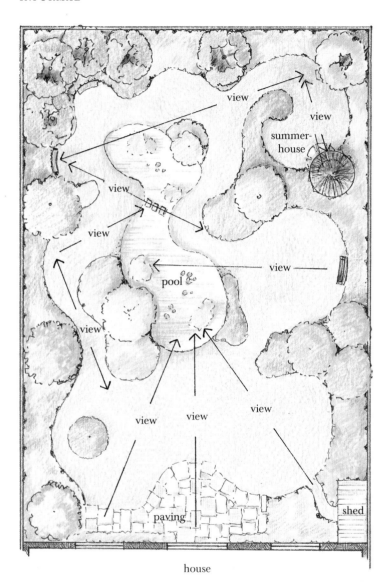

COMBINATION

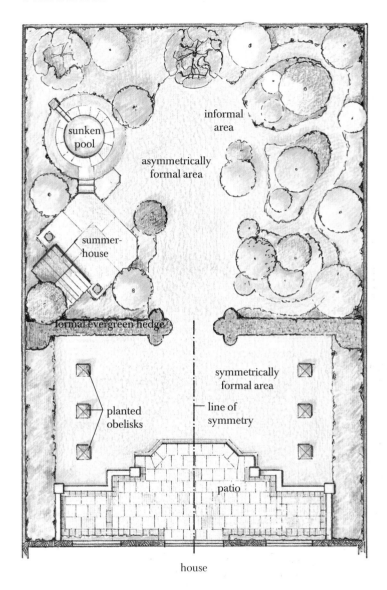

The informal garden is full of shapes that are flowing and organic. There is no symmetry nor any main axes. Instead, the garden reveals constantly changing views as the visitor passes through. Since the informal design is at odds with the formality of this rectangular plot, the design will only be successful if the boundaries are well-concealed by lush and extravagant planting.

This combination garden successfully embraces different garden styles. An evergreen hedge separates the symmetrically formal area from the rest. The top left-hand side of the garden includes formal geometric shapes, but is divided asymmetrically by axes from the summerhouse and the pool. Opposite it, a loose arrangement of trees, shrubs and paths proclaims an informal part of the garden.

ESTABLISHING PRIORITIES

With the basic design principles of unity, balance, interest and rhythm and movement, and a knowledge of garden style at your fingertips, you are ready to think about priorities for your garden. Usually a garden designer uses the client's priorities as one of the starting points for a new garden design. When you are your own garden designer, you wear both designer and client hats. Although your needs and preferences may seem obvious to you, you should still draw up your list of priorities, as a designer would.

TAKE YOUR TIME

Taking your time when drawing up your garden 'wish list' will help you to refine your needs and preferences as well as being essential to ensure your ability to make any changes. In a new house the

rooms you use most may determine which garden views you wish to emphasize. Over the months you may realize that there is traffic noise you want to muffle with clever planting. Or, when bare deciduous trees in winter do not provide the privacy you want, you may consider replacing them with evergreens; but when summer comes around, you might decide you like the dappled light and shade effect of the trees and resist any change at all.

It is also important to ensure that you have seen the plot at all seasons of the year so that when you start to excavate, for example, you do not dig up a dormant and desirable plant. You do not want to plan a scheme around an existing fruit tree only to find when the fruiting season comes around that it is not worth retaining. If you are not sure what is worth keeping and what to dispose of, consider obtaining the services of a trained horticulturist or botanist who will draw up a complete plant profile of your garden, even noting the state of health of the various trees and shrubs. This is especially useful if you are a novice gardener.

DECIDE WHAT YOU WANT

If you have young children, you may decide to have a safe play area. If you love entertaining, you will probably want to devote a part of the garden to outdoor cooking and dining. A plant lover gives priority to a collection of plants, while a conservationist wants a wild garden with a pool for dragonflies and frogs. Consider, too, your lifestyle. If your work week spills over into the weekends, it is unrealistic to have a garden that requires a lot of upkeep. If you are retired, you may have more time for gardening, but might be unable to cope with certain chores. Your final garden design needs to take account of preferences and priorities such as these.

LEFT *A paved garden can be versatile and adaptable. As a starting point, handsome paving, elegant fencing and some well-planted pots are enough to make a tiny city plot attractive. But as the owners' gardening enthusiasm grows, they can fill it with more flowers, rearranging them as they wish.*

ANTICIPATE CHANGE

Gardens change over time and it is important to take this natural evolution into account. If you long for an ornamental pool but worry about the safety of small children, postpone the pool until the children are older, and consider using the area now for a sandpit or lawn. If you hope to be living with this garden when you are elderly, think about the possible value of raised beds for easy maintenance when bending becomes a problem. Plan for a wild area until you can afford the swimming pool, or plant low-upkeep ground cover in a spot that will become a herbaceous border once you have the time to care for one.

SOURCES OF INSPIRATION

You may be an avid gardener or you may never before have owned a garden. Whichever is the case, one way of finding out what you like is to look for photographs that particularly please you in books and magazines of gardens or garden features. Visit plenty of gardens, both public and private, and either buy postcards or take your own pictures. Browse in garden centres and collect catalogues of plants, garden furniture and other accessories that you find attractive. You will gradually build up a collection of inspirational visual references that give you an idea of what you might want.

This is the time to let your imagination run free and draw on as wide a range of sources as you can, even if a feature may seem impossible to achieve in your own small plot. The task of translating the effect to your own garden comes later. Let's say you have an article about a country-house garden with a layout that appeals to you, but it seems far too complicated for your own plot. Don't worry. There may be a detail of a brick path or the way plants drape themselves over a balustrade that conveys something of the look you want to imitate. You may not have room for the long wisteria-covered tunnel pictured in your postcard, but you may be able to adapt the idea to make a smaller archway.

If your garden poses particular problems such as changes of level or excessive shade, use your scrapbook collection to provide solutions. Look out for pictures of steps, terracing, attractive retaining walls, or pleasing ways of planting a slope. Collect articles on shady gardens and pictures of shade-tolerant plantings. Gradually you will compile a reference file of garden details and attractive textural or colour combinations that appeal to you. Gradually, too, an overall mood for your garden will emerge, whether it be formal and symmetrical, or the informal random style of a country garden.

COMPILE YOUR CHECKLIST

Now you have decided what you want from your garden and what design ideas inspire you. The next step is to compile a checklist of these points and arrange them in order of priority. You will quickly see from this list where your preferences lie. At a later stage in your planning you may find that there is no room for some things or that the constraints of the site make certain features impossible to place. Ingenuity may help you to overcome a number of these difficulties, but it will save a lot of time if you have already given some thought to which features you are prepared to let go, and which you absolutely must have at any cost.

To help you categorise your choices, list them under a few main headings, such as decorative features, activities, storage, plants, materials and textures. This will focus your priorities and make sure that you don't leave out anything important.

Decorative features will include ornamental overhead structures such as arches or arbours, and permanent garden furniture, sundials, birdbaths and statuary. Water features come under this heading, too. Most sites, however small, can usually include either a still or moving water feature.

Depending on your own, and your family's interests, the activities heading might embrace cooking and dining outdoors, ball games for the children, swimming, birdwatching and sunbathing. Don't forget to include gardening itself if this is a favourite leisure activity. In that case, you may consider adding structures such as a greenhouse, a cold frame or a potting shed so you can indulge your particular gardening passion.

If you do not have enough space elsewhere, or if you want a storage area that is more conveniently located, you may want to include a site to store gardening tools, barbecue equipment, soft furnishings that cannot be left outside, garden games and toys and pool-cleaning equipment.

The checklist gives you a chance to list specific plants you want to grow: a wonderful rose you admire, or a specimen tree that reminds you of a favourite place. Here, you have the opportunity to give a general planting overview, for masses of evening-scented flowers for instance, or for stunning autumn colour.

The materials and textures heading covers the hard landscaping elements of your garden – stone, brick, wood, metalwork – and the textural effect of these against the plantings. It is handy to illustrate this part of your checklist with items from your scrapbook collection of visual references.

In some cases, things on your checklist may overlap or interconnect. If you long for the climbing rose you once admired, this could look lovely growing over a pergola, or a favourite garden urn could be filled with night-scented flowers and positioned so the smell wafts into the house on the evening air, giving you two features that you like rolled into one.

LEFT *This elegant garden satisfies two main requirements: that there should be plenty of space for entertaining and that mainteance should be kept to a minimum. A warm patio of terracotta tiles is sheltered by ivy-covered walls and a tall hedge, while an olive tree takes up most of the small square bed. There is little upkeep beyond clipping to maintain neatness.*

THE SURVEY

Once you have compiled your checklist, look at the site itself and its unique constraints and possibilities. This is essential for deciding on the best positions for the features you want in your garden. To do this you need to make a complete scale survey of the site. The survey gives all the measurements and positions of the house walls, including the doors and windows that open onto the site. These affect access to the garden and may suggest vantage points for garden views. The survey identifies the measurements and position of boundaries, the main planted features, gates and paths, old garden buildings or the foundations that remain, and septic tanks. The survey must also show changes in level.

On page 22 an imaginary plot is used to show you what is involved in drawing up the survey. The same plot is subsequently used on pages 24-27 to illustrate the next stages – the *analysis* of the site, in which you mark details such as the garden's orientation, soil quality, and the location of underground pipes and cables; the *zoning plan*, in which you roughly mark out where your garden elements might go; the *finished design*, showing the final position and chosen style of each garden element; and the *working plan*, which shows you how to measure and mark out the position of the elements on the ground. These are needed before you can get started on actually digging in and making a new garden.

A well-drawn survey of your site may already exist. If so – and you should check one or two of its measurements for accuracy – it will save you time and effort. But remember to take nothing for granted. Even an apparently regular plot is unlikely to be truly square or rectangular, nor are the walls of the house likely to be square to the boundaries. Our imaginary plot – a neglected garden with a few trees and shrubs – is not quite rectangular. A survey of the site does not exist, so we must start from scratch.

RIGHT *Surveying the garden of a modern house, like this one, with truly rectangular walls set squarely in a rectangular plot can be fairly simple. 'Sighting off' methods, for example (see pages 22-23), can be used. The designer of this garden has been careful to ensure interesting views over the garden from the various view points, both doors and windows, of the house.*

DRAWING UP THE SURVEY

If you are creating your plot survey from scratch, roughly pace out the plot to give you an idea of how the plan will fit on paper. Choose a scale. The most popular scales are 1:200cm (approx. 1/16in:1ft), 1:100cm (approx. 1/8 in:1ft), 1:50cm (approx. 1/4in:1ft) and 1:20cm (approx. 3/8in:1ft). The latter is normally only used for constructional details that require a large scale.

For accurate measuring you need a 30m(100ft) tape for long measurements, a 3m(10ft) retractable steel tape for shorter ones, and, preferably, a helper. You also need pencils, graph paper, a pair of compasses and a directional compass. A scale rule converts your on-site measurements to measurements on the graph paper.

First measure the walls of the house and plot these on the graph paper, indicating any doors and windows and whether they open inwards or outwards. Next, measure the rest of the site. For a house that is set squarely in a square or rectangular plot, you can use the straight lines of the walls for a measuring technique known as 'sighting off'. Measuring by sighting off is fairly straightforward. Stand at one corner of the house and look along the wall. The wall

THE SURVEY

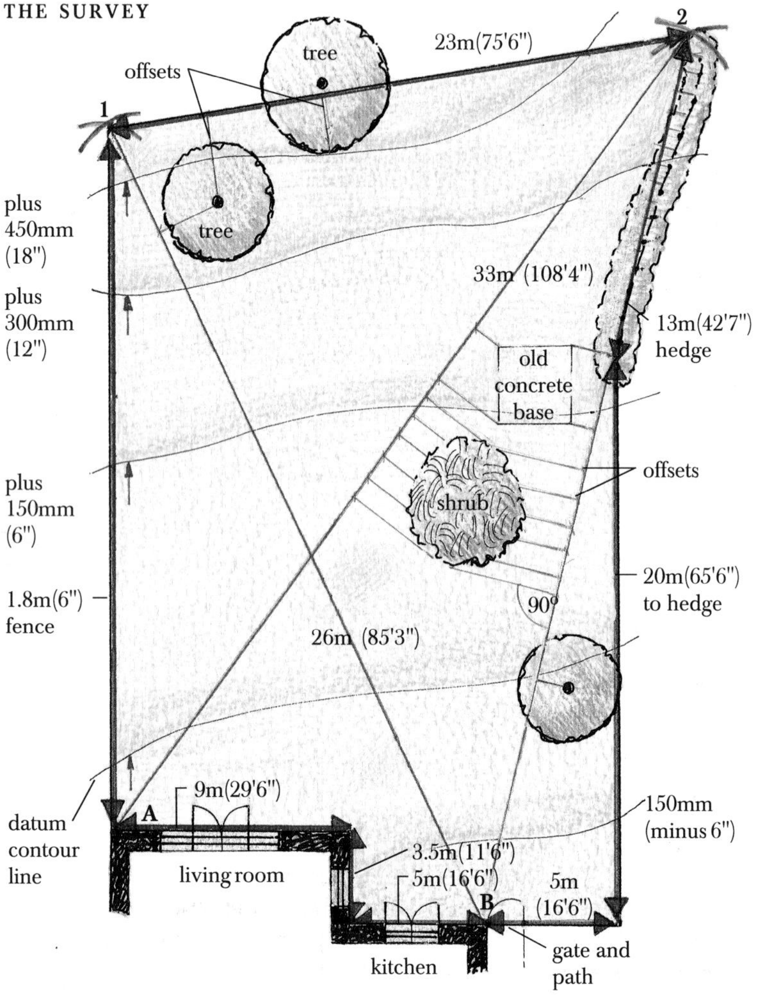

In the survey shown left, boundaries and features have been plotted using TRIANGULATION and OFFSETS. *Changes in level are shown by* CONTOUR LINES.

TRIANGULATION *is used to measure an irregular plot. It means dividing the area to be measured into triangles. Use the house walls as base or datum lines from which to measure the distance to the far corners of the plot.To plot accurately the position of the first corner of the garden* (**1**), *measure the distance on the ground between the corner of the house wall* (**A**) *and that corner of the garden. Scale down this measurement and open a compass to this measure. With the point of the compass at* **A** *on the plan, draw an arc in the direction of point* **1**. *Repeat from point* **B** *along the house wall. The position for* **1** *on the survey is where the two arcs cross. Repeat to plot the position of the second corner of the garden* (**2**). *For straight boundary lines, simply join the points.*

OFFSETS *are measured lines drawn at right angles from a known datum line. They are used to plot curved boundaries or irregular shapes. They are also useful for determining the outlines of ponds or, as shown on the survey here, of dense shrubs or trees, where it is not possible to measure straight through the feature.*

Begin by establishing a straight base line alongside the shrub – here we use the triangulation line from **B** *to* **2** *– then measure at right angles at regular intervals along the base line to the edge of the shrub. Space your offsets along the base line closely for tight intricate shapes, and more widely for shallow even curves. Plot your offset measurements onto the graph paper to draw the outline of the first side of the shrub. Repeat using a second base line, from* **A** *to* **2,** *to plot the outline of the other side of the shrub.*

CONTOUR LINES *join individual measurements of the same height. They are plotted 'plus' (a rise in height) or 'minus' (a descent) from a datum contour line chosen as a base.*

should appear as a fine line. Look beyond the wall to a boundary and instruct your helper to plant a stick or pole at the point where the boundary line and the line of vision cross. Continue around the house, repeating the process at each corner, then measure the distances between the house and each pole and between the poles. Plot these measurements on the graph paper. If the site is irregular, with curved or angled boundaries, then you must use 'triangulation' which is illustrated on the survey on the opposite page.

Changes of level must also be plotted on the survey. If they are not too extreme, measure them as shown below. Choose one height measurement near the house to be a 'datum' or base-line measure. Then take height measurements at various points in the garden and indicate these on your graph paper as a plus or minus figure relative to the datum. Join matching measurements together to give the contour lines. The survey opposite shows that this hypothetical garden slopes upwards from the house.

Small changes of level may make little difference. For steep slopes or where the ground slopes at different rates in more than one direction, consider employing a professional surveyor – it will save the cost of rectifying expensive structural mistakes later on.

DIFFERENT WAYS TO CALCULATE CHANGES IN LEVEL OR FALL OF A SLOPE

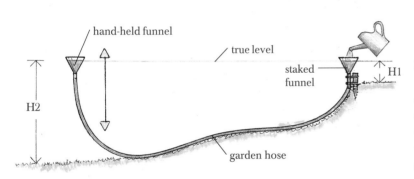

garden hose

brick wall

A brick wall built to a true level (check it with a spirit level) can help to calculate the change in level or fall of a slope. Find the highest point of the slope where a course of bricks starts. Follow this course to the end of the wall. Measure the distance from the ground to this point to give the fall of the slope.

The garden hose method of calculating the fall of a slope is based on the fact that water always finds its true level.

Make a mark at the same level on two identical transparent funnels and insert one into each end of a garden hose. Fix one funnel to a stake at the top of the slope. Hold the other funnel at the lower level. Have a helper pour water into the upper funnel until both funnels are filled to the marks. You will have to move the hand-held funnel up or down until the water is level in both funnels. Measure the height from the mark in the staked upper funnel to the ground (H1), and then have your helper measure from the mark in the hand-held lower funnel to the ground (H2). Subtracting H1 from H2 gives you the fall of the slope.

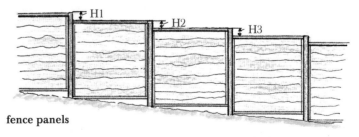

fence panels

Fence panels in stepped formation make it easy to calculate the fall in a slope. Check that the panels are horizontal, using a spirit level. Measure the differences in height between one panel and the next (H1, H2, H3, and so on). Add up all the differences in height (H1+H2+H3+...) to give the slope's fall.

THE ANALYSIS

Following the survey, the next step is to draw up an analysis of the plot. The analysis shows the orientation of the site, areas of prolonged shade or sun, and of dampness or drought. Details such as soil acidity, the location of underground utilities and the direction of prevailing winds are marked. Now the designer takes the opportunity to highlight factors outside the plot that will affect the design, for example, an ugly view that may have to be screened as well as existing elements of planting and landscaping that may have to be altered.

Use a copy of your survey of your site to draw up the analysis. In the example shown, the house faces roughly south so there should not be any areas that are permanently shady. Light and shade greatly affect the character of a plot and what can grow there but remember that the amount of sunlight varies from summer to winter. Although the sun is lower in the sky in winter, some areas may receive more light then, when the deciduous trees are bare. Shade cast by buildings is fixed and must be worked around.

You have little control over climate or the direction of prevailing winds, though building or planting shelter may mitigate their effects. Surroundings, too, are out of your control to some extent, but pleasant surroundings can be embraced as 'borrowed landscape' for your garden, while an unsightly view or neighbours' windows can perhaps be screened.

Test your soil to find its type and structure. Check it at several locations as conditions can vary even over a small area. You may decide to work with your soil type by only using plants that prefer it, or you may decide to take remedial action, improving the soil condition with the use of additives, removing nutrient- (or moisture-) depleting planting or, in extreme cases, improving underground drainage. How to do this and how to plan for irrigation if necessary are dealt with on pages 30-32. Analyse your soil by using one of the simple testing kits sold by garden centres. Most garden soils range from acid (with a pH of about 5), through neutral (pH 6.5) to alkaline (pH 8). Many plants are not fussy about soil acidity, but a choice few will thrive only if the pH conditions are right. Finally, try to mark the position of any undergound pipes or cables so they are not affected by deep cultivation or excavations.

THE SITE ANALYSIS

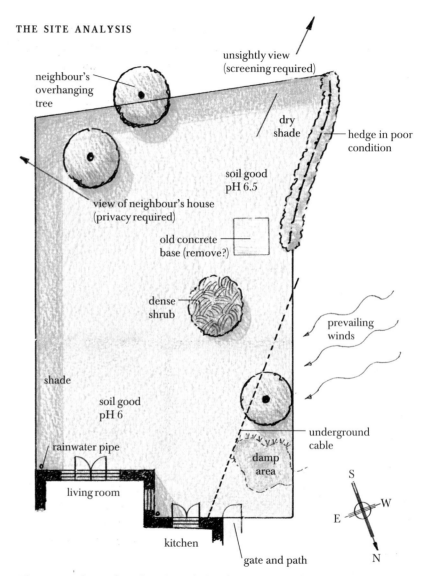

The site analysis of our hypothetical plot includes details of underground utilities and the results of soil analysis. Factors such as areas of shade and the direction of prevailing winds affect the potential use of the garden and so are noted here. Also included are elements outside the plot such as desirable views or views that might be screened.

THE ZONING PLAN

Now you have your survey, site analysis and checklist (see page 20) of the functions you want your garden to fulfil. Our fictional owners would like a children's play area, somewhere to sit both in the sun and the shade, a place to store tools and toys, and a water feature that is at a safe distance from the play area. Now the time has come to see where these features could be positioned. Work with several copies of the site analysis – you will change your mind many times before you arrive at the final layout – and the result will be the zoning plan, sometimes called the functional plan.

One of the best ways to start roughing out the zoning plan is to position the main seating area. Consider if the proposed site is sunny enough or too sunny, if it is or could be made to be sheltered from the wind and from neighbours, and if it has a pleasing view. If you want to use the area for entertaining, make sure there is space for a garden table, chairs and possibly a barbecue, and don't forget easy access to the kitchen.

Consider each element on your checklist in turn. You may find that you have given too much space to one element at the expense of another, or that there are still others that you cannot fit in at all. If this happens, go back to your checklist and your priorities. Could a seating area be made smaller to accommodate, for example, a larger water feature, or could you forgo a secondary seating area in favour of a herb garden? Could the water feature be built in such a way as to incorporate the seating area, or could some seating be placed in along the border?

As you position the various zones in the garden, try to remember that this is not just a one-dimensional plan on paper, but will be viewed by people standing or sitting at various spots. You might make sketches showing different parts of the garden in perspective. Sketching an eye-level view also helps to determine the height and position of screens and other vertical elements.

Remember, too, that there are some features such as arbours, walls or even areas of planting that will cast shade, block views and form their own physical divisions. And think what will happen if you take something away from the site. The removal of an overgrown shrub or unsightly shed will affect the surrounding light, shade and shelter.

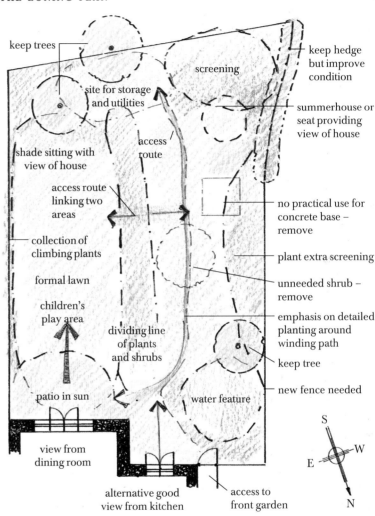

keep trees

screening

keep hedge but improve condition

site for storage and utilities

summerhouse or seat providing view of house

shade sitting with view of house

access route

access route linking two areas

no practical use for concrete base – remove

collection of climbing plants

plant extra screening

formal lawn

unneeded shrub – remove

children's play area

dividing line of plants and shrubs

emphasis on detailed planting around winding path

keep tree

patio in sun

water feature

new fence needed

view from dining room

alternative good view from kitchen

access to front garden

The zoning plan *uses plants and shrubs to divide the hypothetical plot into two areas related to the house windows. To the left, a formal area with seating, a lawn and perhaps space for children's play is suggested. The right side is more informal with a path leading through the planting to a hidden storage area with space for a seat or summerhouse. A water feature near the house makes good use of of damp ground.*

THE FINISHED DESIGN

Once you have drawn up the zoning plan, the next step is to find a style that suits the plot and will pull the different zones together into a harmonious whole. The survey and site analysis may have suggested a suitable style: a four-square regular plot with a north-south orientation and with a central access to the garden would suit a formal style, while an irregular plot surrounded by open country would look best with a loose, informal design. You, of course, may have your own strong preferences. Now, with your knowledge of the basic elements of design, you have to go through the same thought processes as a professional designer to find an appropriate style. You must then choose features, hard surfaces, shapes of beds and borders and so on that fit the style, and then place them in the plot. The result will be the finished design.

The finished design will show the final positions and sizes of each element in the garden: areas of grass and paving, trees and shrubs, rock gardens, vegetable gardens, walls, hedges, fences and trellises, water features, statuary, seating, overhead features such as arbours and pergolas, dining areas with their attendant tables, seating and barbecues, play areas and play equipment, and storage areas. Any changes of level and the need for steps or ramps should be noted on the plan as well as drainage, irrigation and lighting requirements. The finished design must be so accurately drawn that you can calculate the quantities of materials you will need such as turf, paving, brick and so on.

This is the moment to double-check that projected foundations, excavations or new utilities will not interfere with existing underground drains, pipes or wires.

In the hypothetical example we have been following, the design manages to incorporate a combination of styles. A formal design has been chosen for the left-hand side of the garden. The formality is highlighted by a terrace leading onto a spacious rectangular lawned area, all surrounded by hedging. A view from the terrace encompasses a garden seat shaded by a tree. A pretty archway leads through to the right-hand side of the garden, which is more informal. Here, a meandering path winds through a heavily planted area and leads to a summerhouse and hidden storage area, via an ornamental pool and a statue.

THE FINISHED DESIGN

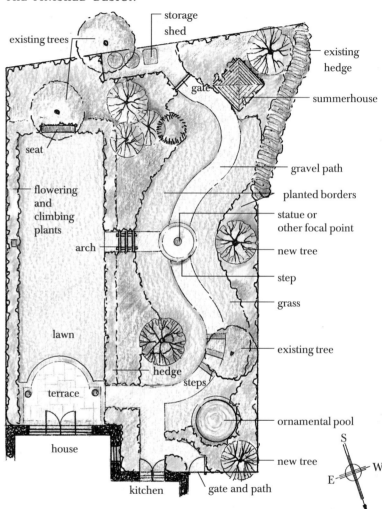

The finished design accommodates existing trees. A neat hedge bordering the lawn with a backing of more informal planting to the west divides the plot. A curving path leads to the storage shed and compost containers, while an ornamental pool occupies the damp low ground near the house. The site's gentle gradient is easily handled by occasional steps in the path. At the rear right of the garden, the shelter provided by the existing hedge is supplemented by planting enclosing a summerhouse.

THE WORKING PLAN

Use your finished design to draw up the working plan. This plan shows the shapes of the main elements required in the garden – paths, patios, pools, and so on – as they are to be marked out on the ground itself, and shows you what measurements you should make in order to mark them out on the ground. Shapes are plotted using offsets – lines drawn at a 90° angle from a known base line to a point to be marked (see page 22). You then scale up the measurements on your working plan and transfer them to the ground for the marking out stage (see page 33). If you have to undertake any major landshaping and drainage, leave the marking out until after they have been done, otherwise any marks you make on the ground will be lost.

WORK SCHEDULE

The final step before you begin work is to plan a logical sequence of it. For instance, you do not want to plant borders and then have to dig them up for the footings of a wall. For long-term implementation of plans, a work schedule is crucial. If a sandpit will later be converted into a pond, ensure access to electricity for the re-circulation pump when shaping the rest of the garden.

For a completely new garden, here is a sample work schedule:

1. Clear plot and remove weeds
2. Shape land and install drainage
3. Mark out the garden's main elements
4. Lay foundations for walls
5. Build walls
6. Lay foundations for horizontal surfaces
7. Lay horizontal surfaces (except the front driveway if your new plan includes the front garden)
8. Replace topsoil
9. Prepare the soil
10. Install lighting and irrigation systems
11. Planting
12. Prepare grassed areas
13. Sow grass or lay turf
14. Complete front driveway (where necessary)

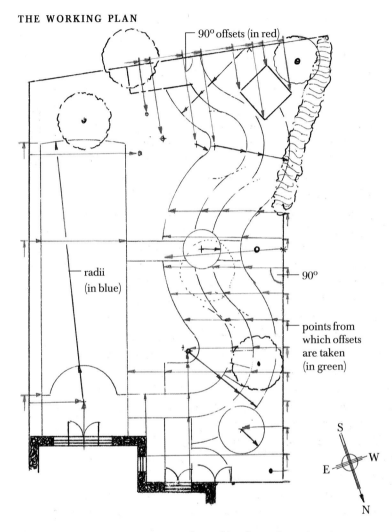

The working plan shows how to plot and mark out the main features that have to be constructed on the ground. The green lines and arrows along the boundaries indicate the points from which the offsets (see pages 22 and 33) are taken. The offsets, shown in red, are measured off at 90° angles to the boundary. These mark the lines of the paths, the centre points for curves, the positions of new trees, the corners of the summerhouse and so on. The blue lines are radii, showing circles and arcs and their centre points.

GETTING STARTED

You now have the finished design, working plan and work schedule. The time has come to get started on reshaping your plot. If you are moving into a newly built house, too often the garden consists of 50mm(2in) of topsoil – the healthy, organic soil full of oxygen that plants will grow in – hiding a mass of rubble and compacted substrate. If the compacted ground is not broken up, you will have drainage problems later on. Once fences and walls have been erected, the job of using mechanical diggers and ensuring the complete removal of garden debris is made much more difficult. For this reason, if your garden is a new one, try to arrange that the ground is properly prepared and a layer at least 450mm(18in) deep of good topsoil is there before you begin.

If your garden is an established one, you should already have taken the precaution of waiting a year to see what the garden offers you throughout the seasons before deciding what plants to remove and what to leave. Before you start clearing, check for any treasures such as ornaments, old bricks, tiles or path edgings that can be reclaimed. The mellow, weathered surfaces of these found objects can bring an instant feeling of maturity to your new garden plan and can help to marry the new elements with the old.

SHAPING AND CONTOURING

You may have decided to change a sloping section of your plot to an area of level ground, perhaps for an ornamental pool or seating area. Or you may want to add interest to a predominantly flat site with a sunken garden or some rolling banks or raised beds. Where such changes of level are required, mark the broad outlines on the

LEFT *The contours in this garden have been shaped to make a lawn that slopes only slightly, while raised beds and steps contain the steeper slopes. The use of old bricks for the retaining walls and steps, together with the massed planting, provide an instant sense of maturity in this new garden.*

ground, then do the necessary reshaping. Once this is complete – for instance, you have levelled out an area for a terrace – you will be ready to mark the final features, such as the position of any terrace walls and the outline of the flower beds. If the planned changes in level are not too dramatic, you may be able to implement them yourself. However, major changes in gradient should always be a matter for professionals and will involve a special preparatory survey.

You also need to determine the logistics of the operation. Earth-moving machinery needs room to manoeuvre, so know ahead of time where soil should be moved to or placed. Soil should not have to be moved more than once or further than necessary. If access to the site is limited, then projects involving the removal or importation of large quantities of soil are a major problem. In these cases 'cut and fill' methods that use the soil cut from a slope in order to create another level area elsewhere along the slope (see right) are the only solution. Loosened excavated soil incorporates air and so can increase in volume by a quarter to a third. When it is deposited in position it must be well mixed and carefully consolidated with the existing surface, one layer at a time, with each layer not exceeding a depth of 150mm(6in). This will prevent slippage and settlement from occurring later.

Remember that topsoil is a precious commodity. Strip it and put it aside before breaking into the subsoil beneath, whether for land-shaping procedures, for the laying of paving or other hard surfaces, or for installing drainage, irrigation or electrical services. You can then replace it, as a separate operation, on the newly contoured land. Plan a storage area for the stripped topsoil, preferably in piles not more than 1m(3ft) high and for as short a time as possible. This will prevent the loss of oxygen that will make the soil unhealthy.

Think about weed clearance at this point, too. If you do not eradicate weeds that spread by underground roots and rhizomes, these will have a field day once the ground has been disturbed, for then every scrap of broken root will sprout a new plant. The more vigorous weeds can even disrupt foundations and other structures. Nowadays many people are reluctant to use chemicals in their gardens, but there are a few stubborn weeds for which this may be the only solution. Take advice from your local garden centre on how to tackle weeds, and always follow the instructions on any herbicides you find you have to use.

ESTABLISHING LEVELS ON SLOPING GROUND

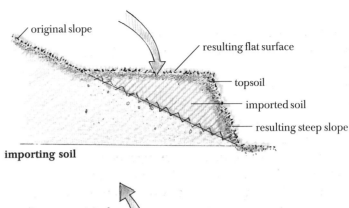

importing soil

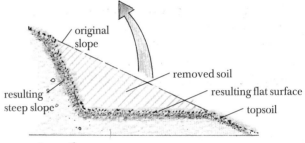

removing soil

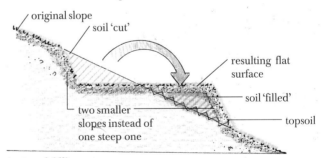

'cut and fill'

Establishing levels on sloping ground *can be accomplished in several ways. Both importing soil (above top) and removing soil (above centre) are only possible where the site is accessible to heavy machinery. The steep banks produced by either method may need a retaining wall. 'Cut and fill' (above) can also be a big operation, but is ideal for smaller adjustments or where there is restricted access. Because the resulting banks are smaller, the problem of soil retention is reduced and costs reduced.*

WATER PROBLEMS

Many gardens either have too much or too little water. If either condition turns out to be a problem on your site, you could solve it by tailoring your garden to the water you have. You could turn a naturally damp patch of ground into a bog-garden or you can plant a dry site with drought-resistant plants. But if you want a planting scheme that requires a radical improvement to the existing drainage or irrigation, you should plan for this from the start.

DRAINAGE

Bad drainage in soil restricts the type of plants you are able to grow and even affects lawns. If the soil is naturally water-retentive, or the water table high, you may need to install land drains – either simple trenches filled with free-draining material or a more complex interlocking pipe system. Examples are illustrated on this page.

To drain efficiently, a hard surface needs a slope of 1:100 (1cm to 1m) or 1:120 (1in to 10ft), though in areas of heavy rainfall a steeper slope is needed. Without an adequate fall, surface water will sit and paving will become slippery underfoot. In addition, the prolonged contact with water will damage the surface. A number of drainage methods for hard surfaces are illustrated on page 31.

INTERLOCKING LAND DRAINS

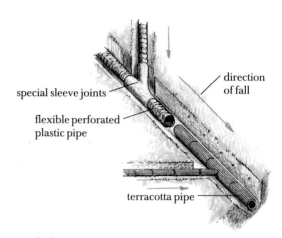

special sleeve joints

flexible perforated plastic pipe

direction of fall

terracotta pipe

Interlocking land drains slope down, carrying excess water away towards a ditch or other outfall. One main pipe made of either perforated plastic or of terracotta is fed by narrower lateral pipes that run into it at angles of approximately 45°, making an alternating or herringbone pattern. The intervals between the lateral pipes are governed by the amount of drainage required – they will be more closely spaced if there is a lot of water to be carried away. The depth of the pipes depends on many factors: natural ground fall (if any), the local water table and soil type.

SIMPLE TRENCHES FILLED WITH FREE-DRAINING MATERIALS

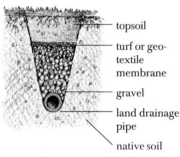

topsoil

turf or geo-textile membrane

gravel

land drainage pipe

native soil

pipe

The pipe system consists of a clay or plastic pipe at the bottom of a fairly narrow trench which is then filled with gravel.

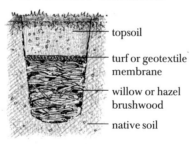

topsoil

turf or geotextile membrane

willow or hazel brushwood

native soil

brushwood

The brushwood method keeps the simple trench clear of stones and debris with a thick layer of willow or hazel brushwood.

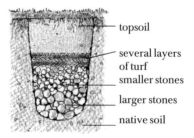

topsoil

several layers of turf

smaller stones

larger stones

native soil

rubble

The rubble method is a simple trench filled with coarse stone or hard rubble graded from larger at the bottom to smaller towards the top.

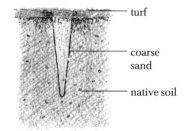

turf

coarse sand

native soil

sand slit

The sand slit method fills a narrow trench or cracks in dried clay soil with coarse sand, aiding drainage and improving the soil.

DRAINAGE METHODS FOR HARD SURFACES

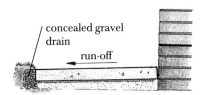

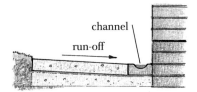

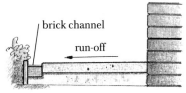

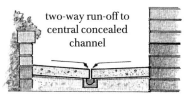

sloped paving

channel

brick channel

centre drain

Sloped paving away from the house wall towards the lawn is a simple drainage method. To prevent water from collecting along the lower edge of the paving, there should be a gravel drain concealed by a covering of turf running between the lawn and the paving.

A channel at the junction of the paving and the wall is necessary where paving must slope towards the house. Here, the water is conducted away to a lower level or drain. The size and depth of the channel depend on the size of the adjacent area of paving and on levels of rainfall.

A brick channel, which could be incorporated as part of a paving pattern, conducts water away from the main area of paving. It is formed by laying an edging of bricks or paving slightly lower than the main paved surface and sloping them towards a lower level or drain.

A centre drain concealed beneath the surface is a solution where a paved area is enclosed on all sides or where falling levels converge. These drains are available as concrete units. For draining larger areas, or where frequent storms are a problem, use a wider drain with a metal grid.

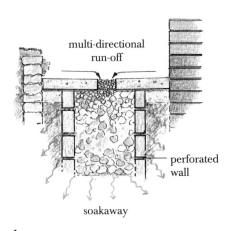

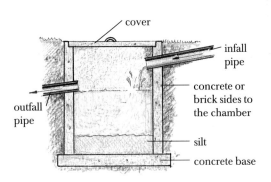

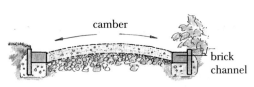

soakaway

silt trap

camber

A soakaway is a cavity under the surface filled with free-draining material. This one has a concrete block or brick wall with many of the joints left open. The soakaway is filled with graded stones with the smaller ones towards the surface. Here, a narrow opening filled with gravel serves as a surface drain, but underground pipes could also be used to direct water away from the surrounding soil to a soakaway.

A silt trap intercepts fine particles of silt or soil in run-off water and stops them from entering the rainwater system. The infall pipe is slightly higher than the outfall pipe, and in normal flow, the silt settles at the bottom of the trap, allowing the clean water to pass into the system. A removable cover permits periodic cleaning of the trap. Trap size depends on the extent of the land-drain system or catchment area, and the silt content of the soil.

A camber is a convex profile or upward curve in a surface and is used where a path is enclosed at both sides and cannot slope either to one side or towards the middle to permit natural surface drainage. To prevent water collecting at either side, a brick gulley or channel on each side incorporates occasional outlets for water.

IRRIGATION

Where your soil does not have enough water, choose an irrigation system tailored to your needs. A perforated pipe or pot drip uses water in the most efficient and least wasteful way, delivering water directly to specific plants, beds or even containers. These systems are particularly useful in areas where water is scarce. A sprinkler system sprays a broad area and is useful for lawns and some crops. However, some water is bound to be lost through evaporation.

Also take into account how frequently you may need to water. You can operate your system manually by linking it directly to the garden tap, or you can install sophisticated electronic controls that need an electricity supply. While they are costly, automatic systems are often the most effective. These apply water at the correct rate and, by operating at night, reduce evaporation. Consult an expert if you are considering a complicated system or if your garden is a large one.

PERFORATED PIPE

Perforated pipe irrigation uses an unobtrusively coloured garden hose punctuated with holes of specific size and spacing, threaded around the base of plants. Cover it with a light mulch to reduce evaporation.

POT DRIP

Pot drip devices are dark-coloured units pushed into the soil to supply water to containers and pots. With automatic controls, they are useful for watering plants when you are away from home.

MINI-SPRINKLERS

Mini-sprinklers are units whose height can be adjusted to suit the particular size and grouping of your plants. If you space them carefully, you can ensure that no area of planting is left unwatered.

POP-UP SPRINKLERS

Pop-up sprinklers use water pressure to cause the watering heads to pop up out of the lawn. When not in use, the heads retract below the surface, out of the way of mowers and other traffic.

LEFT *This versatile and sophisticated perforated pipe system uses porous rubber to let water gently seep into the soil. Lengths of pipe interlock and can be placed in various configurations on or below the surface, allowing water running at low pressure to irrigate specific areas without waste.*

MARKING OUT

Once you have dealt with any land shaping and drainage, you are ready to mark the proposed garden features on the ground. Now you have to scale up your graph paper measurements and transfer them to the ground. You will need the same tape measures as for your survey, plus markers for the ground. The choice here includes: timber stakes (lath) or pegs with a garden line or string; trickled sand or garden lime – easily scuffed underfoot and blurred by heavy rain; and aerosol spray-marking paints – available in various colours enabling you to colour-code the different elements – expensive but long-lasting. Protect the plan with plastic, and be sure to keep it in the correct orientation as you work.

Start by marking on the ground any axes or triangles that you used in the survey. Features such as flower beds, paths, walls and so on, can be marked using offsets measured at 90° from these lines or from a boundary line. You also need to mark the position of excavations for foundations, remembering that a wall may need a foundation trench at least twice as wide as the wall itself. It is helpful to mark such excavations in a different colour.

For circles and regular curves, mark the centre firmly with a peg, and using a marker at the end of a line from this centre point, scribe the curve. You can go over this with a more permanent marker if necessary. Where the shape of a feature such as a flower bed or a pool is freeform, mark the initial measurements with pegs then lay a garden hose along them and use that as a guide to mark the actual outline. Pause now and then to try and envisage how the finished shapes will look. If curves seem out of proportion or a shape is ungainly from a particular angle, it is better to adjust it now rather than after you have started the construction work.

SCRIBING A CIRCLE OR ARC

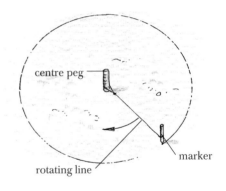

centre peg

marker

rotating line

To scribe a circle or arc, fix a peg at the predetermined centre point. Loosely loop one end of a line over the peg and at the other end attach a marker or chalk at the required radius. Keeping the line and marker as close to the ground as possible, rotate the marker and scribe a mark on the ground.

SCRIBING AN ELLIPSE

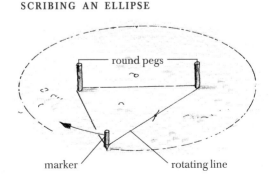

round pegs

marker   rotating line

To scribe an ellipse, fix two round pegs in the ground and loop a length of line around them. With a marker, pull the line into a triangle shape. Keeping the line taut, rotate the marker around the two pegs to scribe the ellipse on the ground. The ellipse's proportions derive from the distance between the two stakes and the length of line: trial and error will produce the desired shape.

MARKING OUT FROM OFFSETS

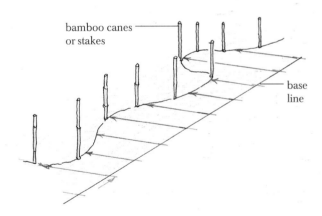

bamboo canes or stakes

base line

Marking out from offsets allows you to plot irregular shapes and isolated points. These are determined in relation to a base line which is marked off at regular intervals (see also pages 22 and 27). Scale up the appropriate measurements from the plan and measure them out on the ground at 90° from the base line. Use bamboo canes or stakes as temporary markers, replacing them with longer-lasting markings if necessary.

HORIZONTAL SURFACES

CHOOSING ATTRACTIVE AND PRACTICAL SURFACING TO SUIT YOUR DESIGN

OPPOSITE *The use of two different but equally handsome surfaces immediately adds interest to a garden. Here, the geometric squares and oblongs of random natural stone and timber decking are an attractive complement to the rounded forms of the planting. The horizontal lines of the decking stretching down the garden give a sensation of extra length to this small space.*

In the most practical sense horizontal surfaces are the paths where you walk, the patios and terraces where you sit and entertain, the pools of space or patches of planting where your eye rests. But horizontal lines and shapes also convey important messages about the garden layout. Straight lines, right angles, geometric curves and smooth surfaces signal a formal design. Looser, naturalistic curves, organic shapes and a lack of deliberate patterning set the keynote for informality.

A path's invitation to explore leads you to step into the garden. If it is successful, its horizontal surfaces help pace your progress and at the same time evoke a mood. A wide path encourages you to saunter, a narrower one to hurry to the end. A landing halfway up a flight of steps offers a breathing space and a chance to turn and enjoy a new view. A paved area with a seat suggests it is time to linger there. While these horizontal surfaces provide you with access to the garden, their pattern or texture is important and can claim your attention as well.

Horizontal surfaces are also functional. Main service routes must be wide and firm enough for mowers and wheelbarrows. Paths and steps near the house should be comfortable for everyone to use – children, the elderly, people carrying loads. Less strategic pathways, those less frequently used, can be narrower and of less substantial construction. Smooth, even paving in sitting areas prevents chairs and tables from rocking irritatingly. An attractively textured surface provides traction on potentially slippery slopes.

A wealth of materials is available to help achieve the effects you prefer. The various surfacing options are discussed in some detail in this section. Always consider not only the visual aspects but the practical ones, such as making sure that routes are convenient and their load-bearing strength adequate. Exploit the choice of textures, patterns, shapes and colours to manipulate space and achieve an integrated design for the garden as a whole.

SPACE AND PROPORTION

Horizontal surfaces, ranging from broad open expanses where the horizontal predominates to secluded intimate spaces that function like outdoor rooms, play an important part in the impression of spaciousness that a garden evokes. Proportions contribute enormously to atmosphere. A garden may feel open and airy in one

area, closed in and protected in another; alternatively, different garden areas might strike various sorts of balance, contrasting some narrower passageways with areas that widen into a clearing and offer a welcome breathing space.

When you made the preliminary zoning plan for your garden (see pages 25), you roughly plotted the major routes around the garden and zoned areas for relaxation and other leisure activities. Now, while you decide the precise extent of each area, the exact gradients and angles to use, and how tightly to draw curves, you must check that the overall balance is right. Spend some time studying your projected layout. Allow your eyes to travel around the space. Note how the shapes on the ground lead the eye into and around the garden. Your glance will follow straight or parallel lines to their conclusion but will explore curves more gently; it will linger in areas that are patterned or hold attractive plants, and it will pause and find relief in quiet pools of space.

CHARACTER UNDERFOOT

Having worked out the broad lines of the design, you now need to decide how to treat these features, perhaps taking a cue from near-by architecture. A tailored, hard-edged, efficient look suits a formal setting. For this, choose crisp geometrical surfacing with clean angles, such as machine-made pavers. Emphasize the outlines with well-defined edgings and kerbs, and use patterns in contrasting colours to pick out details. In gentler versions of formality, plain handsome materials such as stone, brick or wood do not make eye-catching patterns in their own right, but form the 'skeleton' of the design. You then soften this firm structure by letting plants spill over the edges, moss colonize joints, and so on. Alternatively, you can make perfectly functional paths and standing areas using organic or natural materials over suitably prepared foundations, or well-camouflaged structures such as pierced concrete in grass.

LEFT *Wood chips provide an organic and flexible surfacing material that is particularly suitable for informal areas. Here, they go well with log-edged steps to impart a woodland feel to the garden.*

RIGHT *Bricks laid in highly decorative designs add to the lively atmosphere of this small garden. The circular ground pattern encourages the visitor to stop and appreciate the imaginative planting.*

Often a combination of different elements works well, and a change of style can be used deliberately to signal a change of mood or usage as you move into a different part of the garden.

PATTERN AND SCALE

As you select the surfacing material for your paths, bear in mind the distinction between the cosmetic wearing course of paths and paved areas (the gravel, tiles and other materials that you see) and the underlying base courses (the foundations that provide the actual support). Consider the anticipated traffic and the quality of the terrain. Provided that the foundations are adequate, the choice of finishing material is up to you.

Materials can emphasize the shapes in your ground plan and affect the pace at which you tour the garden, visually and literally. Some materials, such as gravel, plain concrete, grass, wood chips or water, are fairly bland or neutral. These visually undemanding materials make excellent foils for more complicated designs.

Some other surfaces – particularly man-made products such as bricks – consist of or can be arranged in parallel lines. These need to be used carefully to enhance the ground plan. Generally, lines that run 'vertically' away from your viewpoint increase a sense of direction; lines that run 'across' the field of vision create a sense of breadth. In addition to patterns based on parallels (such as decking boards), many brick or tile patterns have a one-way bias that will seem to elongate or foreshorten a shape on the ground.

Other patterns have more static qualities. Regular, symmetrical shapes such as squares, circles and hexagons lack obvious directional movement and can have a more restful effect. They work especially well for sitting areas or places where you might linger.

Very decorative patterns, such as concentric circles, usually depend upon small and regularly shaped units, such as bricks, sets or pebbles. These can have great visual impact when juxtaposed with surfaces based on larger, simpler units laid in a grid of squares, or with neutral textures. Achieving successful contrast and harmony between neighbouring surface treatments is as important as choosing patterns of a scale appropriate for the area being covered. Full-size flagstones in a small area may make it look even smaller; a large expanse of small units can look fussy or simply dull.

The most effective horizontal surfaces convey a feeling of being absolutely appropriate to the site. They resolve problems of awkward shapes and instill interest into dull flat rectangles. When considering what sort of effect to choose, spend plenty of time looking at a wide variety of examples. Examine the detail of how the surface is formed and take into account how it works over a larger or smaller area, how it is affected by the shapes in the layout, how it links with neighbouring materials. It is important to see a design in its wider context – and particularly *your* context.

Picture the surface treatments shown here on pages 38-61 adapted to your garden space, perhaps reinterpreted in a different material or arranged in a slightly different way, so that they fit your design like a glove. Study not just the visual qualities of colour and pattern but the 'feel' of the surface, the atmosphere it evokes. Is it in tune with the character of the surrounding walls or fences and with adjacent buildings? Does it convey the sense of restfulness or of movement you are seeking? It is vital to spend some time on this exercise of checking that the treatment you are considering really is the best one to fulfil *your* personal garden vision.

HORIZONTAL PLANTING

Using plants to clothe the garden's horizontal surfaces, like having carpet indoors, softens the ambience as well as providing a really soft surface for play and relaxation. Of course, you must consider wear and tear when deciding whether a carpet – or a covering of plants – is suitable, and be sure to pick an appropriate kind.

Ground-covering plants offer a wealth of design possibilities. They are an attractive solution not only to level areas but also to banks and slopes. They can be used anywhere that calls for plant interest that is neutral and low-key (as opposed to a planned bed or composition of different flowers and foliage). In this kind of planting, the individual plants lose their identity, merging into a continuous low mass. This can be textured or smooth, coarse or fine, depending on what is being grown, but it will provide the ideal contrast to the textures and materials of your hard surfacing.

Ground-covering plants fall into two broad classes. The first consists of resilient types such as grass that you can walk on, like living paving. The second has a primarily visual role, making a smooth transition for the eye from one garden area to another or creating interest at ground level with panels of contrast.

LAWNS

Grass is the ultimate ground-covering plant. In the temperate, maritime climates that suit it best, grass offers a wide spectrum of design effects. High-quality species, immaculately grown and cut short, can make a neutral covering as smooth as baize (or as concrete) and seamlessly link associated shapes on the ground plan. Some gardeners love the perfection of smooth green grass. Others enjoy the sight of daisies and other wildflowers sown amidst a lawn, or less closely mown grass, its surface ruffled by the wind.

Tailor plans for a lawn to your site, taking into account the amount of upkeep you are prepared to expend. Check out local conditions – how your neighbours' lawns fare gives a broad indication of what you can expect – but always base your decisions on the constraints of your own site and your personal requirements. Is the plot overhung by shade trees? How much traffic do you expect? What is the drainage like? Will you be able to water? How often are you prepared to mow? Choose grass varieties and cultivars to give precisely the appearance you seek and to withstand the amount of wear you anticipate. If you are creating a new lawn, seek advice from a reputable local garden centre or consult good gardening books. Plants will fulfil their design purpose only if they are growing well; so be sure to provide the right conditions.

The large family of grasses includes species adapted to hot, dry climates, such as Bermuda grass (*Cynodon dactylon*). Grasses for temperate climates include bent grasses (*Agrostis*), fescues (*Festuca*), perennial ryegrass (*Lolium perenne*) and meadow grasses (*Poa*). Other evergreen creeping plants grow to a turflike mat. Some, such as the bluish-green lippia (*Phyla nodiflora*), are tough and drought resistant. Others are effective for an ornamental lawn, though not tough enough for persistent trampling. For sites in temperate regions that have good drainage, choose between nonflowering chamomiles and the creeping thymes, while for damper sites consider *Cotula squalida*, with fernlike leaves.

RIGHT *This carefully manicured lawn combines an informal shape with an almost geometric sense of order. The smooth expanse of green ties together the surrounding planting and sets off beautifully the glowing white trunks of the silver birches.*

DECORATIVE GROUND COVER

Colour and texture become important when choosing creeping, mat-forming plants to cover the ground. Low-growing, ground-hugging perennial herbaceous plants with interesting foliage colour offer soft leafy textures just a few inches tall, and perhaps the bonus of seasonal flowers. You can mix plants to make tapestry patterns or plan monochrome effects. For reddish tones, consider bugle (*Ajuga reptans*), which has many cultivars in different rich shades of bronze-green and red plus glossy crinkled leaves and blue flower spikes. Choose among varieties of *Lamium maculatum* for greyish-green leaves with a dusty, matte texture. Creeping Jenny (*Lysimachia nummularia*) has smooth, rounded green or golden leaves studded with yellow flowers. Make a soft leafy covering with grey-leaved lamb's ears (the nonflowering *Stachys byzantina* 'Silver Carpet'). London pride (*Saxifraga × urbium*) forms a dense mat of crisp green rosettes.

Many other medium-size perennials spread by runners or self-seed to make soft, leafy ground cover on a slightly larger scale. For example, the foam flower (*Tiarella cordifolia*) is good for shady sites, and hardy cranesbill geraniums do well in both sun and shade. Always check that you have the right conditions for your plants. More woody shrubs and climbers offer a range of stronger textures on a larger, bolder scale. If you want smooth, leathery leaves, consider periwinkles (*Vinca* species) or ivies. Heathers make wiry, dense texturing with their tiny, tough leaves and small flowers. Prostrate junipers and cotoneasters and speading shrubs like hypericum make firm, architectural cover for banks as well as level ground. For a looser, romantic look, climbers such as clematis, honeysuckle and roses can sprawl rather than twining upward.

EVERGREEN GROUND COVER

Evergreen ground cover, *such as dwarf periwinkle* (Vinca minor), *makes a glossy green permanent furnishing at the foot of an evergreen hedge. The shade cast by the hedge is tolerated by vincas, and will visually enrich the glowing blue of the flowers.*

UNDERPLANTING WITH GROUND COVER

Underplanting with ground cover *beneath the canopy of a shapely fruit or ornamental tree can emphasize its attractive qualities. A circle or square of the soft, felt-like leaves of lamb's ears* (Stachys byzantina) *contrasts well with the surrounding green grass.*

SMALL-SCALE ORNAMENT

A small-scale ornament *needs the right setting that carefully chosen planting can provide. Mossy saxifrage makes a good foil for stone textures and forms a neat green foundation to enhance a small feature such as a birdbath. Starry pink or white flowers provide added decoration in summer.*

NATURAL EFFECTS

Many of the plants used for ground cover are natural spreaders. If your design requires crisp dividing lines between panels of planting and hard surfacing, plan to incorporate edgings to prevent underground roots from colonizing adjacent areas. A mowing strip between grass and borders or other structures also helps reduce upkeep. Other plants are inveterate self-seeders and will spread into cracks in paving stones and invade areas of gravel. Some gardeners like the naturalistic effects of moss, and small creeping plants such as thymes, colonizing paving. Plants sprawling over edges and blurring hard outlines soften the geometry of a layout.

They can enliven inanimate surfaces and often lend an atmosphere of mellow maturity to a relatively new site. You can encourage mosses and lichens to grow on stone or imitation stone by painting it with various organic substances, including sour milk, the water in which you have cooked rice, and diluted cow manure. Conversely, you can deter these invaders, and any other ground-covering plants that are in the 'wrong' place, from taking over. You can try removing them manually, but appropriate herbicides are sometimes the only answer. Consider these matters at the planning stage. Establishing plants in the horizontal plane is only the first step. A certain amount of maintenance is always going to be needed to keep them in their place.

NATURAL INFORMALITY

Natural informality *in a garden setting can be enhanced by deliberate planting schemes that echo nature. Choose a carpet of woodland plants to make beautiful low-maintenance ground cover in the dappled shade of a grove of trees.*

RIGHT *Self-seeding ground-cover plants have been encouraged to invade a brick-paved seating area. In keeping with the natural-looking informality of the surrounding planting, they soften the geometric shapes of the cartwheel design.*

FLEXIBLE SURFACES

Flexible surfacing materials range from simple and functional to ornate and decorative, from organic natural substances to highly evolved products, and from the inexpensive to the costly. Most flexible surfacing materials are more economical to install than rigid paving that needs a rigid mortar base. Flexible ground covers include loose materials such as gravel and wood chips; mechanically compacted products such as asphalt; a variety of bricks and blocks 'dry-laid' on a bed of sand; and firm surfaces such as wood.

All these flexible surfaces are capable of slight movement, yielding to vehicular pressure but springing back. Preparation includes thoroughly compacting the native soil at the lowest level and then adding a base layer of clean hardcore. It is sometimes necessary to lay a geotextile membrane to prevent the exchange of rainwater and fine soil particles, which can eventually work their way up to the surface.

SOFTER SURFACES

In some situations solid surfaces are simply unnecessary, particularly for lesser paths in informal or rural gardens. In others, they are best avoided, for example where children play. Wood waste products such as granulated bark are often used in these situations. For a heavy-duty play area with apparatus such as climbing frames, it is worth considering special-purpose safe-play tiles.

GRANULATED BARK AND
WOOD CHIPS

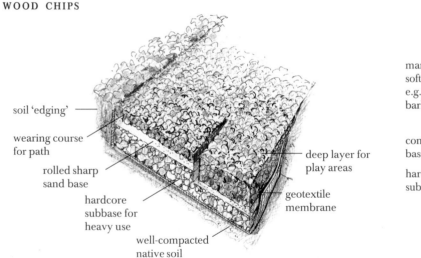

soil 'edging'

wearing course
for path

rolled sharp
sand base

hardcore
subbase for
heavy use

deep layer for
play areas

geotextile
membrane

well-compacted
native soil

SAFE-PLAY SURFACES

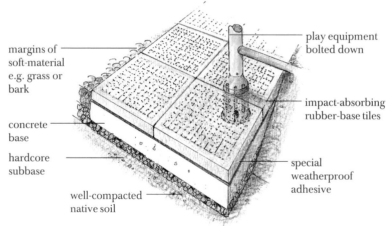

margins of
soft-material
e.g. grass or
bark

concrete
base

hardcore
subbase

well-compacted
native soil

play equipment
bolted down

impact-absorbing
rubber-base tiles

special
weatherproof
adhesive

Granulated bark and wood chips make excellent wearing courses for paths. They are laid on a bed of rolled sharp sand over a gravel subbase, preferably enclosed and retained by a geotextile membrane. Available in various grades, larger fragments are less readily blown about by winds and take longer to break down (as all inevitably will). Bark, with its darker, more muted colour, blends in better with natural surroundings. A depth of 225mm (9in) makes an ideal impact-absorbing surface for play areas.

Safe-play surfaces consist of rubber-base composite tiles ranging in thickness from 25 to 85mm(1 to 3½in). It makes suitably absorbent flooring for anything from a toddler's play area to jungle gyms and sports equipment, which can be bolted into the concrete base. This base must be raked to a smooth flat finish to which the tiles are then fixed with weatherproof adhesive. For additional safety, surrounding areas should be covered with soft materials such as grass or granulated bark.

HARD SURFACES

Gravel is a useful surface, which can look appropriate anywhere in the garden and is equally attractive in formal and informal situations. It encompasses three distinct types: crushed stone, shingle and path gravel. Crushed stone is mechanically broken and graded according to size. Its multifaceted surface may have sharp edges that damage footwear, but it is less likely than the smoother shingle to move about on slopes. Shingle is round, water-worn pebbles from lake beds or the sea, and tends to migrate unless placed on a fairly level surface. Path gravel is another natural material consisting of stones or pebbles with a size range of 1.5-25mm(1/16-1in). Path gravel is held in a matrix of clay-like soil and rolled into a firm layer, usually incorporating a gentle camber to shed surface water.

Asphalt is an ideal surface for driveways and adjacent paths, and for large areas where more complex pavings could be too ornate as well as too expensive. Its neutral texture is an ideal backdrop for plants; a choice of handsome edgings can marry the bland surface with the character of the surroundings. Asphalt is rolled smooth after spreading and needs to be contoured to shed surface water via drainage channels, a task best done by professionals.

Various types and patterns of preformed blocks or pavers in pierced concrete are excellent for use in grassy areas. They are especially useful where access for pedestrians or vehicles is needed but where a completely paved area would be intrusive. They can also be used for occasional parking, supplementing a more conventional driveway. Blocks are first bedded in coarse sand over a firm hardcore base. Then the open cells are filled with soil and seeded with grass or other low-growing plants. The foliage softens the impact of the concrete and can even disguise it, particularly when the area is viewed obliquely.

Dry-laid bricks are a comparatively modern concept in paving. Concrete and cement are used only for the retaining edging, which is positioned first. Bricks are then placed carefully on a very even layer of coarse sand and vibrated by a special mechanical plate. This embeds them in the base and packs sand into the fine cracks of the butt joints. Bricks for this purpose must be very durable and of uniform shape. Their dimensions, and the depth of the hardcore base, depend upon whether the paving is meant for pedestrian or vehicular use. To prevent weeds growing through from below, you can lay a geotextile membrane beneath the hardcore base, bringing it up the sides of the bricks to enclose the whole system.

LEFT *Gravel makes a neutral surface, useful in a variety of situations and suiting formal or informal designs. Here, smooth rounded stones in subtly different shades are placed in a fairly formal setting, contained by geometric lines of brick and inset with square stepping stones.*

Gravel is a versatile material available as angular chippings, rounded pebbles, or a self-binding layer, in shades of greys, whites and honey colours. A wearing course about 25mm(1in) deep is laid over a compacted base of hardcore 100-300mm(4-12in) deep, depending on use. An edging is needed to contain the particles of stone; pressure-treated timber secured with stout stakes makes a simple, functional barrier.

Asphalt forms a fine-textured, functional surface that may be crisply defined by a decorative edging. For pedestrian paths a wearing course laid over hardcore is sufficient. For vehicles a base course of coarser asphalt is necessary.

Pierced concrete pavers are an efficient way of providing a harder surface without interrupting the visual continuity of grass. Blocks are available in various designs and sizes according to their intended use. A good hardcore base is vital, but an edging (shown here with ready-made haunched concrete trim) is not always necessary.

Dry-laid bricks surrounded by a firm edging are embedded in a tamped-down coarse sand base without any cement or concrete. This diagonal herringbone pattern is deliberately chosen to spread the traffic load evenly. Avoid patterns in which the joints follow the direction of traffic because persistent use is likely to cause the bricks to subside along this axis.

GRAVEL

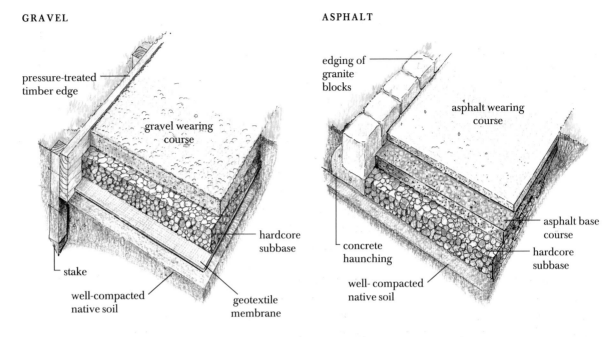

pressure-treated timber edge

gravel wearing course

hardcore subbase

stake

well-compacted native soil

geotextile membrane

ASPHALT

edging of granite blocks

asphalt wearing course

concrete haunching

well-compacted native soil

asphalt base course

hardcore subbase

PIERCED CONCRETE PAVERS

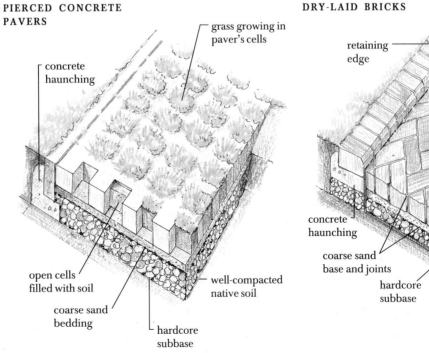

grass growing in paver's cells

concrete haunching

open cells filled with soil

coarse sand bedding

hardcore subbase

well-compacted native soil

DRY-LAID BRICKS

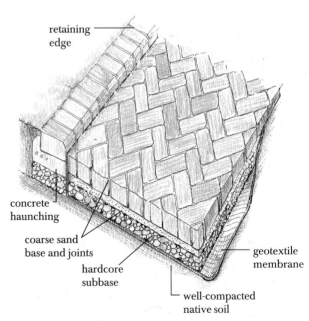

retaining edge

concrete haunching

coarse sand base and joints

hardcore subbase

geotextile membrane

well-compacted native soil

TIMBER

Timber is a beautiful surfacing material with a particular affinity for garden use. Its versatility makes it as well suited to smart tailored decking with sharp outlines in a modern style as to more rustic and informal treatments. The surface can be stained or left natural, smoothly planed or roughly sawn, according to its function and the effect you wish to achieve.

Occasionally the endgrain provides the patterning, with wood sawn into setts or log sections to create a robust, solid look. Often a more extensive horizontal surface with a light but strong feel is built from boards. The linear quality of the natural grain is emphasized when boards are laid parallel, but can be exploited to make many decorative effects. One favourite device is to create square decking modules, which are used almost like giant tiles, both for continuous patio surfacing and as substantial stepping-stones. Timber decking blends well with many styles of architecture and is particularly effective set among trees. It looks and feels warm underfoot, yet does not become as hot as stone or concrete in strong sunlight. Wood is also appropriate for steps, bridges and handrails, so it makes an ideal material for transitions in level and linking the house with the garden.

Hardwoods such as oak or teak (from renewable sources) are best for outdoor use. Softwoods must be pressure-treated with a preservative before use. All timber decking and paving must be mounted on secure foundations with good drainage beneath; boards need strong cross-bracing beneath to keep them from bouncing when walked upon.

LEFT *An elegant timber deck with clean-cut modern lines harmonizes with the serene clarity of the pool. Miscanthus and other ornamental grasses contribute to this graceful composition.*

SIMPLE TIMBER DECKING

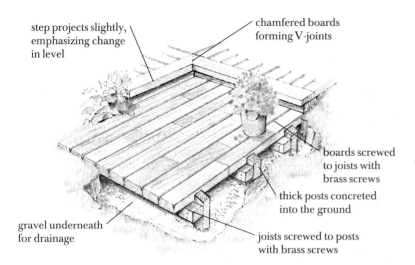

step projects slightly, emphasizing change in level

chamfered boards forming V-joints

boards screwed to joists with brass screws

thick posts concreted into the ground

gravel underneath for drainage

joists screwed to posts with brass screws

Simple timber decking, *made from sturdy planks of random lengths, looks attractive in informal situations, but its geometric lines are also appropriate in a modern, formal design. Chamfered edges create V-joints with shadows that emphasize the direction of the decking. Place a layer of gravel underneath for drainage so that the wood is kept as dry as possible.*

ORNAMENTAL DECKING

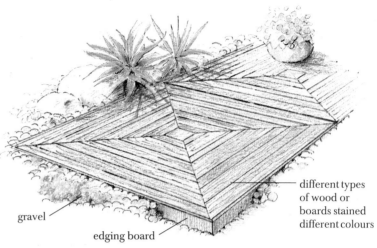

different types of wood or boards stained different colours

gravel

edging board

Ornamental decking *made by juxtaposing different woods exploits the decorative possibilities of different grains and colours. Planks are trimmed to form four triangles, each nailed to support struts beneath and finished with an edging board. Modules can be extended in just one direction to form a path, or in all four directions to make a patio.*

WOOD SETTS

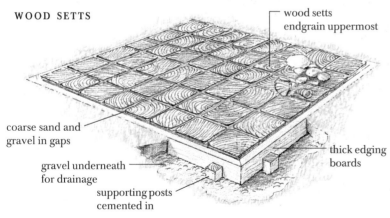

wood setts endgrain uppermost

coarse sand and gravel in gaps

gravel underneath for drainage

supporting posts cemented in

thick edging boards

Wood setts, *100mm(4in) endgrain blocks of hardwood, are set in a coarse sand base over hardcore. The 10mm(½in) gaps between the blocks are packed with consolidated coarse sand and gravel; a layer of gravel underneath provides good drainage. Strong edging boards keep the blocks in place.*

LOG SECTIONS

roughly finished log sections

sand and gravel mix

Log sections, *set in a well-draining, well-compacted mix of sand and gravel, are good for informal or woodland areas. They should be 75mm(3in) to 150mm(6in) thick and pressure-treated with surfaces roughly sawn to make them less slippery when wet. For a more rustic look, fill the joints with granulated tree bark.*

EDGINGS

Apart from their visual contribution in giving definition to a garden design, edgings on paths, driveways and wider paved areas play a multitude of useful roles. One is to contain the lateral spread of certain paving materials. An edging secured in concrete is required to retain a pattern of dry-laid bricks. A less substantial edging keeps loose materials like gravel or bark from straying onto adjacent areas and, conversely, will keep soil in beds and borders from scattering onto paved surfaces.

Edgings also act as useful guidelines. They serve as visual markers in poor light or when snow disguises different surfaces. Along driveways and around parking areas, a low physical barrier such as a kerb, ridge of bricks or row of boulders will act as a warning to a driver in danger of straying onto soft ground.

Different styles of edging add distinction to bland types of paving, and link the materials and the design of horizontal surfaces to other garden elements. You can choose wood or unshaped stones for rustic informal edgings. For more formal situations there are many ready-made units, including period reproductions. The potential for creating attractive edgings from the wide spectrum of bricks, blocks and setts available is infinite. And remember, where edgings border lawns, it is a good idea to keep a narrow grass-free strip alongside the edging to facilitate mowing.

LEFT *Hard-wearing bricks set on end provide an attractive retaining edge to a raised bed. The edging is both neat and functional and contributes to the elegance of the garden design. Together with matching horizontally laid rows of bricks on either side of the random stone path, it emphasizes the sinuous lines of the curved lawn, path and border.*

SLANTED 'ON-EDGE' BRICK

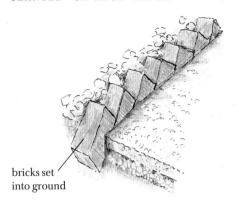

bricks set into ground

Slanted 'on-edge' brick is a traditional edging associated with many styles of architecture and can be achieved with any strong and weatherproof brick or block. The bricks are set into the ground at an angle to project above the paving. They can be fixed by simply compacting soil around them, or they can be set in concrete for a more durable edging.

ROCKS OR BOULDERS

rocks set into ground

Rocks or boulders occur naturally in many soils and make an attractive informal edging. They are best avoided beside a lawn that needs frequent mowing, although a 'wilder' area with longer grass needing only occasional trimming would present fewer problems. Stones of a suitable size can mark the edges of driveways.

CAST CONCRETE KERBS AND EDGINGS

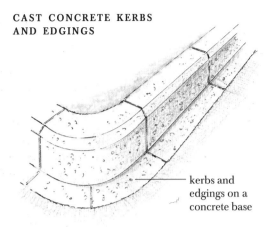

kerbs and edgings on a concrete base

Cast concrete kerbs and edgings are generally used for large driveways and roads. They are available in many sizes and shapes, and for particular sites such as corners and to link changes in level. Traditionally, such units would have been cut from natural stone such as granite, but concrete is more commonly used today.

STOUT WOODEN STAKES

stakes driven into ground

Stout wooden stakes are excellent for informal situations, since it is simple to contour them around curves and they adapt easily to changes of level. Closely spaced round, square or semicircular shapes are driven well into the ground. The wood must be pressure-treated.

CRENELLATED BRICKS

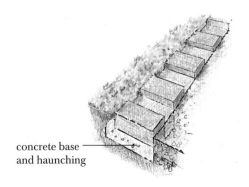

concrete base and haunching

Crenellated bricks provide a good edging for driveways. The bricks are set at alternating heights in a concrete base. The lower bricks are level with the main surface, allowing water to drain away, while the higher ones provide a warning vibration when vehicle tyres run over them.

TERRACOTTA 'ROPE' EDGINGS

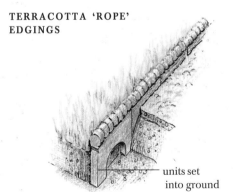

units set into ground

Terracotta 'rope' edgings of fired clay were made in many designs in the 19th century and are especially appropriate for homes of that period. The units may be simply set into a narrow trench that is backfilled with consolidated soil. Manufactured reproductions are available today.

RIGID SURFACES

The more uniform geometrical paving units of this type of surfacing are usually bedded on mortar over a concrete foundation that forms a solid platform. This is particularly necessary for thinner or more brittle units, whether natural stone or man-made products. These depend on a solid underpinning both for the crisp geometry of their layout and for their strength. Most of the more substantial kinds of setts, blocks and flagstones can also be laid in this way as an alternative to the 'flexible' approach of being dry-laid on sand over hardcore and compacted soil.

When choosing rigid surfaces for your garden, you will need to consider the amount of wear and weight they will have to withstand, and whether you need to create an even surface for garden furniture or a texture that will give grip on a slope. Planning for any extensive area of rigid paving must also take special account of surface-water disposal, since what is being created is, in fact, an impervious layer. Make sure the design incorporates suitable gradients and drainage outlets.

NATURAL STONE

In areas where natural stone is part of the landscape, it often sets an architectural keynote for the garden designer. Local stone can govern the style and colour of buildings and walls. In some regions new structures may be required to conform in appearance. Stone also plays a part in areas where river rocks, erratic boulders or rounded flints turn up in the soil and are used for creating drystone walls, edging and markers, if not as actual building materials.

The difficulty of transporting stone limited choice in the past, but

RANDOM STONE OR CRAZY PAVING

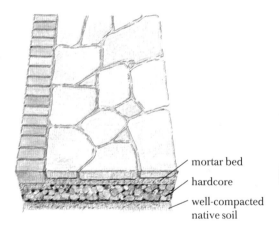

mortar bed
hardcore
well-compacted native soil

Random stone or crazy paving makes jigsaw patterns that exploit the polygonal shapes of flat stones (or broken flagstones). They can be laid leaving a ragged outline or, for a more regular shape, given a tailored edging using, for example, brick. Stones are laid in mortar for stability, and pointed flush with the surface to protect against frost and water damage and for comfort underfoot.

PEBBLES OR COBBLES

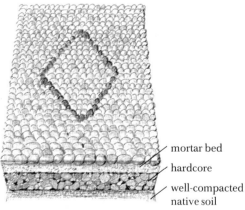

mortar bed
hardcore
well-compacted native soil

Pebbles or cobbles (rounded stones) bedded in mortar provide strong textural interest. The area is surrounded with a temporary wooden framework or permanent edging, and damp stones are pressed into a flexible mortar so even displacement takes place. Small pebbles closely set are relatively comfortable to walk upon; wider-spaced larger pebbles are good-looking but uncomfortable.

KNAPPED FLINTS

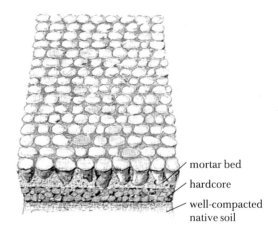

mortar bed
hardcore
well-compacted native soil

Knapped flints (whole flints cut in half) reveal an extremely hard, glassy interior. Laying them like pebbles, flat side facing up, produces a smooth, hardwearing surface. Knapped flints have very sharp edges, and are unsuitable for children's play areas. Bringing the bedding mortar up to the surface offers some protection, and moss (and, in the end, wear) will gradually blunt them.

now stone and its near imitations are fairly universally available, although sometimes costly. The ways in which stone can be used as paving have likewise spread beyond the traditional areas. A classic repertory of shapes and patterns of stone paving harmonizes with many man-made materials, both past and present.

Different types of natural stone vary intrinsically in quality and strength, and their performance is further affected by the way they are cut and laid. Hard stones of uniform consistency are usually cut to size. Stone with a distinct grain can be split into flat blocks, producing a 'riven' natural surface. However, damp and frost may penetrate the grain causing these stones to flake. Laying paving stones with the mortar even with the upper surface helps to prevent water gathering in the joints and entering the stones from the side.

RIGHT *When making a surface from randomly shaped natural stone, it looks best to use mostly large pieces. Here, they combine to create a circle, a naturally restful shape for a seating area.*

SETTS

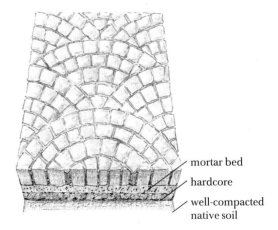

mortar bed
hardcore
well-compacted native soil

Setts *are formed of hard stone, such as granite, cut into variously proportioned cuboid shapes. These can be laid grid-fashion or decoratively, as in the fishscale pattern shown here. Setts are laid in an almost dry mortar and bedded in with a mallet, using a board to achieve an even surface. Joints are then pointed (finished with mortar). Moss softens this somewhat harsh-looking material.*

BLOCKS

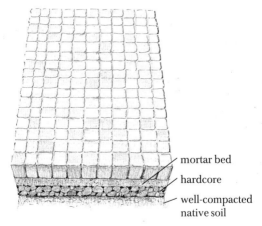

mortar bed
hardcore
well-compacted native soil

Blocks *are stone cubes of uniform size. They are bedded in mortar, traditionally with very narrow joints, to produce small-scale patterns with a relatively smooth finish. Sometimes blocks are butt-jointed (placed close together without mortar between them), with coloured sand brushed into the cracks. The softer stones and marbles are used to great effect in warm, frost-free climates.*

RANDOM STONE LAID ON EDGE

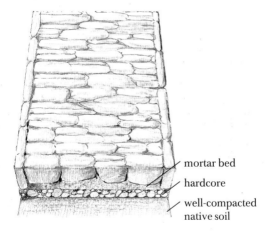

mortar bed
hardcore
well-compacted native soil

Random stone laid on edge *in thin slabs makes a beautifully textured traditional surface with a gently directional random pattern. Only the strongest stone is suitable for this treatment since each piece is set with its more vulnerable side grain exposed to the elements. For strength the stones must be well bedded in, pointed with gritty mortar, and retained between sturdy edgings.*

RECONSTITUTED STONE AND CONCRETE PAVING

Some cement-based synthetic products imitate different kinds of natural stone and the best are almost indistinguishable from the real thing. Others are designed to form a decorative flooring material in their own right. The range of products available spans the whole spectrum of garden styles. There are those suitable for the rustic informality of a cottage garden, while others can provide the neat geometrical shapes required by a modern formal design where patio and courtyard linked with the house. Because they are manufactured in regular preset units, these pavers are relatively straightforward to lay. Individual products can vary in strength as

well as thickness. Check that the quality of the chosen design suits the expected traffic. For vehicular use, you may need a concrete base between the bedding mortar and the hardcore subbase.

Reconstituted stone has a basis of natural stone that has been broken or ground down to an appropriate size and then mixed with cement. The mixture is pressed into a mould to achieve a naturalistic appearance, and the resulting colour is produced by the intrinsic tones of the stone. Concrete pavers are made from crushed stone or aggregate, cement and, in many cases, added pigments. Some are cast in moulds to imitate real stone and some are moulded and hand-textured, for example by brushing the wet concrete while still in the mould to produce a finely grooved and non-slip surface. Other pavers are hydraulically pressed by machine into a variety of finishes and textures.

LEFT *Large reconstituted stone pavers are laid in a square 'Dutch' pattern, their colour lending a feeling of warmth to this modern garden design. The pale stone used for the raised beds and steps provides a neat contrasting edge.*

PAVING STONES WITH HAMMERED SURFACE

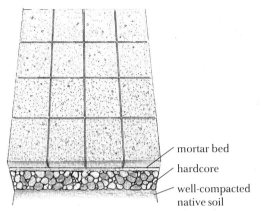

mortar bed
hardcore
well-compacted native soil

Paving stones with hammered surface *set in a grid-fashion make a static pattern. The mechanically hammered finish reveals the aggregate and produces an attractively textured, non-slip surface. Colours depend on the aggregate used.*

BRUSHED FINISH CONCRETE PAVERS

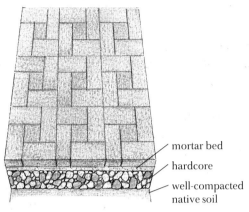

mortar bed
hardcore
well-compacted native soil

Brushed finish concrete pavers *provide a safe, non-slip surface although it is smoother than a hammered texture. This so-called 'Dutch' pattern deploys two sizes of concrete block to make a simple, non-directional pattern.*

COMPOSITE TERRAZZO MARBLE

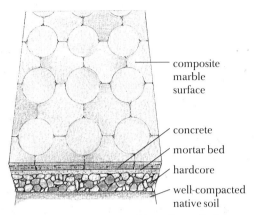

composite marble surface
concrete
mortar bed
hardcore
well-compacted native soil

Composite terrazzo marble *reflects all the sophistication of marble flooring in both style and finish. This polished surface incorporating marble dust is unsuited to icy conditions or sloping sites, but is ideal for sheltered courtyards and patios.*

SLABS WITH STIPPLED FINISH

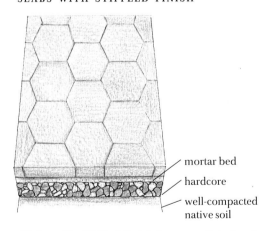

mortar bed
hardcore
well-compacted native soil

Slabs with stippled finish *have a well-textured surface that is non-slip but not too rough to be swept clear. It is produced by passing a heavy steel roller over the wet concrete while in the mould, which lightly 'plucks' the surface. A pattern of hexagons can look static or mildly directional, depending upon the viewpoint.*

IMITATION WEATHERED SETTS

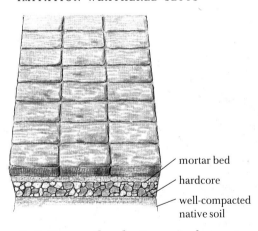

mortar bed
hardcore
well-compacted native soil

Imitation weathered setts *are sturdy concrete blocks moulded to imitate traditional stone setts. Irregularities in the mould and a mix of different colours in the concrete achieves the mottled and weathered effect. Rectangles are uniformly laid out here in a static 'stack bond' pattern. Square setts are also available.*

SLABS WITH BRUSHED FINISH

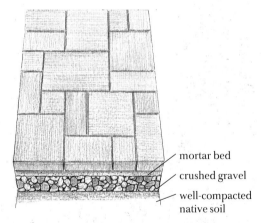

mortar bed
crushed gravel
well-compacted native soil

Slabs with brushed finish *are laid so that the direction of the brush pattern alternates. Rectangular concrete flagstones can also be made to resemble real stone. The 'random pattern' shown here is in fact fairly regular because manufactured slabs are based on multiples such as 215mm(9in) or 300mm(12in).*

BRICKS AND TILES

Bricks are highly popular paving materials. They marry equally well with both natural stone and artificial materials such as concrete or imitation flagstones. They make a marvellous foil for plants, and their scale is capable of a variety of attractive patterns.

Bricks and tiles intended for exterior paving need to be hard-wearing and frostproof where necessary. They should have a non-slip texture although depressed joints help to provide a better foothold. For pedestrian use, laying bricks on a bedding mortar over a hardcore base on well-consolidated native soil is adequate. For vehicles, an additional concrete base is safer, with varieties of brick that are deeper than normal – or normal bricks laid on edge – as a wearing course.

The range of textures, shapes and colours available is wide. Bricks traditionally made of fired clay have a warmth and a pleasantly domestic familiarity; they also keep their colour better than those made from concrete or steam-baked sand and lime mixtures, whose chemical pigments can leach or fade. Where brick is already featured in nearby structures, try to match it closely. Using brick as edgings, in steps, or decoration offers a good way of linking a contrasting new paving material to the surroundings.

Tiles come in a range of shapes and durability. The strongest are quarry tiles, made from unglazed hard-fired clay. They are difficult to cut so are most easily used in rectangular-shaped areas. They can be laid like bricks on bedding mortar. The most fragile, though the most decorative, are glazed ceramic tiles. These are not always frostproof and they need a level concrete base.

BRICK PAVERS

stock or 'wire cut' solid   **halved stable paver**   **Victorian blue diamond**   **chamfered sett**

interlocking brick or block   **quartered stable paver**   **wedge-shaped sett**

Brick pavers, some of which are shown above, come in many styles. As well as traditional oblongs, many special shapes are now available such as interlocking Z-shapes and wedge-shaped setts used to achieve fishscale and other patterns based on concentric rings.

LEFT *Modern bricks are laid in a basketweave pattern with a contrasting stretcher bond design at the lower level. The patterns give an active feel to the ground plan, the small, varying elements contrasting with the large pots and solid shapes of the shrubs.*

STRETCHER BOND

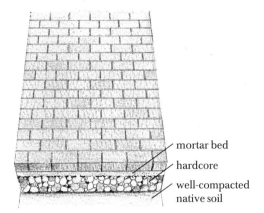

Stretcher bond *is a traditional brick pattern with regular staggered joints. It has a strong directional feel, seemingly widening the ground plan when the uninterrupted 'horizontal' joints are seen to run from side to side as they do here. It also elongates a shape - particularly a path - when these joints 'run away' from view.*

TILE BASKETWEAVE

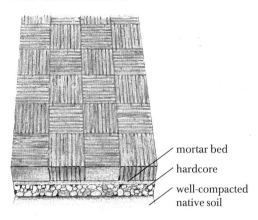

Tile basketweave *patterns can be made from frostproof, hardwearing tiles used on edge, bedded in mortar. This method of laying tiles can achieve a number of attractive patterns, including curves. Narrow joints create the most attractive effects. This basketweave pattern is static and so is eminently suitable for sitting areas.*

STACK BOND BRICKS

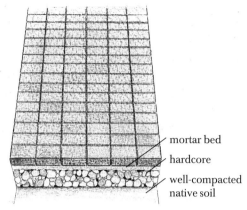

Stack bond bricks *are laid flat (as shown) or on edge with uninterrupted joints in both directions. The result gives a somewhat stark, modern appearance, appropriate for contemporary architecture. This pattern has a static quality when viewed 'across' the bricks, but is strongly directional when the oblongs are seen lengthwise.*

HERRINGBONE BRICK

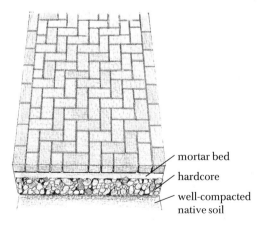

Herringbone brick *patterns can be made by laying the edges of the bricks parallel to the edges of a rectangular paved area, rather than at an angle as shown on page 43. This eliminates the need for triangular 'filler' shapes at the edges and creates a pleasantly 'shifting' effect from all viewpoints.*

DIAGONAL DUTCH

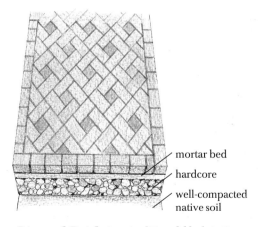

Diagonal Dutch *is a traditional block pattern that carries the eye outward to both left and right. Designers favour it for visually expanding a small enclosed area. It makes a lively pattern for paths and paving with a parallel edging course to contain the angular 'filler' edge pieces.*

QUARTERED STABLE PAVERS

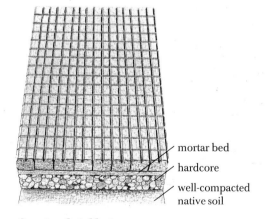

Quartered stable pavers *are very strong engineering bricks designed with the upper surface steeply grooved with V-shaped valleys. They give an attractively 'busy' impression of many small squares or rectangular bricks. The many joints provide an excellent foothold.*

CONCRETE LAID ON SITE

Well-laid and with an imaginative surface treatment, concrete can look surprisingly attractive in a garden setting, dispelling its reputation for being soulless and unsympathetic. Apart from a variety of textures for a non-slip finish, the design can make a virtue out of necessity by incorporating bricks, setts or timber to create attractive detailing, at the same time as providing thermal movement joints. These divisions in the concrete are vital to cope with the natural expansion and contraction of the material: no area of concrete should extend further than about 5m(16ft) in any direction without such joints.

Considerable expertise is needed in laying concrete and curing it properly, apart from any decorative texturing. Some processes are available only from professionals. The semi-fluid consistency of concrete exerts a strong lateral pressure, especially while it is being spread and consolidated, whether by hand tools or machinery, so the area must be well supported by permanent edging or temporary wood formwork.

Like any other paving material, concrete needs a really good, firm base to prevent settlement and, therefore, cracking. When paving is made up of small units, any cracking that occurs usually coincides with the joints and is not obvious unless the settlement is severe. With a relatively smooth continuous surface such as concrete, however, cracks are far more disfiguring. The depths of concrete and mixes will depend on the intended use. A special decorative 'wearing surface' may incorporate coloured pigments. Sometimes it may include different aggregates for decorative effect; these are the small stones, sand or gravel that with cement make up the concrete mix. The special surface will be laid on a layer of ordinary base concrete whose upper surface should be roughened to provide a good 'key', that is, a surface that interlocks well with the layer above.

LEFT *Thermal movement joints are necessary divisions in any large expanse of concrete. In this design they make a decorative pattern on the wide area of concrete that forms the terrace. The graceful geometry of curves and straight lines lend an air of elegance and originality to the garden.*

TAMPED

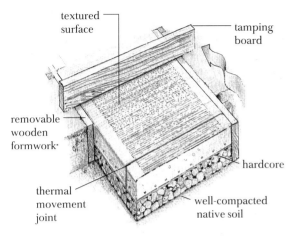

textured surface

tamping board

removable wooden formwork

hardcore

thermal movement joint

well-compacted native soil

Tamped *concrete has a strongly textured surface, providing good traction. The movement of the board creates a ridged linear pattern that is a useful gripping surface for vehicles. Brushing with a hard broom produces a similar but finer texture suitable for foot traffic.*

TROWELLED OR SOFT BRUSHED TEXTURE

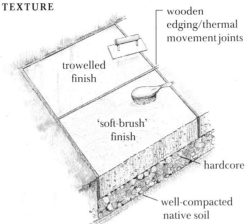

wooden edging/thermal movement joints

trowelled finish

'soft-brush' finish

hardcore

well-compacted native soil

Trowelled or soft brushed texture *are two attractive effects. Trowelling makes a smooth surface best avoided on slopes or where rain or ice can make it slippery. Texturing with a brush offers more grip. Pressure-treated or hardwood boards make patterns and thermal movement joints.*

EXPOSED AGGREGATE

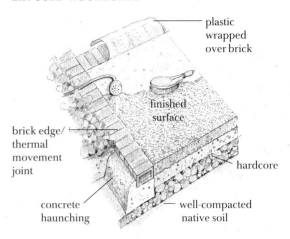

plastic wrapped over brick

finished surface

brick edge/ thermal movement joint

concrete haunching

hardcore

well-compacted native soil

Exposed aggregate *concrete is trowelled smooth and allowed partly to set. The surface cement is then gently brushed and hosed away, exposing but not dislodging the particles of aggregate. Bricks for edging and thermal movement joints are protected from cement stain by plastic that is later cut away.*

MARKED-OUT JOINTS

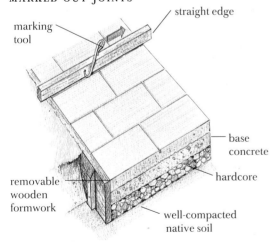

marking tool

straight edge

base concrete

hardcore

removable wooden formwork

well-compacted native soil

Marked-out joints *are made after the concrete is conventionally laid and finished by brushing. While still unset, a metal tool guided by a straight edge is used to impress the surface in a pattern suggesting flagstone paving joints.*

MECHANICALLY IMPRESSED UNITS

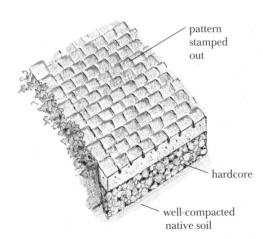

pattern stamped out

hardcore

well-compacted native soil

Mechanically impressed units *can imitate all sorts of paving materials in their many associated patterns, shapes and colours, including flagstones, bricks and setts, shown here in a staggered bond. Machinery stamps the design into the wet concrete.*

RESIN-BONDED AGGREGATE

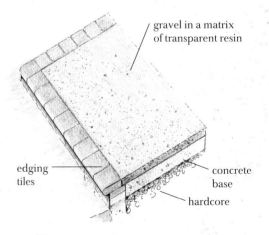

gravel in a matrix of transparent resin

edging tiles

concrete base

hardcore

Resin-bonded aggregate *is a process that creates a permanently shiny but non-slip finish. The concrete base is topped by a surface layer of small rounded aggregate set in a transparent resin. Here, the surface is given an edging of decorative tiles.*

STEPS AND RAMPS

Some of the most interesting gardens are set on different levels and many gardens are approached by steps down – or up – from the house or patio. Steps provide pedestrian access between the different levels but also offer excellent opportunities for strong design statements. The choice of suitable materials is enormous, and the style of a flight of steps can range from the strictly functional to one that has a sculptural elegance, giving the steps a graceful form. Attractive and comfortable steps built in a material and to a design appropriate to the setting can create a successful garden on a problem slope. On a very steep site, steps interspersed with 'landings' may even take the place of the horizontal paths and paved areas that the contours could not accommodate, thus reclaiming what would otherwise be unuseable property. Changes of level on either side of the steps may consist of terracing (hard-edged or informal) or may just consist of slopes masked with planting. The best designed flights of steps will harmoniously integrate all these elements.

Choose materials sympathetic in colour and scale with the surroundings, particularly near the house. In the more remote corners of an informal garden where only intrepid people venture, there is scope for more unusual steps made of logs or hewn out of rocks. But steps for everyday use in the vicinity of the house must be efficient, comfortable and safe. The same priorities apply to the construction of ramps intended for wheeled traffic.

PLANNING STEPS

Steps may run parallel to a slope, approach it at right angles, or both. They may be set into the slope or be designed as a free-standing structure. The amount of space available at the top or bottom of a slope often determines how you position a flight of steps. If the space is restricted at the upper level, the steps may need to project entirely into the area at the bottom of the slope. Conversely, if there is little space at the lower level, then the steps

THE ANATOMY OF A FLIGHT OF STEPS

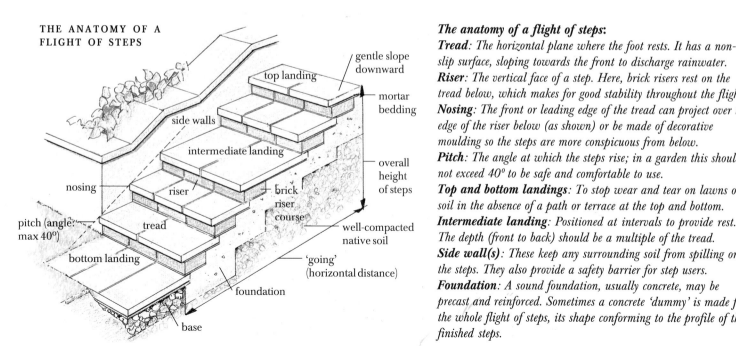

gentle slope downward

mortar bedding

top landing

side walls

intermediate landing

overall height of steps

nosing

riser

brick riser course

pitch (angle: max 40°)

tread

bottom landing

well-compacted native soil

'going' (horizontal distance)

foundation

base

The anatomy of a flight of steps:
Tread: The horizontal plane where the foot rests. It has a non-slip surface, sloping towards the front to discharge rainwater.
Riser: The vertical face of a step. Here, brick risers rest on the tread below, which makes for good stability throughout the flight.
Nosing: The front or leading edge of the tread can project over the edge of the riser below (as shown) or be made of decorative moulding so the steps are more conspicuous from below.
Pitch: The angle at which the steps rise; in a garden this should not exceed 40° to be safe and comfortable to use.
Top and bottom landings: To stop wear and tear on lawns or soil in the absence of a path or terrace at the top and bottom.
Intermediate landing: Positioned at intervals to provide rest. The depth (front to back) should be a multiple of the tread.
Side wall(s): These keep any surrounding soil from spilling onto the steps. They also provide a safety barrier for step users.
Foundation: A sound foundation, usually concrete, may be precast and reinforced. Sometimes a concrete 'dummy' is made for the whole flight of steps, its shape conforming to the profile of the finished steps.

can be set into the slope itself and not project beyond it. The top steps and landing may then 'eat' into the space at the upper level.

The number of steps is determined by the height of the change in level and the horizontal span available to accommodate the steps. As a rule steps in gardens are less steeply pitched than indoor stairs, which often have to be fitted into a confined space and offer a hand rail or bannister in compensation.

Steps must be uniform in height and width. For comfort and safety, a distinct rhythm of gait should be established in ascending or descending any particular flight. This is produced by a constant relationship between the height of the riser and the depth of the tread. If a flight of stairs is particularly long, positioning a landing at every 10 or 12 steps is recommended to provide a physical and mental 'breather'. Provided that the depth of the landing from front-to-back is a multiple of the tread width, the rhythm of gait will be maintained. A further benefit is that intermediate landings make a long flight of steps look much less intimidating.

The lateral width of steps will also vary according to circumstances, but a good rule of thumb is that steps should always be at least as wide as any path leading to or from them. Too narrow a flight of steps tends to instill an uncomfortable feeling of urgency and haste. The wider the steps, the more unhurried and relaxed the progress around the garden.

SAFETY FEATURES

To the elderly or young, just one or two unprotected steps are potentially dangerous, and even able-bodied people enjoy pausing and resting against a solid support. Hand rails, balustrading and side walls are best planned with the steps at the construction stage. Adding them afterwards can present difficulties. Choose materials to complement the steps and the surrounding architecture.

Treads should slope almost imperceptibly to allow rainwater to run off, and have a non-slip finish. To improve visibility, many steps are finished with a slightly projecting nosing that creates a clear shadow-line on the riser below. Choosing materials of contrasting colour as edgings can be decorative as well as making them easily seen. For steps used regularly in poor light or at night, lighting is both flattering and useful. Many types of lighting fixtures can be built into the steps for a streamlined effect.

Riser/tread ratios
The best dimensions for garden steps should be no lower than 100mm(4in) and no higher than 200mm(8in). A good relative proportion between riser and tread is vital for a good rhythm of gait on steps. The shallower the riser, the deeper the tread must be.

RISER	to	TREAD	
mm	inches	mm	inches
100	4	480	19
130	5	430	17
150	6	380	15
180	7	280	11
200	8	230	9

LEFT *Even and regular concrete steps negotiate the steepest section of the slope that leads up the garden from the house. Each tread projects slightly to create the nosing, giving the steps good definition. Brick side walls provide a good safety barrier. As the slope becomes less steep and the garden more informal, the steps give way to a 'stepped path' of gravel, terraced by slabs of concrete.*

ABOVE *Slabs of pale translucent marble lend a sophisticated Mediterranean air to these shallow steps. The risers are faced with a contrasting decorative pattern of small, glazed green tiles which provide both practical definition and elegance.*

ROCK STEPS

Rock steps *made from large rectangular pieces of natural stone climb intriguingly out of sight in a rock garden. Although the proportions of risers and treads diverge from the ideal, such irregularity is acceptable in this kind of a garden context.*

VERTICAL LOG STEPS

Vertical log steps *of naturally durable or preservative-treated timber are excellent for rustic steps in a woodland setting. For stability, each log should be set half its depth in the ground. Roughly sawn horizontal surfaces provide a safe grip.*

SAWN WOOD RISERS

Sawn wood risers – *steps framed by railway sleepers or roughly sawn squared lengths of hard- or pressure-treated wood – look handsome in fairly informal settings. The wood is firmly bolted together or held by stout clamps as shown. An infill of gravel or concrete makes good treads.*

PROJECTING BRICK STEPS

Projecting brick steps *with a hand rail are a good solution when an entire flight of steps projects onto a lower level, and there are no side walls providing a safety barrier. Here, the steps are made from hardwearing and frostproof bricks set on edge to form riser and tread.*

PARTIALLY RECESSED STONE STEPS

Partially recessed stone steps *can be very successful when you do not wish to take up too much space either at the higher or lower level. Natural or reconstituted stone are equally suitable building materials. The treads project slightly beyond the risers to make effective shadow lines.*

FULLY RECESSED STONE STEPS

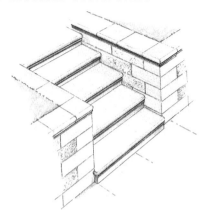

Fully recessed stone steps here make a sophisticated-looking design. The elegant decorated nosings create crisp shadow lines and also make the steps seem wider. The same moulding is repeated in the special capping stones of the adjacent wall, integrating the steps perfectly with their surroundings.

THREE-DIRECTIONAL STONE STEPS

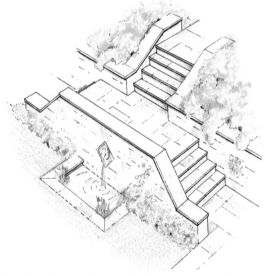

Three-directional stone steps in a symmetrical design suggest elegance and spaciousness, but actually use space economically. The upper flight is recessed, the lower ones projecting, with a sidewall that here accommodates an attractive water feature.

ABOVE *Pieces of random stone with an appropriately rustic air make an informal stairway winding through a woodland garden. The rough appearance of the stones is deceptive, for they have been carefully planned. The top surface is flat, making the tread fairly even, and the upper layer of stones projects slightly for safety, giving the edges good definition.*

CAST CONCRETE STEPS

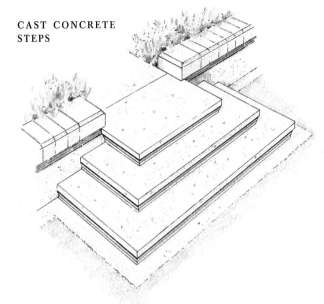

SEMICIRCULAR STEPS

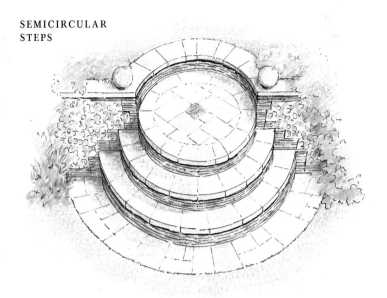

Cast concrete steps that are crisply edged and elegant can be expertly cast on site or built from precast concrete slabs. Here, the nosings and risers are moulded, and a lightly brushed finish exposes the fine aggregates in the concrete. Courses of green glazed tiles emphasize the contemporary, geometric look and the adjacent walls echo the materials of the steps.

Semicircular steps traditionally culminate in a circular top step or landing. This concentric design has a leisurely grandeur – the steps do not rush you in any particular direction. Natural or reconstituted stone treads and landing are married to terracotta tile risers. The same ingredients finish the associated flint walls, providing a feeling of harmony.

HORIZONTAL LOG RISERS

CANTILEVERED STEPS

Horizontal log risers are effective in a natural setting. They are nailed to stout stakes driven well into the ground. Wood preservative helps to prevent the logs from becoming slippery with wear and degradation. The treads, which can vary in width and may slope if necessary, can have a wearing surface of gravel or pine-bark granules or can be made of textured concrete.

Cantilevered steps may be made from strong natural stone or reinforced concrete and are unusual, interesting and functional. They make effective use of a small space but are unsuitable for frequent use by all age groups. Each tread must be very firmly anchored in the retaining wall so as to bear the weight of a person on the step plus the weight of the step itself.

RAMPS

Although they take up more space than steps to cover the same difference in level, ramps are necessary where wheeled traffic is expected. Gradients are usually expressed as a ratio illustrating the vertical change in height to a horizontal change in distance. So, a gradient of 1 in 15 is a rise of 1 centimetre (or 1 inch and so on) for every 15 centimetres (or 15 inches) measured horizontally; 1 in 15 is fine for mowers and wheelbarrows, and a steeper gradient is acceptable for short distances, but a less steep 1 in 20 is preferable for wheelchair users. Where a ramp turns into a bend, the gradient may unavoidably increase, and the gradient of 1 in 20 should be measured from this point. Ramps should be constructed of material that is not slippery underfoot and offers good traction to tyres.

RAMP WITH STEPS

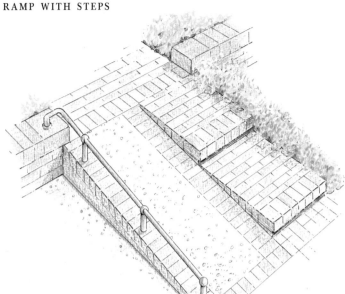

This ramp with steps *has a gradient of 1 in 20. A low rail acts as a safety edging on one side, and the two shallow steps perform the same function on the other. The brick used for the walls and steps edges a panel of exposed sharp-aggregate concrete that gives good grip on the slope.*

LEFT *A flight of steps and a ramp useful for moving garden equipment such as wheelbarrows and mowers fit neatly into a small space. They are made of old bricks to match the terrace, and the sense of continuity between one level and the other is heightened by the the use of a row of contrasting blue-grey bricks to give a neat edging to both the terrace and the ramp.*

VERTICAL ELEMENTS

OPPOSITE *If you treat the vertical elements with a light touch, making them decorative as well as utilitarian, a space can be enclosed to give privacy without becoming too confining. This graceful white-painted wooden fencing creates a charming, secluded refuge from the world outside.*

Seclusion, security and shelter are created by the vertical elements of garden design. Some verticals can form continuous barriers – including the boundaries that surround an enclosed garden and the dividers that separate areas of a larger garden into smaller, individual compartments. As well as plant materials used in hedges of many different styles, these include man-made constructions such as walls and solid fences, and such airy, lighter structures as trellis or railings, and screens or apertures in walls. Vertical elements also include some decorative overhead structures used within the garden. These bring a human scale to spacious gardens and help you feel at home and comfortable in a sweeping land-scape. Sometimes these structures are linear, such as tunnels and covered walkways or pergolas. Others, including arbours, arch-ways and garden buildings, make isolated upright features.

There are many ways of using plants as vertical elements. They can grow as wall-like hedges, or climb and trail to create a screen and provide overhead shelter when trained to grow over wood, brick, metal or stone structures. When choosing plants or hard materials for vertical elements, think of the effect you want to achieve. Take into account the existing appearance of the site, the materials used for nearby buildings, and any local traditions. Then half-close your eyes to help you assess the impact of each vertical surface. Do you want a solid look (a masonry wall or a clipped evergreen hedge), or a lighter-weight and open effect (a trelliswork fence or even a deciduous hedge)? Should the style be geometric and linear, or natural and irregular? Do you seek a crisp, stark structure or one softened with plants? If you want it to consist only of plants, how long are you prepared to wait for them to mature?

DEFINING AREAS

Verticals define the horizontal shapes on the ground plan, but also affect the quality of space they contain. The higher the boundaries, the smaller the enclosed space will appear. This is why enclosed patios and courtyards seem so much like rooms, and narrow paths between tall walls or hedges so much like corridors.

Remember that the ground plan shows only where the vertical elements are positioned and doesn't give the impression of their height. Practise visualizing the plan and gauging the effect of the height and mass of the verticals. You can indicate heights using

SOLID WALL OR FENCE

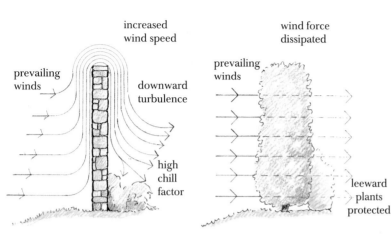

Solid walls or fences may increase wind speeds, causing extreme turbulence and wind chill on the lee side which is damaging to plants. They are also vulnerable to being blown over.

WIND-FILTERING HEDGE

A wind-filtering hedge, the thicker the better, reduces the force of the wind so that plants or people on the lee side are largely unaffected. A hedge is resilient enough to yield and bend with the wind.

SHELTER BELT OF SHRUBS AND TREES

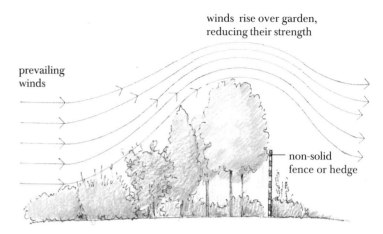

A shelter belt of shrubs and trees is the ideal (but space-consuming) barrier to reduce wind-resistance at exposed sites. On the windward side a bank of planting – with low shrubs graduating upward to trees – deflects the main force of the wind up and over the garden for considerable distances. A pierced fence or screen to leeward filters any residual wind.

bamboo canes and garden line, but you will need to use your imagination to supplement these props. Check that the spaces they enclose are well proportioned.

The smaller the enclosure the more its vertical elements predominate, so greater care needs to go into their design. This is especially true with small gardens in city settings where tall boundaries for security and privacy prevail. In an intimate patio you can be as conscious of the colour and texture of the surrounding wall or fence as you are of the wallpaper of an indoor room. You may want to manipulate it in a similar way. You can lighten a shady area with paint or pale-coloured wood or concrete or create regular patterns with fencing or trellis. You can soften a hard surface with curtains of foliage, or use devices such as mirrors or *trompe l'oeil* to suggest space beyond. One way to counteract the claustrophobia created by a small enclosed space is to erect a non-solid barrier such as trelliswork or a screen of pierced brick or concrete units.

Conversely, large gardens often lack a sense of intimacy and if you introduce vertical structures to enclose spaces their open,

impersonal scale changes. One option is to subdivide the space into individual interconnecting compartments and treat each as a separate garden room. Another is to erect features such as walkways or arbours to give a subtle sense of enclosure and at the same time offer a frame through which to view the world.

SHELTER AND SCREENING

How you plan to use your garden and its unique aspect will suggest your priorities for shelter from the elements. In sunny climates, a leafy arbour or a tree canopy provides shade for outdoor eating. In wetter regions, a summerhouse offers a retreat from a sudden downpour. In temperate areas, consider a draft-proof shelter to take advantage of precious winter sunshine. In exposed gardens, wind is the enemy. Never underestimate the discomfort wind can cause or its destructive effect on plants. Where winds are persistent and strong, it is better to filter their force through more open structures such as fences, pierced walls and a shelter belt of suitably

MIXED INFORMAL SCREEN OF PLANTS

informal grouping of
mixed trees and shrubs
partly hides the building

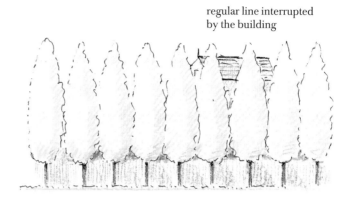

A mixed informal screen of plants can be useful for distracting attention from an eyesore such as a tall building outside the garden. Even in winter bare branches soften and mask hard architectural lines. Informal planting generally hides an unwanted feature more successfully than a straight hedge or a regularly spaced line of trees.

SINGLE-SPECIES TREE SCREEN

regular line interrupted
by the building

A single species tree screen makes a strong design statement especially where conical or columnar shapes are used. Paradoxically, the eye may be drawn to the building beyond because it disrupts the screen's formal rhythm.

resilient plants (or combinations of these). If you try to deflect winds with a solid vertical obstacle this can set up downward turbulence in its lee.

Vertical elements are also useful in hiding or altering views. You may want to screen off an area to make it less exposed to prying eyes, or you may wish to conceal from your own view some unsightly feature outside the garden or an unattractive garden necessity such as a compost heap. If the screen has enough visual interest – it could be an attractive grouping of shrubs or a flowering plant – your attention will be distracted from the offending item.

THE TIME DIMENSION

Planting trees to create a barrier or screen is a long-term project as is establishing any large-scale living vertical feature. Choosing between growing plants and inanimate materials for your vertical elements is thus a question partly of what looks right and pleases you, and partly of how much time you are prepared to wait.

Whereas man-made fences and walls made of concrete units or bricks are comparatively quickly built, planted structures such as hedges take time to achieve the proportions of your garden layout and fulfil the effects you are planning. When they do, they create the feeling of a truly mature and established garden. A natural or imitation stone wall is also a longer-term investment than the instant division of wooden fencing. It, too, takes more time to mature before conveying that feeling of having always been there. Alternatively, stark new brick walls and fences can be teamed with quick-growing climbers, which mellow their impact.

As you look through the following pages, consider the advantages and disadvantages of each kind of structure for your particular setting. But bear in mind this time factor. Look at the range of man-made structures not in isolation, but as foils and partners for glorious plant effects. Planting for a vertical effect is discussed first, followed by a full spectrum of different materials and techniques for man-made walls, fences and screens; decorative structures such as covered walkways and arbours end the chapter.

VERTICAL PLANTING

When you lay out the horizontal plane of your garden you might choose to pave large areas with stone or decking, leaving them almost free of plants. Remember, though, you need at least some plant material growing vertically in order to enjoy the space as a garden. For a minimalist, design requirements might be a tree for height or shade, a clump of screening bamboo, or an evergreen climber providing a curtain or canopy of foliage. What interests us here is those plants that make an architectural contribution to the garden – trees and shrubs with a naturally upright appearance and plants that can be clipped or trained to add to the vertical dimension of the garden.

DESIGNING WITH PLANTS

Building verticals with conventional hard materials such as stone or timber consists of repeating a basic unit. When plants are used in a similar repetitive way they, too, can shape a garden layout. Planting in a continuous line creates a degree of formality, espe-

cially when only one plant species is used. Sometimes the individual plants remain distinct, resulting in a rhythmic pattern like pairs of trees in an avenue. In other cases, plants merge to lose their separate identity as in a hedge. Formality is also achieved when plants of conspicuous outline are used to mark important points in a garden layout, such as the four corners where two paths cross.

A looser grouping of plants can also make an effective garden divider or screen. The more fluid shapes have a more informal effect. And while perennials (non-woody plants) such as tall grasses and shapely specimens such as phormiums can be made to play important structural roles, trees and shrubs make the chief contribution to garden architecture.

Evergreens are the vital ingredient of formal gardens, providing consistent all-year structure. Some conifers such as the pencil-like junipers, some Lawson cypress and Irish yews are naturally formal in their habit, growing into regular cones and spire-like shapes. Planted singly, these plants make emphatic punctuation marks in a design, while a pair flanking an entrance adds importance and

RIGHT *In this formal garden, plants provide year-round architecture, making a satisfying picture in winter as well as at the height of summer. Box makes up the low clipped hedges and the neat little balls in pots, while a variegated holly, trained as a standard, provides a centrepiece. Two cone-shaped yews stand as sentinels to the rest of the garden, and the warmer brown colour of the enclosing beech hedge adds a welcome contrast to the predominant evergreen tones.*

dignity to that feature. Equally useful for establishing a garden's formality are evergreens trimmed into geometric shapes. Yew and box are the classic plants for this purpose because they respond well to clipping and their small leaves create a close-textured, dense surface. Larger-leaved evergreens – laurels, camellias and hollies, for example – can also be pruned and trained into formal blocks and pillars with a glossy, leafy texture.

A regular line of shapely evergreens along the boundary makes a rhythmic backdrop. A row on either side of a main path makes an avenue. However, one of the chief virtues of shrubby evergreens grown in pairs or a row is the way the branches of adjacent plants mesh together to form a continuous, solid-looking surface – a growing building block for you to manipulate in a number of ways. At its simplest this becomes a hedge which you can top with crisp castellations, scalloped curves or ornate finials. Another possibility is to grow evergreens in theatrical Italianate style to frame a series of archways and so create a green colonnade.

Deciduous trees and shrubs contribute to a garden's structure even when they have lost their leaves. In a formal arrangement, the strongly upright trunks and bare branches of free-standing trees sustain the pattern in winter.

HEDGES

For choosing a garden hedge style, the main issues to decide on are its function, size, the degree of formality, its context in the garden, feel and colour. Compare it to planning a wall – is the hedge to be a practical barrier or an ornate statement?

Deciduous hedges look handsome and make effective barriers. Close-growing kinds such as hornbeam and hawthorn can be trimmed to look decidedly formal. For clipping into geometric shapes, the more densely growing, fine-textured plant material is best. Relatively small-leaved evergreens such as yew and box produce the smoothest surface of all and the thickest barriers. Prickly-leaved hollies are among the most impenetrable. You will get a looser sort of formality from larger-leaved evergreens such as laurel, and from deciduous trees and shrubs such as beech and hornbeam. Of course from a distance such a hedge looks smooth. You can choose the uniform look of a single-species hedge or the tapestry effect of combining different species.

Plants of freer growth habit can make hedges when closely planted in a line. You might consider bamboos and tall grasses or various types of roses or low-growing shrubs such as lavender.

TALL GRASSY PLANTS

Tall grassy plants can make good screens and barriers. Some grasses and their relatives, bamboos, make dense windbreaks, their leaves affording a pleasing rustling accompaniment in the background. Beware of the invasive tendencies of some species.

FORMAL HEDGE

A formal hedge lends an air of elegance to a garden. Small-leaved evergreens such as yew and box are best for clipping into decorative geometric shapes. All hedges should be clipped slightly narrower at the top, so that sunlight can reach all parts.

These last two groups do not necessarily need clipping, but most need some kind of annual pruning or they become leggy. Different types of rose make varying hedges from impenetrable barriers to low edgings. Box and certain berberis species have dwarf forms useful for low ornamental hedges.

When you have decided what genus you want (and checked that your conditions suit it), choose your species carefully. Conifers vary tremendously in their growth rate. Some are notoriously rampant while others are too slow-growing to meld into a satisfactory hedge. Check how much and how frequently to clip them: little and often is the usual rule.

The various traditional ways of training trees or climbing plants offer wonderful examples of architectural hedging and always add romance and distinction to a site. Among them is the ancient practice of pleaching, or training growing branches to interweave, to produce overhead archways, tunnels or allées, and aerial hedges on stilts. More two-dimensional are palisades, using climbing roses for example, while apples or pears grown in espaliers and cordons make delicate screens of shapely branches, adorned with pale flowers in spring and crops in due season.

PLEACHED ALLÉE OR TUNNEL

In a pleached allée or tunnel the young branches are trained to meet overhead – this also makes an attractive archway in a single pair of trees. Pleaching involves allowing young deciduous trees to grow with clean trunks to a predetermined height, above which the branches are tied to a frame so that they interweave to form architectural shapes. The frame may be removed later.

STILT HEDGE

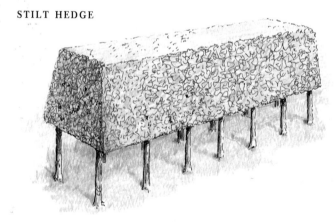

A stilt hedge can be formed from pleached trees such as limes, beeches or hornbeams. To pleach trees, the young side branches are first trained along a series of parallel wires or battens until they overlap. Regular pruning and tying in of branches encourages the heads to thicken and form a box-like shape; eventually the framework of supports is dismantled.

PALISADE

A palisade is also achieved by pleaching young branches above a uniform height. Lower branches are removed and side branches are trained to interweave. By careful pruning and training you can create a graceful row of arches that frames the view beyond.

DECORATING VERTICAL STRUCTURES

Climbing and trailing plants are unsurpassed in their capacity for bringing inanimate surfaces to life. There are flowering plants, plants with fruits, plants with daytime or evening fragrance, a range of evergreens, and many predominantly foliage plants, often with leaf variegation or ravishing autumn colour. These can all be used to adorn hard vertical structures in the garden.

Plants have evolved various mechanisms to hoist themselves upwards towards the light and anchor themselves to their hosts – aerial roots (ivy, climbing hydrangea), twining stems (honeysuckle, wisteria), coiling tendrils (passion flower, grapevine, annual sweetpeas), or twisting leaf-stems (clematis). Some climbing plants (jasmine, bougainvillea) have lax branches that scramble over or through hosts and need some guidance and tying in to a support.

Plants with aerial roots cling to the relatively smooth surfaces of walls, stout fences and host tree trunks. A few climbers like parthenocissus need the initial support of a cane or wire, but once in contact with a surface develop adhesive tips to the tendrils and become self-clinging. Make sure your walls are sound before you allow these climbers to colonize them since their roots can loosen crumbling mortar and cause structural damage. Other plants call for additional supports. Tie in lax branches of scramblers like jasmine to rustproof nails driven into the wall or fence posts at strategic points. Create a fine framework for plants with twining stems and coiling or twisting tendrils by stretching a series of horizontal wires between pairs of nails. Consider putting up a ready-made grid of wire or plastic mesh or a panel of wooden trellis. The former is lightweight but functional and is best when covered as quickly as possible by planting; trellis, however, can be decorative in its own right or complemented with plants.

True climbing plants come into their own in conjunction with openwork styles of fencing, including trellis panels and overhead features such as archways, arbours and pergolas, where their coiling stems and twining tendrils easily find a grip. However, it is crucial to match your supporting framework to the size and vigour of your chosen climber, so be sure your ornamental structure is designed to provide long-lasting support.

ABOVE *Honeysuckle makes a perfect, light-toned decorative effect for a series of dark ironwork arches that cover a walkway between two prettily planted borders. The pale yellow of the honeysuckle flowers harmonizes with the yellow and blue planting scheme. Their sweet fragrance perfumes the air at head-height as visitors walk below.*

WALLS

There is a lot more to designing a garden wall than calculating its dimensions and selecting a material that looks appropriate in the context of your house and garden.

Two basic wall types concern the gardener: freestanding and retaining walls, both of which may still need professional planning and building. When freestanding walls are also boundary walls, local planning regulations must be heeded. (Construction of the third wall type, the load-bearing walls of a garden shed or summer-house are like, those of a house, the province of an architect or building engineer and are outside the scope of this book.)

TYPICAL FREESTANDING WALL

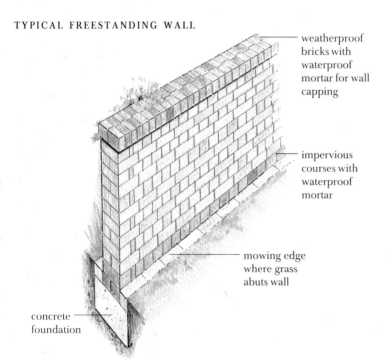

weatherproof bricks with waterproof mortar for wall capping

impervious courses with waterproof mortar

mowing edge where grass abuts wall

concrete foundation

A typical freestanding wall's height relates to its thickness. A short stretch of wall needs no reinforcements or piers, though piers are useful in allowing a higher wall to be relatively thinner. Any wall needs protection from wet weather, so here a protective capping is fixed with waterproof mortar and courses of impervious bricks at the base prevent dampness from rising.

Whether you are copying an existing wall, re-creating a local style, or have a free hand to build in whatever material you choose, an understanding of wall construction helps you decide on the best effects for your garden. Look at different walls for inspiration and note any special features. Many apparently decorative elements have an important function. For instance, a contrasting capping that makes an attractive finishing touch must be designed with waterproof materials which protect the wall from the damaging effects of weather. Special coping bricks or blocks are often used for this purpose. You may see vertical piers interspersed in the predominantly horizontal lines of a brick wall. Like the buttresses of a cathedral, they are there for strength, but the best designs make these structural elements a satisfying part of the garden design.

A wall's strength may not be evident from its appearance. For example, it should have a first-class foundation (see pages 74-75), and there may be internal reinforcing rods. Various invisible strategies prevent weather damage, from damp-proofing to thermal movement joints.

The design aspect of walls is thus inseparable from making them structurally sound. So it is worth knowing some technicalities even if you put the job in the hands of professionals.

FREESTANDING WALLS

These structures generally don't have a load to support other than their own weight but must be designed for stability, especially when subjected to high winds or any other lateral pressure. Carefully calculate proportions of thickness in relation to height. As a rule of thumb, a wall 230mm(9in) thick should be no more than 2-3m(6ft 6in-9ft 9in) tall without being reinforced. One way is to build supporting piles at predetermined intervals, which form part of the design. An invisible alternative is to embed reinforcing bars in the foundation. These rods pass vertically upwards through the interior of the wall. The foundation itself, normally of concrete, usually starts150mm(6in) below the ground surface (see page 74).

Any wall will last longer if kept as dry as possible. Deterioration takes place in structures that are permanently damp, especially if they freeze. (House walls are usually protected from rising damp by a dampproof course near the bottom. This is not an option in freestanding walls because it physically separates the upper part of the wall from its base and makes it unstable.) The solution is to incorporate courses of impervious and frostproof brick, stone or other material at the bottom of the wall, preferably joined with a mortar mix that is itself waterproof. A similar treatment at the top of the wall prevents water penetration from above. Alternatives include decorative cappings or courses of impervious tile or slate.

WALL WITH PIER SUPPORTS

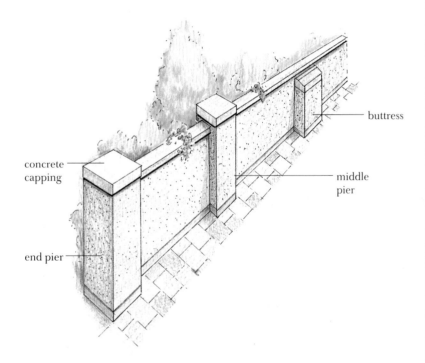

buttress

concrete capping

middle pier

end pier

This wall with pier supports shows three types of supporting pile in a mortar-covered wall with concrete cappings. The end and middle piers have been constructed and bonded so that they straddle the wall they help to support. (Where an end pier serves as a gatepost it may need the reinforcement of a steel rod passing through its centre into the foundation below.) The buttress is bonded to the wall to reinforce it on one side only. In a boundary wall, this is traditionally the side facing the owner's land.

ABOVE *This is a fine freestanding serpentine wall, where the radius of the curves is great enough to allow the 'Flemish bond' brick pattern to be used (see page 79). For tighter curves, either specially curved bricks or a 'header only' bond would be required (see page 78). Special ridged capping tiles protect this wall.*

RETAINING WALLS

Occasionally retaining walls are built around raised garden ponds and raised beds, but their chief use occurs where a sloping site is terraced. Since the main load-bearing pressure comes not downwards but sideways, pay particular attention to the foundations and also to the nature of the ground behind, below and in front of the wall. Take into account the soil type. If the soil behind the wall is water retentive, incorporate drainage (see below) to prevent water build-up from adding extra weight at the rear. A 'toe' of foundation extending from the rear of the wall allows the weight of soil above it to help hold the whole structure in place.

It is important to decide how to treat the area in front of the wall. Paving it or putting in a lawn will leave the ground relatively undisturbed, but if you decide to cultivate it the top few inches of loosened soil may allow the wall to shift forwards. A deeper

LEFT *Colourfully planted dry stone walls retain the terracing in a sloping garden. Stone walls such as these look very natural and suit an informal setting. They rapidly acquire the patina of age, and are the ideal host for rock plants and ferns.*

TYPICAL RETAINING WALL

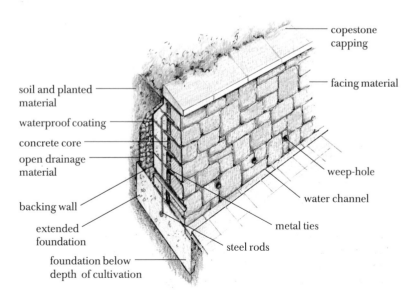

soil and planted material

waterproof coating

concrete core

open drainage material

backing wall

extended foundation

foundation below depth of cultivation

copestone capping

facing material

weep-hole

water channel

metal ties

steel rods

A typical retaining wall *is strengthened by its 'toe' or extended foundation and steel reinforcing rods placed at regular intervals. Foundation depth will depend on whether the soil in front of the wall is well-consolidated or undisturbed or is to be planted. Linked to the concrete backing wall by reinforcing metal ties, the stone facing slopes gently backwards, giving added stability. A layer of tanking (a waterproof coat) at the rear and a capping of sloping copestones protect the wall from water damage. Drainage measures, such as stones placed behind the wall and weep-holes through it with a water channel below, prevent water from building up behind the wall.*

foundation will counteract this. Foundations rely on the support of the soil surrounding them. Make sure the foundation for a retaining wall behind a bed or border lies below the depth of cultivation.

As a rule, the thickness of a retaining wall should be about one-third of the height. Any wall higher than 600mm(2ft) should be checked if not designed by a building engineer.

Occasionally retaining walls consist of dry materials such as stone. These are best kept low and are self-draining provided they are sufficiently thick. More often in garden contexts, retaining walls are built of a single material or use a concrete backing for strength and a cosmetic facing material is added. Some walls are vertical, but others are 'battered', that is, they slope gently backwards. This lowers the centre of gravity and adds stability. The degree of slope is usually about 1 in 12 – that is, 25mm(1in) off the perpendicular for every 300mm(1ft) the wall rises.

The stability of all retaining walls relies on the degree to which you can keep them dry at the rear, so reduce any water pressure to the minimum. Include a layer of open drainage material behind the wall and lay a horizontal row of pipes (known as weep-holes) near the base of the wall to bring the water to a drainage system at the front. Giving the back of the wall a tanking or waterproof coat of cement, plastic or bitumen will prevent water from passing through the wall itself and disfiguring its face with lime salts or algae marks, but this is partly a matter of climate and preference.

INCORPORATING WALL JOINTS

To accommodate the natural expansion and contraction of building materials in different atmospheric conditions, mortar-bonded walls must be designed with gaps called thermal movement joints, of approximately 10mm(⅜in). These gaps allow each wall panel to expand and contract independently. If the individual panels overlap, it means you can build a freestanding wall higher than it could be if built as a single unit because the vertical overlaps act like supporting piles to give greater stability.

In concrete walls built in place, the thermal movement joints allow for initial shrinkage as the concrete sets. Walls built of concrete blocks or reconstituted stone require joints at intervals equivalent to approximately two to two-and-a-half times the wall's height. As a general guide, thermal movement joints should be positioned no more than 6m(20ft) from a corner and no more than 12m(40ft) apart in the main body of the wall. Brick walls need joints about every 3-4m(10-12ft). The exact measurements to suit your specific circumstances should be checked by a building engineer.

Sections of wall can be linked together with specially made expanded metal wall ties rather than by bonding the building units (see pages 78-79). However, both metal ties and stark vertical gaps in a garden wall can be unsightly unless they are an integral part of the design, are camouflaged by plants, or are disguised by some intrinsic part of the wall's structure such as a pile or overlap.

WALL BUILT IN SECTIONS

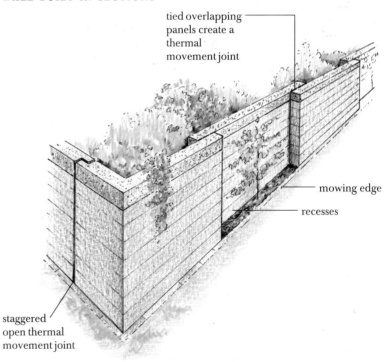

tied overlapping panels create a thermal movement joint

mowing edge

recesses

staggered open thermal movement joint

This wall built in sections incorporates two types of thermal movement joints. One is the gaps at the overlaps joined with metal ties. The resulting recesses provide frames for plants such as wall-trained flowering shrubs or fruit trees. The other is simply a staggered vertical gap. It is impossible to see through and makes the wall exceptionally stable. The building materials are painted concrete blockwork with a textured concrete capping.

FOUNDATIONS

Unless firm bedrock lies just below the surface of the soil to provide a naturally stable foundation, you will need a good-quality concrete foundation or footing for mortar-bonded garden walls. The foundation must be substantial enough to prevent the structure from being affected by any subterranean movement. Its dimensions depend upon the weight and thickness of the wall and the nature of the soil. It should also extend below the frost line for the area. Strip foundation is used for freestanding walls and, in a slightly modified version, for retaining walls – the concrete below a retaining wall often extends to the rear to form a 'toe' (see page 71). A raft, or spread, foundation is more often used for buildings or walled enclosures and provides both foundations and floor. It offers a useful alternative to the strip principle in less stable soils.

Concrete for a strip foundation is laid in a flat-bottomed, vertically sided trench which follows the route of the proposed wall. The strip is stepped where the wall crosses the contours of sloping ground. The width of the strip is usually twice that of the wall. The wall is built along the centre of the strip. The depth of the strip is a different matter altogether: it is calculated according to the specific soil type, bearing in mind the height and weight of the wall.

Soils that are themselves stable and supportive need the shallowest foundation. For a 1m(40in) wall in hard gravelly soils and undisturbed hard limestone (disturbed limestone is anything but stable when it is wet), you need concrete that is 300-600mm(1-2ft) deep. For the same wall, you need concrete 600-900mm(2-3ft) deep in stiff clay that is hard and unmouldable when wet. Sand and flexible clays are notoriously unstable. Some flexible clay soils require a foundation that is deeper than the height of the wall itself. The golden rule is never to leave foundation depths to chance. If in any doubt, check with a building engineer.

Raft or platform foundations consist of a large slab of concrete that rests or 'floats' on the ground, spreading its own weight and that of the structure it supports over its entire area. Raft foundations extend downwards at the periphery in what is known as a downstand, encapsulating a hardcore layer and adding stability. Depending on the anticipated weight they will bear, raft foundations are sometimes reinforced with steel rods which extend beyond the wall base line by a minimum of half the wall thickness.

RIGHT *This retaining wall provides both a backdrop and a ledge for plants. Where the ground in front of such a wall is composed of loose soil, its foundation needs to be deeper than usual or pressure from behind could cause the wall to shift forwards.*

STRIP FOUNDATION

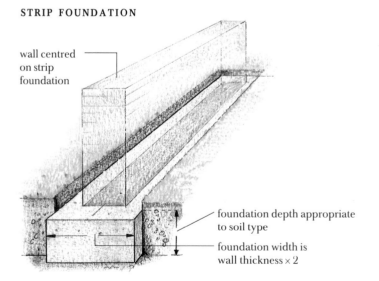

wall centred on strip foundation

foundation depth appropriate to soil type

foundation width is wall thickness × 2

A strip foundation is a strip of concrete that follows the line of a freestanding wall. It should be twice as wide as the thickness of the wall. Its depth is calculated according to the soil type, as shown on the opposite page.

FOUNDATION DEPTHS

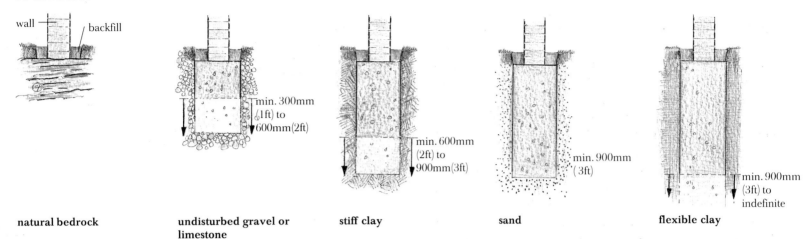

natural bedrock   undisturbed gravel or limestone   stiff clay   sand   flexible clay

Foundation depths are shown here for bedrock and different kinds of subsoil, giving the approximate depths of concrete that are needed to support a 1m(40in) high wall.

RAFT (OR SPREAD) FOUNDATION

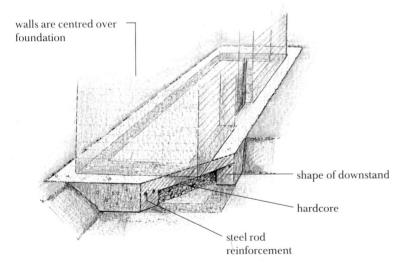

A raft (or spread) foundation is a platform of concrete extending over the entire area of a walled enclosure, spreading the total weight of both raft and wall evenly. Reinforcements and a downstand, or deeper layer of concrete at the edges, add stability.

STEPPED STRIP FOUNDATION

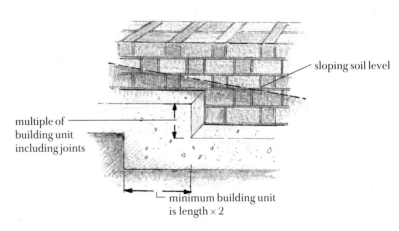

A stepped strip foundation is used where the ground level slopes. The concrete strip is stepped down to conform with the gradient. Calculate the dimensions of the steps as exact multiples of the building unit used in the wall plus any mortar joints.

BRICK WALLS

The choice of brick for your garden wall is just the beginning of the decision process. What kind of brick? What colour? Does it need to match or to complement existing architecture? What kind of pattern or bond? What degree of strength is required? Is there a local tradition to conform to? What style of capping, and what colour and finish of mortar? And you will have to consider weatherproofing properties as well as aesthetic ones.

Brick walls owe their appearance partly to the quality of the units from which they are built and partly to the pattern or bond used in their construction. Bricks are made in a variety of materials and their sizes are standardized to plus or minus 2-3mm(¹⁄₁₆-¹⁄₈in) in any dimension. Before mass production, however, even standard bricks varied considerably in size. Their quality and color depended on the local clay used with different batches showing differences in their firing. Such irregularities are seen in the surface of old brick walls, softening their impact; in contrast, modern bricks create a crisper, more uniform look. Bear in mind these

qualities when deciding on the materials and bond for they will affect the atmosphere you are seeking to create.

You can underline the wall's style with a capping, or protective top layer, of weatherproof bricks or tiles. Special sloping capping bricks called copings are also available.

Choose the bond for your wall for its pleasing appearance, but also for its strength. Different bonds are illustrated on pages 78–79. The strongest brick walls have units arranged in such a way that all the perpendicular mortar joints between them are bridged by the courses above and below, avoiding potentially weak uninterrupted joints running through the wall. Some brick bonds have evolved because of their intrinsic strength, others as local traditions. Among them are the garden bonds, developed for freestanding garden walls that were fair-faced on both sides, relatively quick to construct, and useful for dealing with the irregular sizes of old handmade bricks. Garden bonds call for fewer uniform bricks of the exact length to pass from one face of a wall to the other. They are characterized by their greater number of stretcher (long side) courses in relation to header (short side) courses. You can subtly enhance the texture of the bond by the way you choose to finish the jointing between the courses of bricks.

JOINTING AND POINTING

The way the mortar joints are finished – jointed and pointed – has a profound effect on the appearance of any wall. The treatments can range from unobtrusive finishes of mortar coloured to match brickwork, to highly dramatic contrasting effects and textured profiles that create pronounced patterns and shadow-lines. Some are more cosmetic than practical, and in exposed gardens you should always make sure the finish is weatherproof. An inappropriate pointing style is also a sure give-away when you are trying to copy or replace an old wall, so examine any original models carefully at the outset of building.

Always choose mortar appropriate to the building materials you have chosen. The rule is that above damp-proof course level the mortar should always be weaker on setting than the building units. This makes it more flexible so that if any movement occurs, the remedy is to repair the mortar (often just by repointing) rather than to replace entire building units that have cracked.

PROPORTIONS OF A BRICK

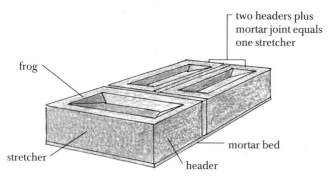

two headers plus
mortar joint equals
one stretcher

frog

stretcher

header

mortar bed

Proportions of a brick *are made so that the stretcher (the long side) equals the length of two headers (the short side) plus a perpendicular mortar joint. For purposes of calculation, four bricks plus four mortar joints stacked vertically equal 300mm(1ft) in height. Brick sizes vary, but a modern standard brick has a 215mm(8½in) stretcher, a 100mm(4in) header and a depth of 65mm(2½in). This allows for mortar joints of 10mm(³⁄₈in) for bedding and perpendicular joints.*

The difference between jointing and pointing is one of timing. Jointing is done as the wall is being constructed, and consists of finishing the mortar as it exudes from each course of bricks. Pointing is done as a separate operation on a finished wall, and is appropriate where, for example, a wall is to be finished with a more expensive mortar than that used for constructing it. As in repointing, it is also used where the joints of a wall need repairing. Joints are a standard 10mm(⅜in).

Some popular finishes of brick mortar joints appear in cross-section below. They are shown in contrasting colours for clarity and to illustrate how mortar colour affects the tonal values of the bricks. They also demonstrate how various profiles can emphasize or underplay the pattern of the joints.

RIGHT *In this low wall built of new bricks, the mortar joints have been slightly indented in a 'bucket-handle' style. The jointing has been very carefully executed and its neat appearance perfectly suits the modern, clean-lined look of the wall.*

BRICK MORTAR JOINTS

flush

Flush *is a bland finish that pitches rainwater straight off the wall and is excellent for exposed situations. Usually done by striking excess mortar off with a trowel, it can also be textured with a piece of wood or hessian.*

once-weathered

Once-weathered *has a sloping profile which helps water to drain off. The 2-3mm(¹/₁₆-⅛in) recess at the top creates shadow-lines under each course; vertical joints are sometimes struck flush so that the horizontal lines are emphasized.*

keyed

Keyed *is a more deeply impressed finish using a narrow curved tool. Keying makes attractive pronounced shadow-lines but is unsuitable for exposed sites.*

overpointed

Overpointed *has the mortar spread over the brick's faces. It gives good protection and weathers to an attractive rustic appearance. You can match mortar and brick colour or add texture by rubbing with hessian.*

bucket handle

Bucket handle *has a curving profile achieved with a rounded tool – originally a galvanized bucket handle. It gently emphasizes the shapes of individual bricks and is weatherproof.*

recessed

Recessed *is done with a special recessing tool that pushes the mortar back squarely between the bricks. Strong shadow-lines emphasize the brick courses dramatically. This is useful only in sheltered sites.*

LEFT *This attractive freestanding brick wall built in Flemish bond provides a perfect backdrop for climbing roses. In its role here of dividing the plot into separate areas, its height and design lend an air of substance to the garden, enhanced by the double arch in the same bricks.*

STRETCHER BOND

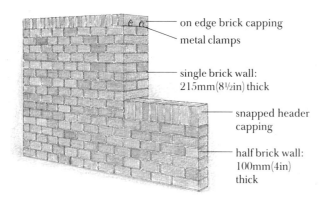

on edge brick capping

metal clamps

single brick wall: 215mm(8½in) thick

snapped header capping

half brick wall: 100mm(4in) thick

Stretcher bond *construction shows the long or stretcher face of the bricks. The perpendicular joints are centred on the stretchers. The taller section is one brick length thick. Invisible metal ties are placed in the mortar at intervals; the end brick is tied in with metal clamps. The lower section is a half brick thick, suitable only for low walls. Its stopped end uses half bricks and its capping is also made of half or 'snapped' bricks, the cut face set downward.*

HEADER BOND

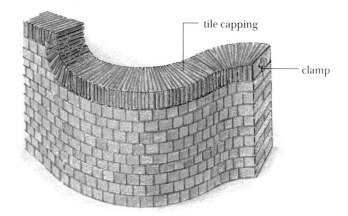

tile capping

clamp

Header bond, *with the short face visible, is useful for working around curves. Special curved bricks are available, but curves with an internal radius no smaller than 1.8m(6ft) can be achieved fairly smoothly using headers only in a single brick wall. The perpendicular mortar joints will inevitably be slightly wider at the convex face than on the concave side. Tiles on edge make a versatile capping for a curved wall.*

ENGLISH GARDEN BOND

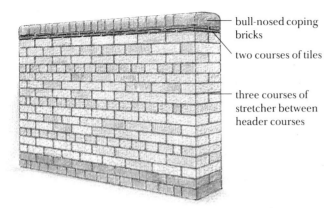

bull-nosed coping bricks

two courses of tiles

three courses of stretcher between header courses

English garden bond *has three (or any odd number of) stretcher courses sandwiched between single header courses. This ties the faces of the wall together. Two courses of tiles set flush with the wall face (the tiles could project), and a row of bull-nosed (rounded profile) coping bricks cap this wall.*

ENGLISH BOND

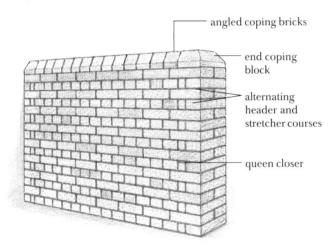

angled coping bricks

end coping block

alternating header and stretcher courses

queen closer

English bond *is used where strength is a high priority since it has the minimum of uninterrupted internal joints. It consists of alternating courses of headers and stretchers. To support and bridge the perpendicular joints between the stretchers at either end, a queen closer (a lengthwise cut brick) is inserted one brick in from each end. Here, special angled coping bricks protect the wall. A wider matching end block gives stability.*

FLEMISH GARDEN (SUSSEX) BOND

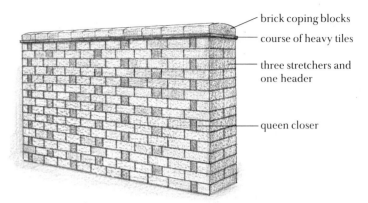

brick coping blocks

course of heavy tiles

three stretchers and one header

queen closer

Flemish garden (Sussex) bond *has a header between three stretchers. This attractive pattern features headers centred over the central stretcher brick. The capping is a single course of projecting heavy tiles beneath a row of brick copings. Queen closers (bricks cut in half lengthwise) at either end achieve the correct bond.*

FLEMISH BOND

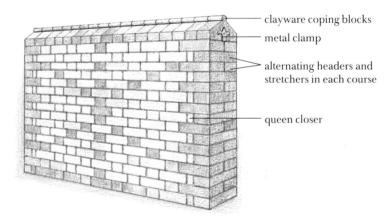

clayware coping blocks

metal clamp

alternating headers and stretchers in each course

queen closer

Flemish bond, *with stretchers and headers alternating in each course, gives a strong, more decorative wall. It requires queen closers (lengthwise cut bricks) in alternate courses to stagger the perpendicular joints. Traditionally, darker-coloured headers were used to make patterns; nowadays bricks of a different colour can be used for similar effects. Here, an ornamental baked blue clayware coping caps the wall, which contains some matching headers.*

NATURAL STONE WALLS

A stone wall gives a garden a marvellous sense of permanence. When choosing such a time-honoured building material, you will find that traditional styles are impossible to ignore. The multiplicity of stone types and of ways in which the stones are dressed or used in their natural state have given rise to a wide range of bonds.

The style of a stone wall can range from the ultimate in architectural formality through a variety of local vernacular forms to a random style using rustic dry stone or boulders. In the past, because only the best-quality stone tailored into geometrical blocks was transported any distance (and then only to construct the grandest edifices), it is walls of old stone that give a sense of place and relate best to their landscape. You worked with what you could find locally. If you lived in a region where good stone was quarried, even humble gardens might have regular neat stone walls. In some areas the stone was only partially cut to an even face, or not at all, creating walls with a coarser finish. Poorer qualities of stone might be built into free-standing structures using a dry stone technique, or mortared into walls with dressed stone (or brick) to give the ends, the corners and the capping stability. If there was no stone, you

used timber, made bricks, or built with mud to make walls of adobe, and so on. Interpreting this in today's terms, if there is no local tradition to follow and you want to use stone, choose a tailored, understated style of stone wall rather than a more fanciful structure that may look alien in its surroundings.

The principle of bonding a stone wall is the same as for brick – that at every opportunity a perpendicular joint should be bridged top and bottom by a stone. Unless you use expensive specially sawed stone blocks, the different sizes and shapes of the individual pieces make building stone walls somewhat more challenging.

As with brick you need to tie the two faces of the wall together. For this, bonders are placed at approximate intervals of 1 sq m (or 1 sq yard) on either face of the wall. These consist of stones long enough to penetrate about two-thirds of the width of the wall. The alternative is to use a long stone called a through-stone, which is more often associated with building dry stone walls. The length of these stones is equal to the thickness of the wall, and so they appear on both of the wall's faces.

When finishing the joints of a stone wall, you can either emphasize the shapes of the individual stones with deeply recessed joints, or bind them into a unified surface by bringing the mortar

STONE JOINT FINISHES

snail-trail

Snail-trail *makes a network of lines, creating the illusion that each stone is cut to match its neighbours. While the mortar is wet use a tool or small trowel to mark parallel lines along the joints, leaving a smooth intact band of mortar.*

round recessed

Round recessed *uses a wet pebble (or a bent pipe or plastic hose) to impress the wet mortar to a fairly deep recess. This makes strong shadow-lines between each stone.*

twice-weathered

Twice-weathered *gives a bird beak effect achieved using a pointed trowel to shape the mortar. This needs to be done expertly to look attractive.*

brushed

Brushed *finish is the one most commonly used in rustic styles of wall. Just before the mortar finally sets, remove the excess with a stiff wire brush.*

square recessed

Square recessed *finish is best used in conjunction with square or rectangular stones, and is made with a special tool. It gives dramatic shadow-lines.*

turf

Turf joints, *when soil or turf replaces mortar, are applicable only in rock gardens, or for a dry stone wall planted with a hedge. Ensure that soil in the jointing connects with the wall's earth core to keep plant roots moist.*

level with the face of the stones. Mortar and stone harmonize better when the mortar mix includes a good proportion of ground-up matching stone. Stone wall joints at 10-25mm(⅜-1in) are usually wider than those in brick walls.

As when using stone for paving, bear in mind whether your stone has any natural grain that is liable to crack if exposed to rain and frost. Generally, lay striated stone so that the grain runs horizontally. In cases where the grain runs vertically (such as the slate herringbone bond on page 82), make sure it has a capping of protective stones.

RIGHT *This mixed rubble and flint wall, with its simple water-proof mortar capping, has a traditional if rough-and-ready appearance. It looks well in informal situations such as this wild part of the garden where snowdrops have been allowed to naturalize themselves in a grassy area, and where small-leaved ivy is beginning to colonize the wall itself.*

UNCOURSED RANDOM RUBBLE WALL

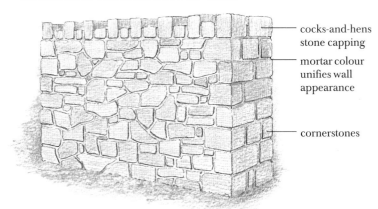

— cocks-and-hens stone capping

— mortar colour unifies wall appearance

— cornerstones

This uncoursed random rubble wall *uses honey-coloured sandstone rock of naturally random shape and size. The flatter side of each stone is used for the facing. Since the stones are uncoursed there are no horizontal lines. The result is an attractive chaos of shapes controlled by the more rectangular large stones used as cornerstones. More regular alternating stones are used for the capping in a style known as cocks-and-hens.*

COURSED RANDOM RUBBLE WALL

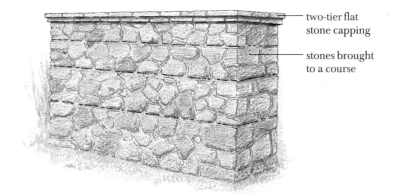

— two-tier flat stone capping

— stones brought to a course

This coursed random rubble wall *is of red sandstone. Here, the irregular pieces of stone are periodically brought to courses to give a more regular, layered effect. However, the rounded profiles of the stones give the face of the wall a strongly textured and rustic look. Following tradition, the bands of stone are deepest at the bottom and shallower towards the top. Pronounced shadow-lines are created by the two-tiers of flat capping stones.*

RANDOM HORIZONTAL THIN SECTION RUBBLE WALL

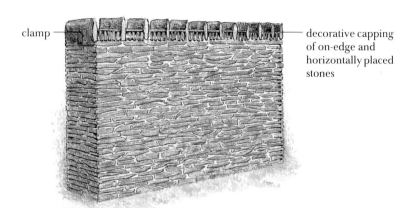

clamp

decorative capping of on-edge and horizontally placed stones

A random horizontal thin section rubble wall uses uncoursed stones that occur in thin strata such as slate and shale to give a naturally horizontal appearance. This deep grey-blue slate evokes the feeling of ripples on water. A clamp secures the decorative capping at the end.

THIN SECTION VERTICAL WALL

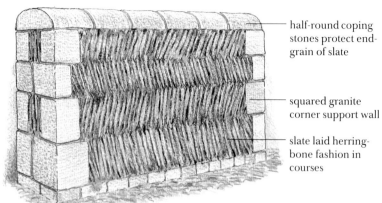

half-round coping stones protect end-grain of slate

squared granite corner support wall

slate laid herring-bone fashion in courses

This thin section vertical wall incorporates fairly equal-sized pieces of local stone occuring in thin strata with a stronger stone. The courses of vertical slivers of slate are arranged in an attractive shifting herringbone pattern and held in place by the coping and corner stones.

RANDOM SQUARED RUBBLE WALL

dressed stone coping blocks

stones left uncoursed

In a random squared rubble wall, a sophisticated version of the uncoursed random rubble wall on page 81, each square or oblong stone is a different size but they are cut at right angles. The larger corner stones are 'tooled'– their surfaces textured with marks made by tools. The dressed stone coping is a traditional shape often reproduced in imitation stone.

COURSED RANDOM SQUARED RUBBLE WALL

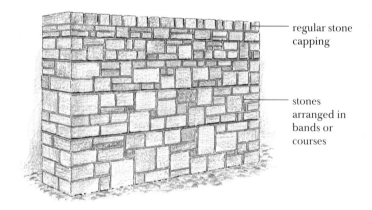

regular stone capping

stones arranged in bands or courses

In a coursed random squared rubble wall bands of random-sized square-cut stones are brought to the same level to form a distinct course before the next band is constructed. Deeper stones are placed at the bottom and narrower ones at the top, creating an interesting yet low-key effect. The simple capping uses matching stones cut to uniform thickness.

POLYGONAL RUBBLE WALL

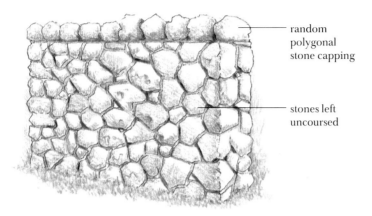

random polygonal stone capping

stones left uncoursed

A polygonal rubble wall is built from uncoursed hard, multi-faceted stone pieces. Some types of stone occur in deep seams and have to be blasted from the quarry thus producing their uneven appearance. Built into a wall the rocks produce an irregular surface full of character.

BOULDER WALL

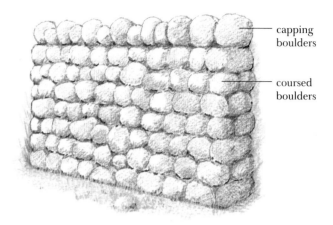

capping boulders

coursed boulders

A boulder wall is an obvious choice in areas in which water- or weather-worn boulders of fairly uniform size are plentiful. The more or less regular line of capping boulders sets the style. To ensure stability with these smooth rounded shapes, first dampen the boulders and key, or set, them well into the mortar.

KNAPPED FLINT WALL

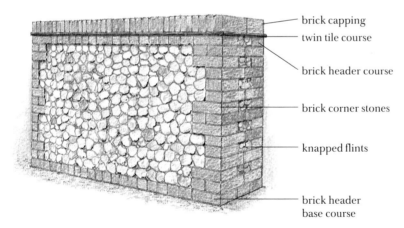

brick capping

twin tile course

brick header course

brick corner stones

knapped flints

brick header base course

A knapped flint wall in an attractive brick framework is traditional in areas where flints are common. The irregular flints are bonded in a lime mortar, which protects the body of the wall and contributes to the visual contrast. The flints are 'knapped' – a face cut flat and squarish, exposing the shiny interior. Whole or water-worn flints could be used to create a more uneven surface.

DRY STONE WALL

capping stones

cover band

slope

band of long through stones

wider base footing courses in trench

Dry stone walls traditionally follow land contours. They are built without mortar above a stone footing in an excavated trench. Local styles vary, but such walls are always thick relative to their height. Bonding stones are placed at regular intervals, either two-thirds of the wall's width or as 'through stones'. For extra stability, stones may be set sloping downward and inward.

CONCRETE BLOCKWORK WALLS

Concrete blocks often imitate various forms of natural stone used for walls, but an undisguised block or unit of concrete can make a handsome effect in the garden, particularly when linked with modern architecture. The endless permutations of texture, colour and shape allow you to design walls that are anything from unobtrusively functional to positively attention-seeking, and you can tailor the finish to tone with the surroundings.

Walls made of concrete blockwork need to take into account thermal movement, especially initial shrinkage. The greater the number of units in a wall area, the smaller the problem since the effects of expansion and contraction are to some extent absorbed by the frequent joints. Be sure to use a cement specially formulated for concrete blocks to make up a suitably soft and flexible mortar. Choose a style of jointing or pointing appropriate to the form of the block. Blocks resembling natural stone clearly call for authentic stone or rubble type joints. Clean mechanical shapes look better with more formal or minimal jointing.

Where two blockwork walls join at right angles, they are normally bonded. If walls meet at an intermediate T-junction, the two walls are 'butt-jointed' (side to end) and linked with specially manufactured metal rods or ties. This allows movement to take place without loss of structural strength. If piers are necessary to strengthen a blockwork wall, place them at intervals not exceeding twice the wall's height and make them at least twice the thickness of the main wall. Vertical thermal movement joints will also be needed (see the illustration for a wall built in sections on page 73).

LEFT *White-painted square concrete blocks are used for this high wall separating different compartments of a garden. The wall gives a dramatic, modern air to the garden and makes a good foil for tall plants, foliage and colourful irises.*

PLAIN CONCRETE BLOCKS

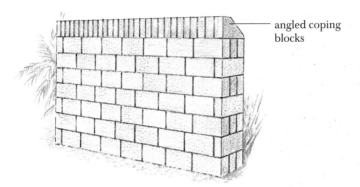

angled coping blocks

Plain concrete blocks *made from fine-grade aggregate have a smooth texture. The attractive shifting appearance of the face derives from the bond – successive rows overlap by one-third of a brick. Each unit is one-third of its length (the proportion of header to stretcher in a standard brick is one-half). Cross bonds stretch from one face to the other only at the wall ends, so parallel blocks would have to be linked internally with metal rods.*

IMITATION HIGH RELIEF STONE BLOCKS

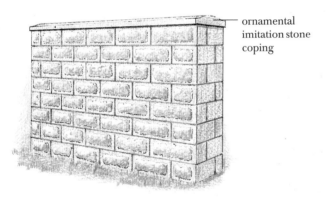

ornamental imitation stone coping

Imitation high relief stone blocks *copy a classic style of dressing or cutting natural stone. The face of each unit has a high-relief finish with the uneven convex centre surrounded by a smoother, tooled frame. Manufacturers of these blocks often imitate stone from specific sources and concrete block walls offer a fair approximation of a real stone wall at considerably less cost.*

CHAMFERED PROFILE BLOCKS

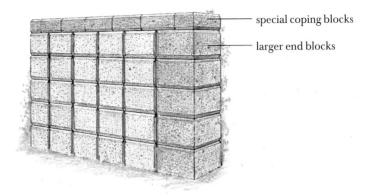

special coping blocks

larger end blocks

Chamfered profile blocks *demonstrate the versatility of concrete. Wall blocks and coping blocks of many sizes and shapes come in a range of predetermined colours and finishes. These blocks are textured by washing away surface cement to expose the aggregate. The chamfered edges, cut at an angle of $45°$, make a strong grid of shadow-lines, but the blocks do not bond or interlock and need internal reinforcing with metal rods.*

CONCRETE UNIT WALL

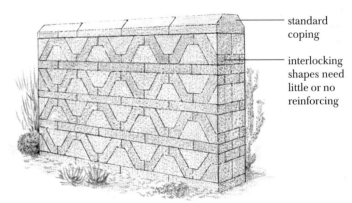

standard coping

interlocking shapes need little or no reinforcing

A concrete unit wall *may be designed and cast in a variety of interlocking shapes. Here three basic units combine with a standard coping in a lively and intriguing pattern. Narrow joints emphasize the design. Earth colours and a textured finish conjure a contemporary style. Make sure such assertive designs don't clash with nearby architecture.*

CAST CONCRETE WALLS

Panels of precast concrete and concrete poured on site into formwork, a mould of timber or board, offer further scope for interesting wall surfaces, often with an abstract feel.

Cast concrete works best in a modern setting where it doesn't conflict with more traditional materials and styles. It is most successful in dry climates because in areas of higher humidity disfiguring stains or algae are sometimes a problem. As with concrete blockwork, a range of different textures and colours is available, though where sunlight is intense some pigments may fade. You can also apply special concrete paints to improve or change the concrete's appearance or to ensure that it links with existing building materials or garden schemes.

For a particularly fine or detailed finish, sections are usually precast and then fixed to piers in their final position, either forming segments of the structure itself or are affixed to a backing, a supporting wall, of cheaper material. Precasting is normally done in horizontal moulds under carefully controlled conditions. Concrete poured at the site is cast in vertical moulds. Steel reinforcing bars can be incorporated for extra strength, and this stronger concrete is especially useful for retaining walls.

Special equipment and skills necessary for handling poured concrete put all but the simplest forms beyond the scope of most do-it-yourself garden designers. Complex patterns may need professionally made moulds. The concrete mix is specially formulated to be fluid in use yet strong when set, and must be well compacted and/or mechanically vibrated to remove air-pockets. A release agent ensures that the formwork is removed from the set concrete with minimal damage to finely detailed surfaces. You also need to allow for shrinkage once it sets and provide the usual thermal movement joints (see page 73).

RIGHT *A dramatic white wall acts as a good foil to spiky architectural foliage. Here the starkness of the wall – and the house behind – make a strong statement in a semi-arid setting. Concrete walls such as these are usually cast on site. The matching trelliswork is made of steel and painted white.*

POURED CONCRETE PANELS FROM TIMBER FORMS

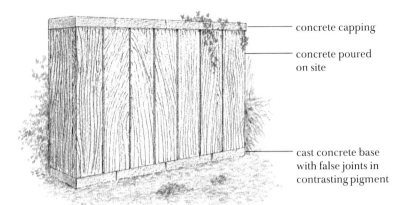

- concrete capping
- concrete poured on site
- cast concrete base with false joints in contrasting pigment

Poured concrete panels from timber forms *feature the texture of the rough-sawed planks used as the mould. The finish is appropriate to both rustic and urban settings. Each vertical section must be poured in a single operation. Horizontal forms would allow the concrete to be poured in layers corresponding to a panel width. The base is cast separately first, the capping last.*

MOULDED ABSTRACT SHAPES

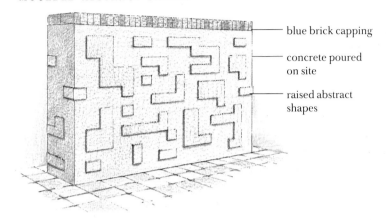

- blue brick capping
- concrete poured on site
- raised abstract shapes

Moulded abstract shapes *are made from a smooth concrete mix poured on site into a mould incorporating recessed abstract shapes. Raised motifs such as these can also be made as precast slabs and then fixed to a backing or supporting wall. The top here is finished with a row of blue clay engineering bricks, but could equally be cast in a contrasting-toned concrete.*

PRECAST AGGREGATE PANELS

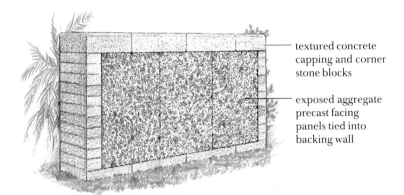

- textured concrete capping and corner stone blocks
- exposed aggregate precast facing panels tied into backing wall

Here, precast aggregate panels *are used as facing with lightly textured blocks for contrast, combining two construction methods. The base, the corner stones and the capping blocks frame an invisible backing wall built in standard blockwork. The precast facing panels need to be attached to the backing wall by means of ties or rods and also mortared in.*

RECESSED DIAMOND PATTERNS

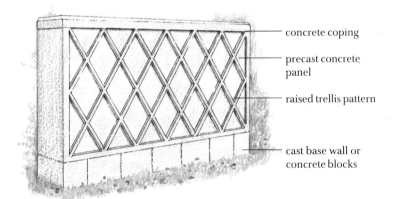

- concrete coping
- precast concrete panel
- raised trellis pattern
- cast base wall or concrete blocks

Recessed diamond patterns *are cast in a smooth concrete mix. The raised trellis-like pattern is achieved by means of a timber form incorporating a series of diamond shapes in relief. (Remember that the formwork or mould is always a negative of the finished wall face.) Patterns like this are best cast on site for a precast wall of this size would be difficult to transport.*

TIMBER WALLS

Timber makes an unusual but striking material for walls. It is a natural design choice for a garden made in a woodland clearing or where a group of trees forms a backdrop inside or outside the garden boundary. It could also offer a small consolation for the loss of one of your own trees, perhaps – provided the wood is of a suitably durable genus such as chestnut or oak.

Except in the form of a trellis or fence, timber is more often used for retaining than for freestanding walls. Apart from playing an obvious role in changes of level on a sloping site, timber can make an ideal frame for raised beds. Provide good foundations for timber walls as for masonry walls.

Choose a finish to suit the garden. Unless you want the most rustic of settings, this will almost invariably mean removing the bark and losing the rounded profile of the parent tree. Four-square planed planks stained with a translucent or opaque colour are sophisticated enough for a style-conscious town garden. Rough-sawn or hewn finishes have a more chunky, homespun quality. You can colour this wood, leave it in a natural state, or improve on nature with transparent stains or etching to enhance the grain.

To be viable, timber walls need to match brick or stone in bulk and mass. Most wood is bought already preserved (either by steeping in preservative or by the vacuum or pressure-treatment methods) to make it durable and resistant to weather and insect or fungal attack. Otherwise wood can be treated with preservative as necessary, but remember, the drier it can be kept, the longer it will last. While many wooden walls or fences can be constructed by the homeowner, construction of timber crib walling (shown far right below) is better left to a professional.

LEFT *Here, the robustly made wooden retaining wall which serves as a planting area, the steps and the deck have been designed as a uniform and satisfying whole. Hardwoods, though not cheap, are extremely durable in garden structures. They also have an integral warmth and an affinity with a wide variety of settings and plants and look particularly good in modern garden designs.*

VERTICAL SQUARE-SAWN TIMBERS

plank set in stone or concrete

Vertical square-sawn timbers in the main section of this retaining wall are protected with a capping board. For strength, set the planks in the ground to a quarter or a third of their depth in well-consolidated stone or concrete. The joints between the butted planks allow water to percolate through from the soil behind, but for better drainage drill a series of 25mm(1in) weep-holes near the wall's base. A 100-150mm(4-6in) thick layer of gravel separates the timber from the soil.

HORIZONTAL SQUARE-SAWN TIMBERS

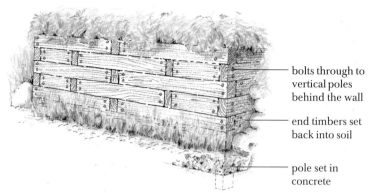

bolts through to vertical poles behind the wall

end timbers set back into soil

pole set in concrete

Horizontal square-sawn planks are used in a simple retaining wall for stability. Timbers project backward into the soil at right angles to the face of the wall. The end-grain forms an attractive counterpoint to the horizontal lines. Bolts screwed into holes secure the visible horizontal components to unseen vertical poles behind the timber wall. These poles are placed well below ground level, preferably in concrete. Good drainage is needed to keep this wall stable and prolong its life.

TREE TRUNK WALL

wood base set well into the ground

A tree trunk wall isn't sophisticated-looking, it's simply a series of sawn logs of varying length and diameter set firmly into the ground at different heights. The bark confirms the rustic effect, though you could use peeled, treated wood instead, but this would lack the casual simplicity. Walls such as these make good screening for utility areas. Children love them so consider using them to surround play equipment.

TIMBER CRIB RETAINING WALL

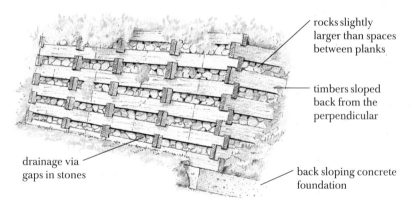

rocks slightly larger than spaces between planks

timbers sloped back from the perpendicular

drainage via gaps in stones

back sloping concrete foundation

Timber crib retaining walling, sold in kit form, is ideal for a sloping terrain. It is based on interlocking horizontal timbers set parallel and sloped backward. As the wall is constructed, the spaces between the rows of timbers are filled with rocks just larger than the gaps between the front timbers. A concrete foundation provides a level starting surface, necessary since the system relies on its own weight and super-efficient drainage to retain the soil.

FENCES

The choice of style, stature and materials for fencing depends on the prevailing architecture and on where in the garden the fence runs, and also on whether it is intended to keep people and animals in or out. Fences are generally a quicker and less costly option than building a wall or growing a hedge. In fact, a simple post-and-rail fence may provide a temporary solution while you take your time deciding on a more permanent barrier. A well-built fence can last a lifetime, but keep in mind that any wood will need periodic applications of preservative or paint, while a wall once built needs little attention.

Some fences merely mark a boundary or internal garden division and need little intrinsic strength, but others must be designed to withstand horses and cattle. In these cases, match high-quality materials, including the fence supports, to a suitable design. Even the most functional fences can be attractive, and many can be camouflaged or made more effective with plant material.

Palisades or palings form a more or less continuous pattern of vertical units; other fences are based on boards or panels of varying length, suspended between posts that form part of the rhythm of the design. Plan the intervals of such fences carefully to work well in your situation. Try to avoid awkwardly stepped fences on slopes and remember that complex formal designs based on broad pattern repeats require a level, regular site. The more elaborate the design, the more important it is to base it on even divisions.

PICKET FENCES

Nothing epitomizes a country garden better than a picket fence. Whether plain or decorative, part of its charm is to offer tantalizing glimpses of the garden within and play host to climbers, particularly roses. Picket fences are also functional: the vertical gaps filter the wind, making them a better choice than more solid fencing for exposed sites. A tall, substantially built fence with a pointed or spiked top makes an effective security barrier.

Scale the fence to suit the garden. Posts must be of sufficient size to accommodate the combined thickness of pickets and rails, and should be spaced at intervals of about 1.8m(6ft). Width, thickness, height and spacing of pickets depend upon individual requirements. You could use boards from 10mm(³⁄₈in) to 25mm(1in) thick, for example. The stouter and more closely spaced the pickets, the stronger the fence (and the higher the costs). If you want a light, decorative-looking fence for separating an internal garden area, achieve this effect by choosing lighter and wider-spaced pickets.

Strong supporting posts, usually square or rectangular in section, should be set well into the ground in consolidated stone or concrete. Two or more horizontal rails, called arris rails, which are often triangular-shaped in section, are fixed into the posts, and the vertical pickets are attached to these using rust- and corrosion-proof nails or screws. The posts and arris rails always run on the owner's side of the fence.

Leave the wood in its natural state – treated with preservative unless a hardwood – or choose a stain or colour to suit the surroundings. Paint will need freshening every other year, or you could opt for one of the many pigmented preservatives available today. If possible, have all the posts, rails and pickets pre-treated before construction to make them more durable.

POST FIXINGS

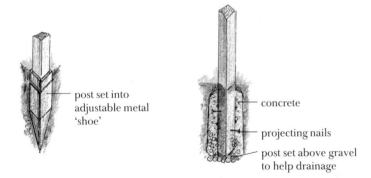

post set into adjustable metal 'shoe'

concrete

projecting nails

post set above gravel to help drainage

Post fixings *need care to ensure that all fences and gates are stable. Set supporting posts into the ground firmly either by using a metal post 'shoe' or set directly into concrete. Setting a shoe in concrete is also preferable as a shoe sometimes twists if driven directly into the ground, making alignment of posts difficult.*

ACORN-TOPPED PICKETS AND POSTS

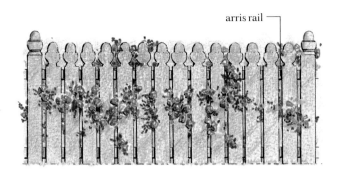

arris rail

Acorn-topped pickets and posts use a traditional motif cut in outline on the pickets and turned into a handsome finial to crown the square-sectioned posts. The dark red tones of sweet-smelling 'Etoile de Holland' roses make a bold statement against this green painted fence.

POINTED (OR ARROW) PICKETS

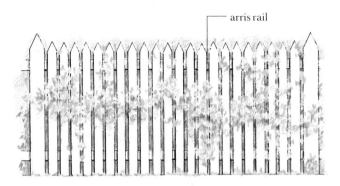

arris rail

Pointed (or arrow) pickets, where pickets and matching posts have pointed tops, are classically simple. They provide good security as long as they are too closely set to offer any foothold on the arris rails. Here, smart white paint shows up a yellow rose such as 'Golden Showers', which thrives in light shade.

CONCAVE-TOPPED DOUBLE PICKETS

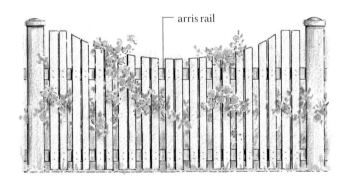

arris rail

These concave-topped double pickets have round posts with decorative caps supporting pickets arranged in twos, with wider spaces separating each pair. The tops of the pickets form a graceful curve. A washed-out blue-green preservative makes an ideal foil for an apricot rose such as the scented 'Gloire de Dijon', which is trained through and over the fence.

CHEVRON AND DIAMOND PIERCED PICKETS

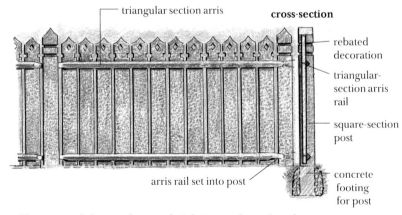

triangular section arris

cross-section

rebated decoration

triangular-section arris rail

square-section post

arris rail set into post

concrete footing for post

Chevron and diamond pierced pickets are shown here from the rear. Stout square posts set well into the ground are made stable with compacted stone or, preferably, concrete. Two triangular arris rails are set with a mortise joint into the posts and the pickets are screwed to them. A dark chestnut-coloured wood preservative emphasizes the fence's decorative qualities.

PALISADES

A palisade is essentially a row of closely set vertical poles or stakes. They may be peeled or have their bark still on; they are either placed into the ground individually or fixed to arris rails that are supported by posts preferably set in concrete (see *pointed palisade* below). Designs are traditionally plain and functional, often with pointed tops conveying a 'keep out' message. To viewers inside the garden, the arris rails offer some relief to the uncompromisingly upright effect of the wall itself. The rounded shape of the poles sets up a satisfying rhythm of vertical shadow-lines, and this can be exploited by some decorative treatments.

RIGHT *A traditional palisade is here made by placing individual poles in the ground. It makes a charming support for the rambling rose 'New Dawn' and a backdrop for a herbaceous border containing love-in-a-mist and phormiums. The straight-topped poles soften the traditional stockade appearance.*

POINTED PALISADE

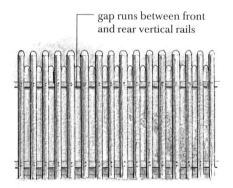

cross-section

half-round arris rails

post set in concrete

*A **pointed palisade** is shown in its original simple form with the tops of the poles sharpened to points and the bark left intact. This fence has an earthy, practical quality that suits it to garden boundaries in today's equivalent of frontier territory, where potential intruders are to be deterred. The impact can be softened by trimming the poles into perfect, smooth rounds.*

DECORATIVE PALISADE

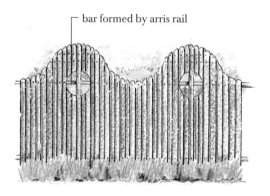

bar formed by arris rail

*A **decorative palisade** has the top trimmed to a wave pattern, and the individual stakes, stripped of bark, have been finished with rounded rather than pointed tops to create a more friendly impression. Circular windows have been cut into the upward curves of the palisade, their horizontal bars formed by the half-round supporting arris rail running along the back of the fence.*

HIT-AND-MISS PALISADE

gap runs between front and rear vertical rails

Hit-and-miss palisade *is a simple application of the principle seen in the post and rail fences in which poles are alternated at the front and rear of the support to filter wind while screening the view. Here, the verticals are half-round halved stakes in two lengths attached on either side of rectangular horizontal rails. The stakes are peeled with rounded tops.*

BAMBOO

Versatile bamboo offers refreshing alternatives to less heavy-duty forms of wooden fencing. It is intrinsically decorative. In its natural state the smooth, graceful stems are relieved at intervals with attractive nodal marks and slight ridges, and its textural qualities are brought out by a variety of manufacturing techniques. Large poles, smaller canes and branching stems combine with canes that have been halved, split or flattened to make a diversity of styles.

The plainer forms of fencing have a handsome, neutral quality that can look good in a wide spectrum of contexts – urban or rural, formal or informal, large or small scale. A few are based on simple oriental screens, while others are very decorative.

RIGHT *Slender canes of bamboo, tied together with wire and braced by more substantial horizontal canes, give this fence a delicate, screen-like appearance. Bamboo also complements the oriental style of the layout and planting of the garden.*

WOVEN BAMBOO

decorated lead or zinc post caps

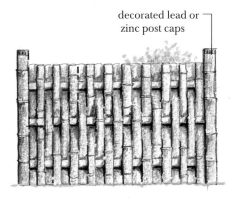

*A **woven bamboo** fence of large poles split in half lengthways and woven makes a heavily textured fence. The panels are attached to sturdy posts, which are sealed against the weather by ornamental metal caps. Plain, earthy textures and sculptural plant shapes would complement this robust fencing in a town or country garden.*

VERTICAL BAMBOO

bamboo capping

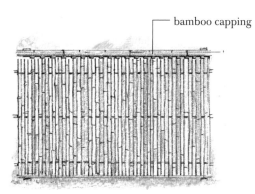

Vertical bamboo *is a simple and popular fencing material, neutral in texture and suitable for many styles of garden. It consists of stout bamboo uprights tied together with natural fibre or wires with horizontal bracing canes at the rear. The support posts are stout stakes of bamboo or other durable timber.*

TIED BAMBOO

fibre ties

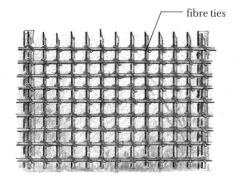

Tied bamboo *consists of an attractive lattice of equally spaced upright and horizontal canes bound with natural fibre ties. Here, the cane tops are cut to sharp points to give greater security. For lower fences or internal garden screens, you could cut the tops flat. Stakes driven well into the ground support the fence sections.*

POST AND RAIL FENCING

Post and rail (or post and board) fencing offers variations on the theme of extending or fixing individual pieces of wood between a series of posts set securely into the ground. In this category come some of the most practical kinds of stockproof fencing for gardens next to a paddock or pasture. Build these of sturdy timbers, with the posts well set in concrete if necessary, to withstand the considerable pressure that horses and cattle may impose. The rustic look of split wood offers an alternative to the handsome, functional lines of sawn timbers. In more domestic settings, you can opt for overtly decorative effects. Hardwood rails may be left untreated, but softwood needs preservative treatment.

SAWN POST AND RAIL

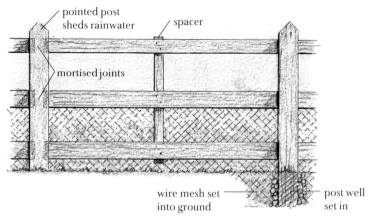

Sawn post and rail fence pieces are sawn to precise dimensions, resulting in smooth, even surfaces. The rails are mortised into the posts, their number and spacing depending on what needs to be kept out. You can add an intermediate vertical spacer between the supporting posts for extra stability. To exclude smaller animals or poultry, attach wire mesh to a horizontal rail, sinking it below ground level to foil burrowers such as rabbits.

SPLIT RAIL

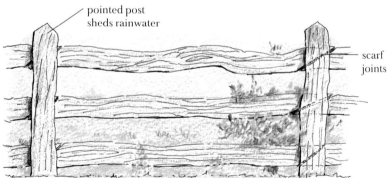

Split rail fences are eminently suited to a rustic setting. Hardwood is split into appropriate dimensions to make strong square-section posts and thick rails which retain the wavy profiles of the parent tree. The rail ends are cut at angles to make overlapping joints known as scarf joints in the vertical slots cut through the posts.

ABOVE *The elegant design of this white-painted fence perfectly suits the town garden setting. Two lengths of thin vertical board are arranged alternately in sections between the posts, and boards and posts are topped with stylish horizontal capping.*

HIT-AND-MISS

cross-section

alternating
boards
either side

concrete foundation appropriate
for all solid fences

Hit-and-miss fences have horizontal planks attached to alternate sides of the vertical posts. Visually the fence forms a solid barrier offering complete privacy, but the gaps between the boards filter the wind and make this a good choice for enclosure in exposed sites. In a variation on the hit-and-miss theme, the alternating boards are arranged vertically, and fixed on either side of horizontal rails.

DECORATED VERTICAL BOARD

base board

Decorated vertical board demonstrates how traditional principles can be adapted to create original fencing. Spaced vertical boards placed over a base board are finished with an elegant curved capping which might complement adjacent architecture. The posts' rounded tops echo this curve. This fence is painted white, but you could choose any high-quality finish that harmonizes with your surroundings.

DIAGONAL BOARDS

protective capping

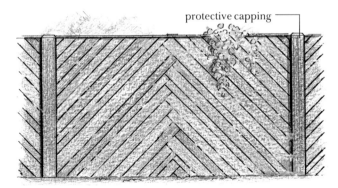

Diagonal boards display the texture of timber well. Boards or slats of unequal width are arranged diagonally and attached to unseen horizontal arris rails at the rear. Adjacent strips of wood here are treated with different-toned preservatives, though a single colour could be used. A horizontal wood capping protects the end-grain of the diagonal boards and provides a neat finish.

CONCERTINA SPLIT POLES

pole set in
ground

Concertina split poles are a useful lightweight fencing. They can be bought ready-made and look good in many situations. The sections of fence will open and close like a concertina, so that the diamond trellis can vary in height. The half-round split poles, which are bought pinned together, are driven into the ground to support the latticework.

PANEL FENCES AND PALINGS

With the exception of the chestnut palings, which are made in a strip and sold in rolls, these traditional fences are manufactured in panel sections which are designed to be attached to evenly spaced posts. Many of them are time-honoured designs derived from the woven hedge fences called hurdles that farmers used as permanent or temporary barriers. While some of them remain best suited to a rural setting, most of the slat and closeboard panel fences look equally good in urban gardens.

SPLIT CHESTNUT PALING

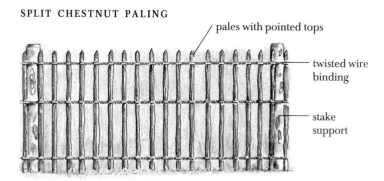

pales with pointed tops

twisted wire binding

stake support

Split chestnut paling uses straight branches split into pales or stakes of roughly triangular section measuring about 25-30mm (1-1¼in) on each face and cut to a point. Twisted wire binds the pales into a strip which is wired to supporting round or square posts driven into the ground. Sold in rolls, palings can be used as a temporary fence while building a wall or waiting for a hedge to grow. A particular advantage of palings is that they can be deployed around tight curves.

HAZEL WATTLE

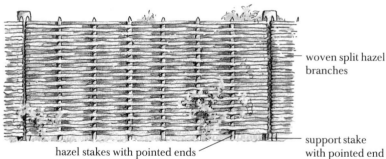

woven split hazel branches

hazel stakes with pointed ends

support stake with pointed end

Hazel wattle fencing, is made from a frame of stakes interwoven with flexible split hazel branches about 25mm(1in) thick. Each wattle panel is normally attached to strong pointed support stakes driven into the ground. The original use of these light portable fences was for temporary pens for herding sheep. Available in various sizes, and with a life of about eight years, they make ideal instant furnishing for a new garden where more permanent barriers will eventually be erected.

ABOVE *A gently zigzagging fence protects the peonies from the play area. This simple panel fence with overlapping horizontal slats has a vertical batten in the centre of the panels for additional strength.*

OSIER WATTLE

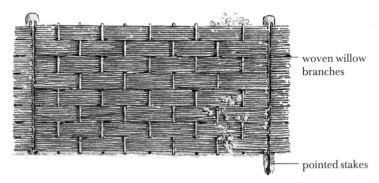

woven willow branches

pointed stakes

Osier wattle fencing is similar to hazel wattle, but derives from low-lying areas abundant in osiers – a species of willow specially cultivated and 'coppiced' (cut back and regrown) for its wand-like branches. The suppler, thinner osier branches are used whole and woven in blocks rather than individually, producing an attractive basketweave pattern. Osier's finer texture gives a less rough-and-ready character than its hazel equivalent; consider it for shelter around a sitting area.

INTERWOVEN SLATS

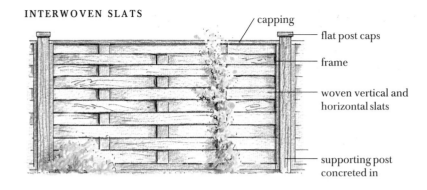

capping

flat post caps

frame

woven vertical and horizontal slats

supporting post concreted in

Interwoven slats of wood about 65mm(2½in) wide make up the main weave in these mass-produced panels. The surrounding frame is additionally braced by vertical battens at the rear. The supports may be capped timber or slotted concrete posts, both concreted in. The quality of this kind of fencing varies from extremely good to very poor, with flimsy slats weakened by frequent knots in the wood. Different-sized panels are available, and the wood is amenable to a wide range of coloured stains.

OVERLAP PANELS

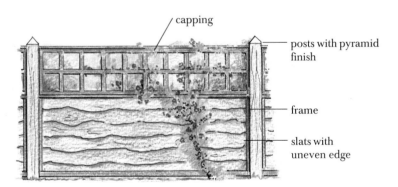

capping

posts with pyramid finish

frame

slats with uneven edge

Overlap panel fences are widely available in a range of sizes and qualities. The panels are in many ways similar to the interwoven slat style of fencing. The slats overlap horizontally in the frame against vertical battens at the rear. The slats sometimes have straight edges, but more often are used as sawn from the wood. The resulting uneven or 'waney' edge gives a decorative, rustic look. Here, an overlap panel is topped with a section of square trellis, relieving the hard line of the fence top.

CLOSEBOARD

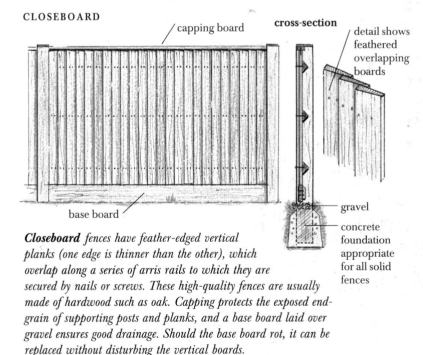

capping board

cross-section

detail shows feathered overlapping boards

base board

gravel

concrete foundation appropriate for all solid fences

Closeboard fences have feather-edged vertical planks (one edge is thinner than the other), which overlap along a series of arris rails to which they are secured by nails or screws. These high-quality fences are usually made of hardwood such as oak. Capping protects the exposed end-grain of supporting posts and planks, and a base board laid over gravel ensures good drainage. Should the base board rot, it can be replaced without disturbing the vertical boards.

METAL FENCES AND RAILINGS

At the other extreme from split rail or panel fences are the imposing façades of wrought iron railings which guard the boundaries of many urban and country gardens or decorate balconies. Designs may be specific to a local historical style, so try to maintain the integrity of a period house. Look at neighbouring architecture that retains its original ironwork and choose your own appropriately. Where you are not bound by a need for authenticity, choose a plain, unassuming design or break new ground with an entirely modern effect. Occasionally a handsome period design works in a bland modern context as a decorative feature, so check with architectural salvage companies for interesting pieces. Reproductions offer an alternative. Period cast-iron designs are reproduced in newer alloys, but most need regular maintenance with paint. Other options are black, brown or green vinyl-coated fences.

Metal fences, from wire netting to chain link, offer the ultimate in utilitarian design. They are useful where gardens border countryside or no-man's-land, or as a boundary for internal garden divisions such as tennis courts and other special games areas.

CHAIN LINK FENCES

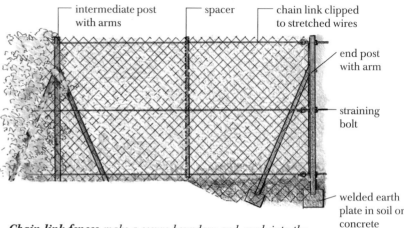

Chain link fences make a secure boundary and, sunk into the ground, provide a barrier against burrowing animals. Vinyl-coated fences in dark green or black blend with the background better than a galvanized finish, and planting an evergreen such as ivy gives further disguise. Posts may be of wood, concrete or angle-iron as shown here. Welded earth plates give stability.

ABOVE *Painted metal railings can look attractive in their own right, but they also make an excellent support for sun-loving clematis (here, C. alpina 'Frances Rivis') and other climbers, especially when flower and railing colour harmonize.*

CONTINUOUS BAR FENCE

cross-sections

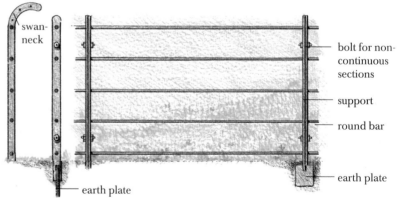

Continuous bar fences of long railings drawn through holes drilled in vertical supports were traditional on country estates and farms. They were erected on site by blacksmiths. Now, they are sold in sections and bolted together. Uprights sometimes have a curving swan-neck threaded with wire or barbed wire.

LOOPED IRON RAILINGS

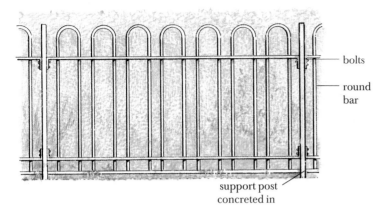

bolts

round bar

support post concreted in

Looped iron railings *are graceful either on their own or in conjunction with a hedge. These looped iron round bars are also known as unclimbable railings because they are spaced too narrowly for anyone to gain a foothold. They pass through horizontal strips which are in turn bolted to steel supporting posts. These are concreted into the ground for stability.*

DECORATIVE FORGED FENCING

brick column on foundation

Decorative forged fencing *often uses flowers and plant forms for inspiration; here, a modern interpretation reminiscent of Art Nouveau spans the spaces between supporting brick columns. Individual panels made in beaten and forged steel or bronze are handmade by commission, and make an effective barrier and a bold design statement.*

'ROMANESQUE' RAILINGS

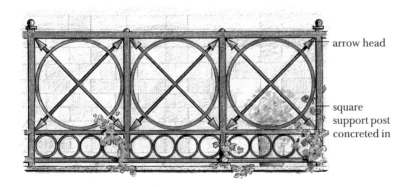

arrow head

square support post concreted in

'Romanesque' railings *use a repeating motif made of steel rods typical of a style used for balconies and street level railings. Cast iron has a similar though often rather heavier decorative effect. Paint in a colour to match adjoining woodwork or in handsome shades of black or dark green.*

SPEAR-HEADED RAILINGS

cast-iron or aluminium head

round support post concreted in

intermediate support post

Spear-headed railings *have a surprising affinity with evergreen hedging or other adjacent plant material. The traditional iron bars with cast-iron heads are now more often made in cast aluminium. However, when painted (black is the traditional colour) these are indistinguishable from the real thing.*

GATES AND APERTURES

Gates, grilles and open screens offer access to what lies beyond a solid wall or fence. When well-designed as a handsome piece of garden furnishing, these apertures add to the atmosphere, whether they provide a way through, an invitation to explore or just a tantalizing glimpse of the garden. Screens, including trelliswork, are valuable where a solid vertical structure would seem too enclosing (for example in small spaces), yet where some measure of protection is desirable. Another advantage is their wind-filtering role, making them particularly useful in open windswept areas. In more confined spaces they help to counteract turbulence.

SCREENS

The degree of openness of a screen depends on its design: the size of the apertures, the thickness of the units and the angle at which it is viewed. Some screens have apertures so small that anything on the far side is virtually indistinguishable. Yet all screens counteract a sense of claustrophobia by suggesting space beyond. They also hide unsightly features such as compost heaps or dustbins.

Materials for ready-made screens are as varied as those for walls and should be chosen to harmonize with nearby structures. They can be decorative in their own right, or sober and functional, perhaps serving as support for plants. As for walls, a deep foundation approximately twice the width of the supporting structure is essential for freestanding screens. Damp-proofing of two courses of engineering bricks at the foot of brick base walls is advisable.

For exposed terraces, balconies and roof gardens, toughened glass is a good screening material. It combines the benefits of an uninterrupted view with protection from wind. The glass may be tinted and/or textured, and could incorporate an ultra-violet screen. When glass is used anywhere, strict safety rules apply and the framing and fixings must be dealt with by a professional.

PIERCED BRICK

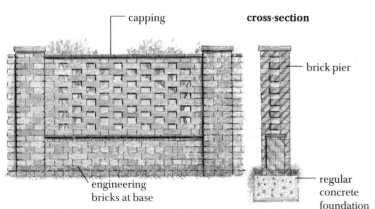

Pierced brick screens are constructed like a normal wall between supporting piers with capping that is both functional and decorative. As the section shows, the upper screen portion is only one brick thick, viable provided the work is well bonded or mechanically tied in to the piers. The screen effect is achieved by omitting the headers from a Flemish bond pattern (see page 79).

PIERCED CONCRETE UNITS

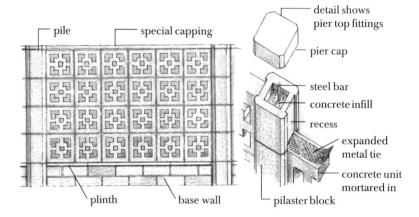

Pierced concrete units in various colours, textures and patterns are complete in themselves (as shown here), or are based on units of four. Since the units are stacked in a potentially weak construction with uninterrupted horizontal and vertical joints, expanded metal ties are laid between courses and tie the units into the piers, made from pre-constructed concrete pilaster blocks.

RIDGE TILES

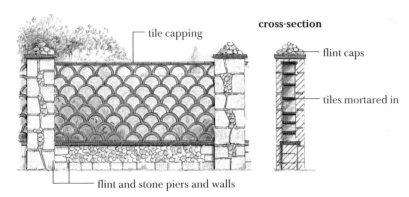

cross-section

TERRACOTTA UNITS

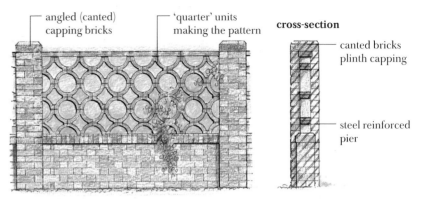

cross-section

Ridge tiles *make a highly decorative screen when mortar-bonded and arranged in alternating rows in a fishscale pattern. The supporting base wall and piles combine natural stone with knapped or whole flints, and are capped with tiles that match the ridge tiles for a harmonious effect. Whole flints attached with mortar decorate the pier caps.*

Terracotta units *are available in a number of styles. The example here is based on a single curved unit with flattened ends. When mortared together, four units make a circle that alternates with the negative shape of a curved diamond. Piers and a low base wall, to protect the terracotta from damp and mud splashing, are essential.*

TIMBER BOARDS

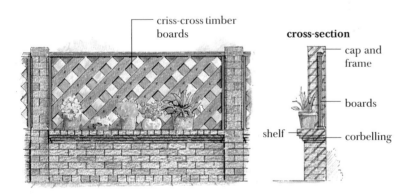

cross-section

ALUMINIUM-FRAMED GLASS

Timber boards *may be fixed together with studs in a simple criss-cross pattern like a substantial trellis. The dark green paint has a stylish look, but alternative treatments with less upkeep include staining or using more weather-resistant wood such as pressure-treated timber. Properly framed and capped, these boards are supported between brick piers on a low wall. Tiles have been corbelled, or stepped, outward to support a raised plant shelf.*

Aluminium-framed glass *allows a view to be enjoyed while providing a protective screen. The height of the toughened glass will vary according to circumstances. Here, it is designed to shelter people seated on a balcony. A handrail is provided for convenience and additional safety. The supports are fibreglass columns, but they could be made of timber or stone, which in turn hold up a timber beam garlanded with a climbing plant.*

GATES

Like the door to your house, a gate is a focal point of the design. Some gates are dictated by existing vertical structures on either side. Iron railings and picket fences, for instance, usually have matching gates since those made of a different material or in a different style would clash. Masonry walls of brick, stone, concrete, stucco and so on provide opportunities for specially created gates.

The design, material and finish of gates is best linked with any nearby architecture. Timber offers many styles, traditional and innovative, from adaptations of functional field gates to solid, door-like constructions, and with the natural look of wood or various painted finishes. Choose gate fixtures such as catches, hinges and locks to harmonize with the overall effect. Metal, the principal alternative, does not have the domestic connotations of timber, but is by no means limited to traditional ironwork styles. You can finish light modern steel and aluminium structures in paint colours or in a range of metallic effects such as bronze.

Hanging a gate or pair of gates is a skilled operation, and the larger the gate, the greater the skill needed. Even a small gate exerts considerable forces on the supporting posts or columns, so these need to be strong and properly placed on a foundation. You should set timber supports well down into concrete. Build stone or brick piers around a central steel bar or girder set into the concrete foundation. A gatepost or pier has to move only the merest fraction to make a gate crooked, and therefore unable to function properly.

LEFT *Acorn-topped pickets and gate are charmingly curved to echo the curves of the filigree panels of the verandah beyond. With a little creative thought, this simple fence and matching gate are given great style, enhanced by the grand supporting posts with finial tops.*

ARCHED WINDOW GATE

An arched window gate has a sense of mystery increased by the step-down approach. The tongue-and-groove structure gives a solid look, emphasized by the plain stuccoed wall. A graceful focal point is created by the echoing curves of door, wall and window.

JAPANESE STYLE TWO-LEAF GATE

This Japanese-style two-leaf gate is made of light wood. The frame is painted and the panels are stained to show off the grain. The shell-shaped windows permit a glimpse of the interior. Plain rendered walls on either side enhance the simplicity of the design.

WOODEN GATE WITH TUDOR TOP

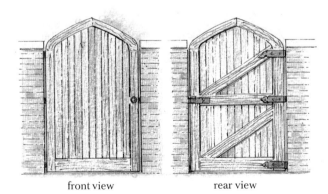

front view   rear view

A wooden gate with Tudor top made of brown-stained timber has vertical tongue-and-groove boards set in a frame. Diagonal cross-bracing on the rear prevents distortion. The shaped top lends a note of distinction and looks good in many situations. A gate such as this needs the support of strong side walls. The hinges are of a size and strength to bear the considerable weight.

SIX-BARRED FIELD GATE

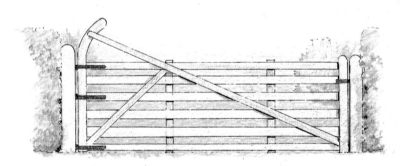

A six-barred field gate is a traditional type of gate which varies with locality. Five or six horizontal bars are supported diagonally (and sometimes vertically). Stout supporting posts at either end and substantial hinges bear the considerable weight of the gate. Elegant versions of field gates have strayed from the countryside into the suburbs to grace driveways.

DOUBLE METAL GATES

Double metal gates *for a main entrance can be elegant and utilitarian. The modern equivalents of wrought iron are usually welded tubular or square-section steel. The weight of such large gates means that they need to be hinged to steel girders embedded in the centre of the supporting columns or piers.*

MOON GATE

This moon gate *with long strap hinges is finished with bronze-patina-effect paint. Opened, it forms a simple circle of space; closed, it gives a contemplative, mantra-like focus. The three long hinges on one side are necessary to support and open the gate and also form part of the design.*

SQUARE-SECTION METAL GATES

Square-section metal gates *offer glimpses into the garden beyond and use square-section steel (metal that in cross-section has a square shape) to advantage. The angled top is appropriate to both the trellis design and the metal itself, as curves in steel are difficult to achieve without distortion.*

ORNAMENTAL GATES WITH A CANOPY

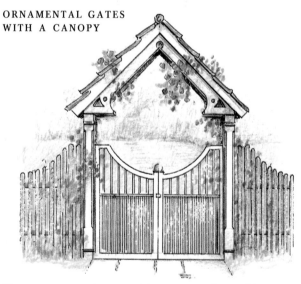

These ornamental gates with a canopy *show a Victorian-style exuberance that can be entirely appropriate in the right context. These gates continue the picket fence theme, but the detailing of the canopy's tiles and the decoration of its wooden frame should repeat those on the house. The canopy requires substantial support posts.*

GRILLES AND WINDOWS

Like non-solid gates and trelliswork, grilles and window-like apertures in walls permit tempting glimpses of what lies beyond, and also make a tall, functional barrier look lighter and more interesting. In the southern United States, Central and South America, southern Europe and Middle Eastern countries, metal window grilles are an important part of the local architecture, improving security while allowing ventilation. In their material and styling grilles have much in common with metalwork gates. Some of the most interesting and appropriate grilles result from a reinterpretation of the traditional styles in modern materials such as square-section steel, which has a square shape in cross-section. Otherwise, grilles for modern gardens may break new ground, creating designs perfectly integrated with their surroundings.

RIGHT *An opening behind an attractive stone seat lightens the solidity of this mellow stone wall and provides tantalizing views of the garden. The opening, which is entirely of stone, resembles a castle window and suits the ancient appearance of the wall.*

VERTICAL PANELS WITH A SINUOUS MOTIF

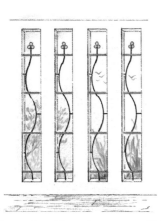

Vertical panels with a sinuous motif *introduce an elegant vertical emphasis into a stuccoed wall. The sinuous metal strips topped with a trefoil make an allusion to the Art Nouveau style, which is perfectly suited to a garden setting.*

SQUARE-SECTION METAL GRILLE

This square-section metal grille *has an intricate outline contained by the wall design. Square-section steel is ideal for designs based on squares and diagonals. The silhouetted cat motif could be another design element of choice.*

CURVILINEAR GRILLES

Curvilinear grilles *use patterns based on circles and curves, echoed by semi-circular capping tiles along the wall. The spiralling shapes on the left have an airy, traditional feel, while the overlapping circles are more modern.*

DECORATIVE STRUCTURES

To be outdoors in the open air but at the same time enclosed and surrounded by plants is one of the pleasures of a garden arbour, pergola, arched walkway, gazebo or summerhouse. Looking out from within, the device of a rectangular or arched frame draws attention to the view of the garden or vista beyond. This frame can also support a range of climbing plants, many with beautiful scented flowers that will be at the right height to delight the senses.

Bold linear structures are garden dividers on a grand scale and need plenty of space. Because they are almost always based on straight lines, they are an integral part of the geometry of the garden layout. When a pergola encloses a path, for example, it becomes a key feature. In a large formal layout, this could be placed along a central path. In a small or narrow garden, it would be better along a side path running parallel to (and balanced by) a boundary wall.

Large garden structures have to be built to withstand wind, weather and the weight of plant mass. They should be proportioned to the scale of the garden. The building principles for pergolas and tunnels can be applied to many other garden constructions. Instead of a long series of arches, you could design a small square feature where two paths cross. A slightly larger version, made of two or three spans of horizontals over uprights, creates a shady sitting area; when built against a boundary or house wall, it becomes an outdoor room. Pergolas, trelliswork and other structures can be adapted for *trompe l'oeil* effects to increase the sense of space. Where space is limited, a decorative structure can be in two rather than three dimensions. You can make an attractive airy screen or garden divider from a line of uprights linked with looped ropes that will support climbing plants.

LEFT *This substantial pergola supports climbing roses which give welcome dappled shade to the stone patio. Its clean lines and light colour give the whole structure a fresh and airy feeling. The moulded tops of the uprights add just a touch of elegance.*

PERGOLAS

Pergolas originated as a framework for climbing plants such as grapevines. Some are designed on a massive scale with stout masonry columns and sturdy overhead beams. More compact versions work in smaller gardens. In a very small plot it is best to modify a pergola-type construction and run it along a boundary wall because a large structure placed in the centre of a small area could cramp the space. You can scale down the elements of a pergola only so far: the proportions are always ruled by the height, which must be tall enough to allow an adult to walk upright.

The width of a pergola or tunnel depends on the space available and the effect you want. A minimum of about 1.5m(5ft) allows two people to walk comfortably through side by side. For a really grand layout multiply this by up to three, though this width calls for a massive structure with 4.5m(15ft) cross-beams. Remember that the uprights, beams and cross-beams that form the roof all need visually to balance one another.

Landscape designers often use a cube system to work out the distance between the uprights, but the main concern is proportion. Close spacing of the uprights makes the pergola more tunnel-like, while wider spacings create the appearance of a series of broad windows. Overhead beams rest on the uprights with cross-beams in between. Increasing the frequency of the cross-beams provides extra support for trailing plants and creates more shade beneath. It is also a useful device for insuring privacy for a sitting area overlooked by high buildings.

A pergola covered with plants can be very heavy. This means that the uprights supporting the horizontal beams, which in turn hold the plants, must be very strong and need solid foundations (see page 108). The beams and cross-beams forming the roof must be firmly secured to one another and to the tops of the uprights.

LARGE SCALE PERGOLA

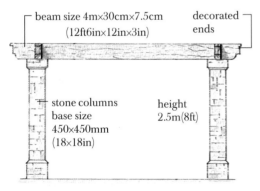

beam size 4m×30cm×7.5cm (12ft6in×12in×3in)   decorated ends

stone columns base size 450×450mm (18×18in)   height 2.5m(8ft)

front elevation

MEDIUM SCALE PERGOLA

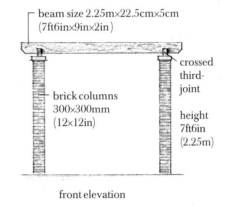

beam size 2.25m×22.5cm×5cm (7ft6in×9in×2in)

crossed third-joint

brick columns 300×300mm (12×12in)   height 7ft6in (2.25m)

front elevation

SMALL SCALE PERGOLA

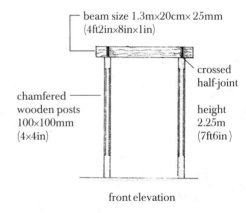

beam size 1.3m×20cm× 25mm (4ft2in×8in×1in)

crossed half-joint

chamfered wooden posts 100×100mm (4×4in)   height 2.25m (7ft6in)

front elevation

(dimensions for all uprights and horizontals are approximate)

A large scale pergola is wide enough for two or three people to walk through abreast or to pass comfortably in opposite directions. Thick stone columns balance the substantial cross-beams visually and are strong enough to bear the considerable weight of beams and plants. Both columns and beams with their decorative ends have a monumental quality suitable for grander sites.

A medium scale pergola, roughly square in section, is wide enough for people to walk through comfortably side by side. Brick columns (no less than a brick-and-a-half thick) make simple uprights. The cross-beams are cut to one-third their depth (crossed third-jointed) and slotted over the beams which raises them, adding lightness to the design. The chamfered ends enhance this effect.

A small scale pergola with its more upright proportions has a less leisurely feel, yet it has space for two people to pass in opposite directions. Built all in wood, its simplicity suits the compact scale so that attention can be focused on the climbing plants that will partly obscure it. The beams and cross-beams are cut to half their thickness (crossed half-jointed) for a level appearance.

PERGOLA POSTS

Pergola posts, columns or uprights are usually more visible than the overhead beams, so the material and style you choose for them contributes most to the pergola's character. Wood, metal, brick or stone can all be used to match nearby or existing garden architecture or to provide their own architectural keynote. You can make your pergola monumental or elegant, traditional or contemporary, rustic or refined. The style and size of the supports will suggest – or even dictate – the size of the roof beams.

SQUARE-SECTION WOODEN POST

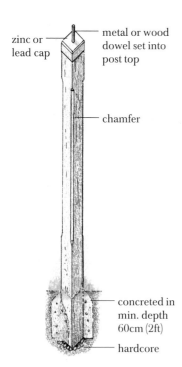

zinc or lead cap

metal or wood dowel set into post top

chamfer

concreted in min. depth 60cm (2ft)

hardcore

BRICK OR STONE COLUMN

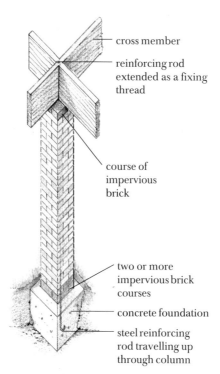

cross member

reinforcing rod extended as a fixing thread

course of impervious brick

two or more impervious brick courses

concrete foundation

steel reinforcing rod travelling up through column

ABOVE *A pergola shades an open walkway with the dramatic autumn colours of crimson glory vine* (Vitis coignetiae). *Here, classical round stone columns with capitals and plinths set on square bases support substantial wooden beams. The shaped ends of the beams and extended cross-beams emphasize this pergola's width and grandeur.*

A square-section wooden post *support is set in concrete. The projecting metal or wood dowel at the top is for securing the overhead beams. A zinc or lead cap at the top of the post protects it from moisture. Chamfered edging gives a lighter, more elegant feel to a square post.*

A brick or stone column *must have a concrete foundation suited to the soil type and the overall weight of the structure. A reinforcing rod at the centre extends at the top to double as a dowel for the cross-beams. The masonry courses are built up gradually, allowing time for the mortar to harden.*

Pergola uprights use different materials from tree trunks to brick, welded metalwork or local stone in any number of ways. You may also choose from reproduction materials – aluminium replacing cast iron, and concrete or fibreglass replacing stone. For a more elegant post, add a plinth, or base, at the bottom and a capital at the top. Mouldings, rebates (decoratively cut grooves). and chamfered (angled) edges also add a touch of flair. Metal dowels can be set into the top of the posts to serve as fixings for the cross-beams – the end of the dowel may be threaded to take a nut.

PERGOLA UPRIGHTS

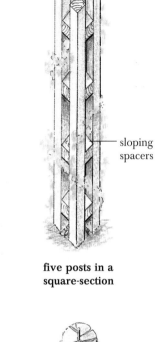

sloping spacers

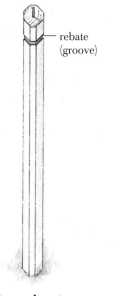

rebate (groove)

tree trunks with bark

five posts in a square-section

octagonal post with rebate

cast iron or aluminium

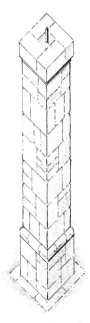

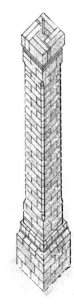

welded square-section metal

classical column (concrete, fibreglass or stone)

reconstituted stone blocks

thin-section local stone

brick half-rounds

chamfered corner bricks

PERGOLA ROOF CONSTRUCTION

The overhead structure of a pergola, or pergola roof, is usually made from timber poles or planks, or less frequently, from metal girders. The style and weight of the roof, or support, beams and the cross-beams is determined by the posts. They may be shaped at the ends and chamfered for a lighter decorative finish, or left four-square and chunky to emphasize their strength and mass. The illustrations show a few of the many techniques for creating a pergola roof. In the first two, shown below, the options for fixing the right-hand side of a pergola roof against a wall are illustrated.

RIGHT *A rustic pergola creation perfectly complements its setting and echoes the tall background trees. Straight trunks form a substantial roof while 'arches' at the ends are fashioned from curving trunks.*

CROSSED HALF-JOINTING

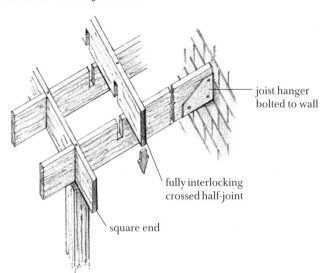

joist hanger bolted to wall

fully interlocking crossed half-joint

square end

Crossed half-jointing *consists of equal thickness boards running in both directions. Slots are cut halfway through each board so that they fully interlock, all finishing at a common level. The plain solid look is underscored by the square-cut ends.*

PARTIALLY CROSSED JOINTING

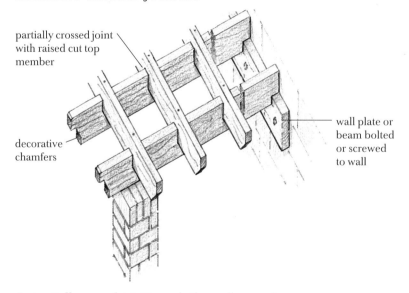

partially crossed joint with raised cut top member

decorative chamfers

wall plate or beam bolted or screwed to wall

In partially crossed jointing *only the smaller cross-beams are cut so they sit higher than the beams. To increase privacy from above, space the cross members close together. Viewed obliquely, the pergola roof will reveal little of what is below.*

LATERALS NAILED OR SCREWED TO STOUT BEAMS

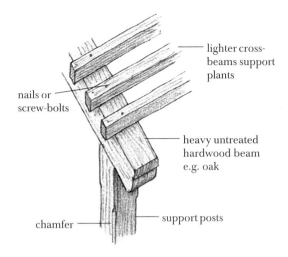

lighter cross-beams support plants

nails or screw-bolts

heavy untreated hardwood beam e.g. oak

chamfer

support posts

Laterals nailed or screwed to stout beams *are an alternative to using joints. Strong but lightweight cross-beams bridge a wide gap between uprights, distributing the weight of the plants more evenly over their greater area than a few stout cross-beams would.*

STOUT CROSSED HALF-JOINTS WITH OGEE ENDS

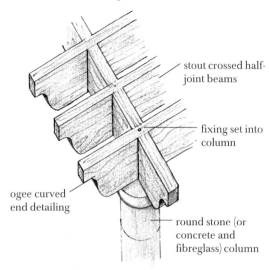

stout crossed half-joint beams

fixing set into column

ogee curved end detailing

round stone (or concrete and fibreglass) column

Stout crossed half-joints with ogee ends *create a stylish pergola supported by slender stone or stone-effect columns. The S-shaped (ogee) curved beam ends add distinction to this simple design, although in a rustic setting, the curve could appear fussy.*

RUSTIC POLES

cross poles nailed or screwed to support poles

angled brace

Rustic poles *are most effective in a rural or country-style garden. Though pretty, this pergola will be relatively short-lived since it is made entirely of untreated branches retaining the bark.*

CAST METAL ARCHES

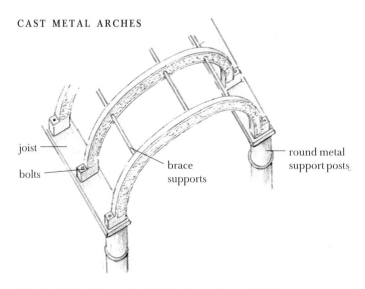

joist

bolts

brace supports

round metal support posts

Cast metal arches *and support posts can be made in bronze, aluminium, or steel. These decorative arches are bolted over metal joists to make an unusual yet striking pergola or tunnel.*

ARCHED WALKS AND TUNNELS

When you want a long decorative structure that combines a plant display with geometric forms, consider creating an arched walkway or tunnel. Either will add distinction to a larger garden. Whether off-the-shelf or specially designed, made of metal or timber, these are a series of linked arches which form a continuous linear structure. While they have an airy, open construction, they impart a more closed feeling than a pergola. As you stroll within a tunnel, the dappled sunlight (or perhaps moonlight) filtering through a light mesh of overhead arches and leafy branches adds to the charm. When planning where to position one in your garden, place it so that framed in the arch of light at the far end there is an enticing focal point such as a seat, statue or urn of flowers to tempt you through and reward you at the end of your passage.

METAL TUNNEL WITH OGEE TOP

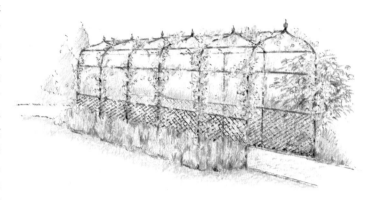

A metal tunnel with ogee top is one of several garden arch and tunnel systems that you buy and assemble yourself. Various sizes and designs are available in round or square coated steel tubes. The upright supporting pieces can either be set directly into the soil or for greater security concreted in. The wire mesh grid at the base plays host to climbers which obscure it.

SAPLING TUNNEL

A sapling tunnel is made from two rows of closely planted young trees which are trained and pleached (see page 68) to meet overhead. Flowering trees such as laburnum look stunning in spring. Pears, with spring blossom and clusters of fruit in autumn are also ideal candidates. The shape is established by tying the branches to a wire framework, but eventually the trees become self-supporting. Regular pruning and shaping is vital.

TIMBER ARCHED WALK

This timber arched walk is made of durable hardwood or treated softwood with some horizontals of steel tubing. It has carefully proportioned posts and boards and the corners of the stout uprights are chamfered for visual lightness. The tubing makes an attractive contrast to the timber, adds structural strength and provides extra plant support.

SWAGS AND PILLARS

Among the most romantic of garden structures, pillars draped with swags form part of the function of a pergola, but because they are two-dimensional they are more likely to be feasible in a smaller-sized garden. Choose decorative uprights of timber, metal or masonry in a style to suit the setting. Position them at regular intervals along a path or behind some low planting where they frame a series of windows overlooking the garden.

The horizontals are made of looping ropes or chains, which act as hosts for vigorous climbing plants such as rambler roses. Judge the scale and proportions of the elements to suit the space. You could even erect parallel rows of swags and pillars on either side of a path for a roofless pergola effect.

RIGHT *Roses are trained along ropes which are strung from regularly placed groupings of posts to fill in the spaces in between. The device of rope swags and posts is useful for creating a vista down a garden path to a focal point.*

DOUBLE ROPE SWAGS

Double rope swags *are made from white-painted posts with cap and ball finials and double rows of matching white rope. Ropes for swags need to be chunky if they are not to look out of scale, and use synthetic fibres which are longerlasting. The same approach can be used for fencing around a tennis court to conceal the functional uprights and help disguise the wire netting (see page 168).*

BRICK COLUMNS AND CHAINS

Brick columns and chains *suit a spacious garden. Masonry columns conjure a sense of strength and permanence. New bricks suit some garden styles, but here the square columns are built with time-worn bricks. The detailing at top and bottom of the columns harmonizes with nearby walls. The swags consist of bronze-effect chains. Use unobtrusive fixings for the plants: dark- or brick-coloured wires are less conspicuous than white or green.*

TRELLIS

Traditional trellis can be described as an openwork type of fence panel composed of a grid or lattice of wooden slats attached to a frame. The use of supporting posts, the choice of timber and its finish and the relatively instant results are all comparable to panel fences. But whereas a fence is primarily a barrier, a trellis tends more towards the role of a screen, providing a measure of shelter and disguise without completely blocking air and light.

Trellis always retains a deliberately artful, architectural quality that enhances a garden. It is thus especially important to choose a style and colour that links well with nearby buildings: ensure that painted trellis does not clash with the brick or stone of the wall behind. Once the trellis is covered with climbers it will have less visual impact, but be careful that the red of your favourite rose does not clash with the brickwork behind it instead.

A wide range of ready-made units is available or designs can be tailor-made. Highly ornamental designs – especially those incorporating curves – can cost as much as walls of equal size and also need to be maintained regularly with paint or preservatives. A substantial structure of trellis panels supported on tall posts and finished with a handsome capping can make a functional enclosure, but the effect remains decorative. But even simple rectangles of ready-made trellis from your garden centre have charm since a mundane view becomes enchanted when glimpsed through a mesh of criss-crossing timber and trailing flowers and foliage.

Trellis traditionally acts as a support for plants but should also itself look attractive in its context. You need to balance these two considerations, taking into account the style and intricacy of your trellis design and the habit and vigour of your climbing and twining plants. If you merely want a support for a permanent curtain of foliage, choose a plain robust design of treated timber that will need minimal upkeep. But if you want to enjoy the design of the trelliswork itself, take care not to overwhelm it with greenery.

ORNATE SLATS WITH CUTOUT ANGLES

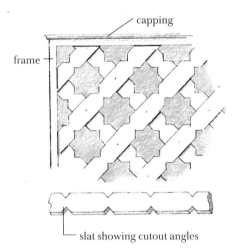

ORNATE SLATS WITH CUTOUT SEMICIRCLES

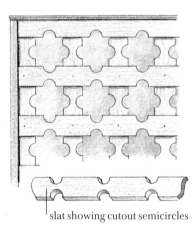

FRETWORK TRELLIS

Ornate slats with cutout angles *show how simple shaping of slats results in more complex trellis patterning. Here, V-shapes are cut into diagonal trellis slats at appropriate distances. This turns square apertures into eight-pointed stars, a pattern often found in Oriental architecture.*

Ornate slats with cutout semicircles *show a more static pattern achieved with horizontally and vertically placed slats. Here, semicircles are cut into the slats at an appropriate distance, depending how 'open' you wish the screen to be. The resulting pattern is a pleasing square-in-a-circle effect.*

Fretwork trellis *can be created by any competent craftsperson as an alternative to joining slats. Cut patterns into single sheets of wood, plywood or a composite material based on timber and resin. The design could be different for each panel or continuous and part of a greater pattern.*

DIAMOND TRELLIS WITH ARCH

A diamond trellis with arch *frames a distant seat. The pyramid-shaped caps of the posts echo the pitched outline of the trellis itself. The arch is made of laminated or curved thin-section timber. Any climbing plants grown here should be light and delicate, and in keeping with their support.*

CONTRASTING TRELLIS PANELS

Contrasting trellis panels *orchestrate different patterns into architectural features. A courtyard can be defined by simple grids of trellis. Here, a central window-like panel of star design has a Moorish feel, emphasized by the ogee curves at the top. A low wall supports the trellis, enclosing an intimate but airy space.*

DIAGONAL OVER SQUARE TRELLIS

Diagonal over square trellis *makes a strong architectural structure. As with an interior dado rail, the vertical weight and proportions are carefully balanced. A central window (which could be a mirror) creates a feature below the curved capping.*

CURVED TRELLIS PANELS

These curved trellis panels *have rectangular apertures in proportion to the overall shape. The curved cappings set up a graceful rhythm, punctuated by the centre roundel. The design and rich lacquer-red colouring are Japanese in inspiration.*

ABOVE *A roofed trellis arch is the starting point for this delightful mural illusion in an old town garden. The stone steps, the position of the wooden basket or trug, the glimpsed painted pot of lilies and the angle of the painted door all lead the eye through to the broad terrace of a palace in a dream-like setting beyond.*

TROMPE L'OEIL

Meaning 'to trick the eye', *trompe l'oeil* is a time-honoured tactic or technique intended to convince the viewer that false objects such as those depicted in a mural painting are 'real', or that a real object is larger, more spacious or at a greater distance than is actually the case. *Trompe l'oeil* was practised by the Ancient Greeks, who tapered the columns of their temples to make them narrower at the top, thus giving the illusion of greater height. Architects and painters have exploited the rules of perspective to create similar trick effects ever since.

A simple instance of *trompe l'oeil* in garden design is to narrow a path or border as it recedes. By exaggerating the natural perspective, this suggests that a greater distance is involved. Of course, this phenomenon works only from one viewpoint – it looks distinctly peculiar when seen in reverse – and even then the trick must be staged with the utmost care if it is not to look ridiculous: all the uprights and other elements in the feature or garden 'picture' must obey the same rules of adjusted perspective. It always helps to keep the elements of the design very simple with just enough geometry to convey the message succinctly. Colours, too, need to be carefully chosen to underline the spatial effects – misty blues, greens and greys to suggest distance, and brighter reds, whites and yellows to bring the foreground nearer.

Trompe l'oeil devices are particularly successful and appropriate in small to medium-size gardens. Where space is at a premium, ways of making the plot look larger are always appreciated. It is also easier to stage-manage artificial effects in a small area where people can be directed to approach the feature from the correct angle for viewing. Discreetly placed mirrors are useful devices for giving an illusion of greater space and depth, and combine well with trellis, gates (to make mirror or false gateways as shown opposite) and small water features (see for example the photograph of the small city garden on page 196).

FALSE PERSPECTIVE WALL TRELLIS

A false perspective wall trellis creates a three-dimensional illusion. Slats narrowing towards the centre represent the view into a tunnel, while the brick arch suggests the tunnel entrance. A focal point of misty blue flowers in a small terracotta flat-backed pot suggest distance. Diagonal trellis on either side sustains the theme, and plants link it to the nearby garden.

PAINTED MURALS

Painted murals create scenic illusions, introduce space and bring light and airiness to areas such as an enclosed basement. Stick to a simple theme with uncomplicated shapes, and use exterior paints on a smooth, stable surface. Strategically placed foreground plants enliven and lend credence to the illusion.

EXAGGERATED PERSPECTIVE

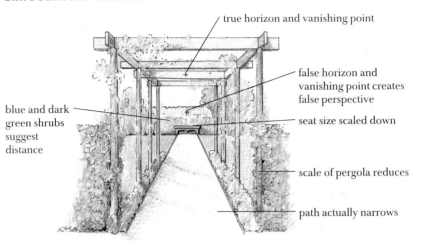

true horizon and vanishing point

false horizon and vanishing point creates false perspective

blue and dark green shrubs suggest distance

seat size scaled down

scale of pergola reduces

path actually narrows

Exaggerated perspective increases distance across a garden by falsifying several elements. The plain gravel pathway physically narrows towards the far side while the classical seat is undersized. The surrounding grey-blue and dark green plants exaggerate the sense of distance. The pergola's posts and cross-beams progressively get smaller and closer together as they recede.

MIRROR GATEWAY

cross-section

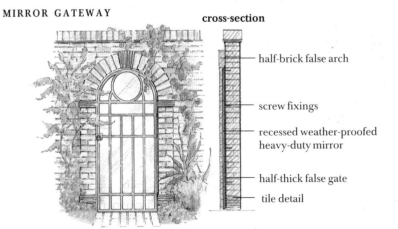

half-brick false arch

screw fixings

recessed weather-proofed heavy-duty mirror

half-thick false gate

tile detail

A mirror gateway is a great space-enhancer. Here, an exterior-quality mirror secured to a blank wall is surrounded by a false arch of half-bricks (full size when reflected). The reflection of plants and path create a feeling of depth. The half-thick false gate across the archway makes the illusion more convincing.

GARDEN BUILDINGS

Designing a small building for the garden is an opportunity to let creativity reign. While you may want to acknowledge aspects of nearby architecture, you can draw on all sorts of additional factors. For one thing, because it is outdoors you have a whole repertory of plant materials at your disposal – if not an arbour of living trees or a topiary gazebo or hut, then perhaps a curtain of climbing plants on a host framework of ornamental ironwork or trellis. Plant products, too, make sympathetic building materials, from rustic timber and clapboard to woven hazel or bamboo. Building with those materials that contrast with the main house may be more successful than using bricks that do not quite match. They certainly blend in better with more informal or rural settings.

There are many sources of inspiration, from Japanese teahouses to thatched huts from South Sea islands, and from log cabins to Moorish kiosks. Gardens dating from the eighteenth or nineteenth centuries have a wealth of architecture, from mass-produced Victorian gazebos and glasshouses, available nowadays as reproductions in pre-assembled kits, to individualistic huts, shelters and summerhouses with features you can borrow and adapt for yourself. Eccentricity has always been an endearing trait in garden buildings, and books on old gardens provide ideas for follies, ruins, hermit-inhabited grottoes and other characterful items to tuck away in appropriate corners.

Designs for more orthodox garden buildings depend on their purpose – whether you simply want somewhere sheltered to sit and enjoy the view, or have more practical priorities such as storing

LEFT *The golden hop and clematis are among the climbers that festoon this leafy bower with its green curtain backdrop of* Jasminum officinale. *The pergola-type roof appears to hang freely because the supporting columns are well disguised with flowers and foliage. The prim white seat and rounds of box add a degree of order to the lush scene.*

ARBOUR OF WOVEN BRANCHES

An arbour of woven branches *makes a friendly shelter. It is made by weaving branches of hazel or willow, adapting the method used for fencing (see page 96). The braided edgings and trim around the window are reminiscent of basketwork. Natural materials such as these make this an ideal arbour for an informal setting – or a hide for watching events in a wildlife garden.*

seats and barbecue equipment or servicing sports activities. In a range of complexity come primitive shelters such as arbours and bowers, small garden structures such as pavilions and gazebos, and summerhouses – complete with utilities. Finally, there are greenhouses designed specifically for plants. (Conservatories, regarded as extensions of the house, are outside the scope of this book.)

Plan a building that fulfils your purpose, but also bear in mind its value as a focal point to be seen and appreciated for its visual contribution to the scene. Gazebos are often purely ornamental, placed in the garden as an eye-catcher or perhaps to house or frame a sculpture. But their original function in the garden was to offer a view over the garden or a landscape beyond it.

Apart from the fun of choosing and designing your garden building, there is the question of what you choose to call it. The most sophisticated summerhouses are sometimes referred to by their owners as the shed, hut or cabin; simpler shelters might be dignified by the name of pavilion or gazebo. A pavilion is technically a tent or a portable shelter, but nowadays the term implies a utilitarian purpose, a place where you take refreshment or shower after a game. Applied to a slightly quirky garden building, it still has a note of romance. An arbour was originally a bower formed by closely planted shrubs and trees with their overhead branches intertwined or woven into trelliswork. Today its meaning has expanded to include any sitting area where the roof is formed mainly of leafy plants. So keep an open mind as you survey the examples on the following pages and in manufacturers' catalogues. It is not the name that matters but whether the structure will work for you in your garden.

NATURAL TREE ARBOUR

TRELLIS ARBOUR

GROTTO

A natural tree arbour *can be formed from a ring of closely planted light trees such as birch or aspen. Their attractive trunks form the walls and their branches meet overhead to make a leafy ceiling. For a more solid, formal effect choose a denser-growing tree such as beech and pleach the branches together (see page 68). The curved bench of rustic wood sustains the woodland theme.*

A trellis arbour *with pale turquoise-stained trellis, a slatted roof and built-in seating has a degree of sophistication. Pink roses scrambling over and through it contrast with the colour of the trellis and conjure an atmosphere of old-fashioned romance. Choose scented flowers to grow over and around a structure of this kind to refresh and delight people seated within.*

This grotto *is formed in a deep recess in a rock garden. The outside is made with large rocks and the interior is lined with pebbles and shells. A grotesque mask formed from shells functions as a waterspout, the water falling prettily into a shell bowl from where it overflows into a shallow pool. Features such as this are easy to create using an artificial water source and a pump.*

ABOVE *An arched wooden frame among tall shady trees makes an open pavilion for a fair weather setting. The deck, which extends out from the brick patio of the house, is made of matching wood, unifying the whole design. The low walls of squared trellis add style and privacy. The lop-leaved palms provide additional shade and softer curving forms.*

STONE AND LOG PAVILION

This stone and log pavilion *has been made from materials gathered locally, giving it an immediate connection to its rural surroundings. The spaced logs arranged in diagonal patterns give the heavy hut-like structure a lighter, decorative quality.*

TWIN BATHING PAVILIONS

Twin bathing pavilions *make an imposing approach to the swimming pool and serve a useful purpose as dressing rooms and storage space. Bronzed or tinted glass domes provide interior light. This exotic design, giving an impression of both bright light and deep shade, is in keeping with a sunny, arid climate.*

RIGHT *This gazebo, sheltering a graceful statue surrounded by roses, lilies and lavender, makes a major focal point. Its white colour, softened with weathering, harmonizes with the statue. It would also look good painted grey, green, black or a colour chosen to link it with nearby architecture, foliage, or flower tones. The paired supports are of square-sawn wood and the closely spaced slatted timber roofing is topped with an ornate finial.*

OCTAGONAL WOODEN GAZEBO

An octagonal wooden gazebo *is reminiscent of a pavilion in an Oriental miniature painting. Its light framework could be constructed of metal. Individual styling and colour offer unlimited scope to suit your own setting.*

CUSTOM-MADE STEEL GAZEBO

A custom-made steel gazebo *in dark green coated or enamelled steel has a handsome square design – a series of diamonds and octagons on side walls with an open roof made of square-section tubes. The high natural rock bank makes a dramatic backdrop.*

DOMED METAL GAZEBO

A domed metal gazebo *of ornate but traditional design is enhanced by a bronze verdigris finish. A focal point in itself, the open archways also frame views in different directions. Its essential formality makes it ideal for a small geometric garden layout.*

RUSTIC RETREAT ARBOUR

ROTATING SUMMERHOUSE

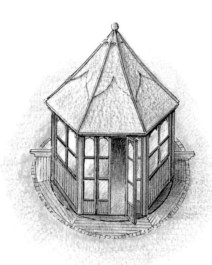

A rustic retreat arbour uses the natural shapes of tree trunks in this woodland garden shelter. Poles form the walls and ceiling. Encourage climbers such as clematis or honeysuckle to swathe the structure with softening greenery.

This rotating summerhouse, which could be six- or eight-sided, is mounted on a platform over roller bearings. This means it can be turned either manually by handles (as shown), or electronically. This ingenious idea gives a choice of view and allows you to take advantage of sunshine or shade in different seasons and at different times of day.

ABOVE *A fine old circular white clapboard summerhouse has slender arched windows and a lead roof with upcurved ends, giving it a quaint, fairy-tale charm. The triangular lead panels of the turreted roof are riveted to metal supports. The turret is topped with an elegant lance for a finial.*

READY-MADE CEDAR CHALET

This ready-made cedar chalet is typical of a range of pre-fabricated wooden summerhouses. You can choose different stylistic details for windows and doors, and enhance the structure with awnings and deckings to suit the site. The flat roof, covered with a material such as bitumastic felt, has a slight pitch to shed rainwater. The chalet stands on a base of poured concrete or gravel.

OCTAGONAL GREENHOUSE

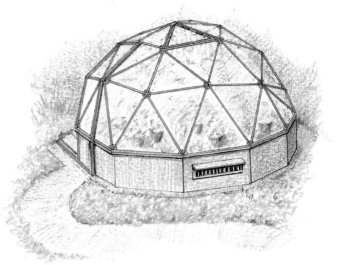

LEAN-TO GREENHOUSE

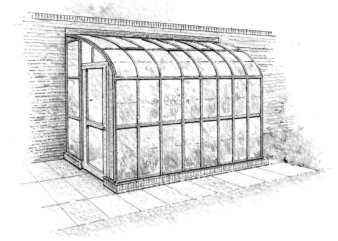

An octagonal greenhouse, *like most multi-sided greenhouses, is economical in terms of space and looks good from every direction. Working well with traditional and modern settings, it is attractive enough for a central position in the herb or vegetable garden or to feature on the patio. The choice is either aluminium or cedar construction. This example has an adjustable air vent at the roof apex and is fitted with a sliding door.*

Lean-to greenhouse *designs are space-effective and can put a house wall to good use. Keeping a greenhouse cool can sometimes cost more than heating it, so choose a sunny location only if you can provide efficient shading and ventilation systems. High-quality models come in anodized steel or aluminium in a choice of colours. Matching the brick of the base wall to that of the wall behind marries the greenhouse to its setting.*

ORNAMENTAL VICTORIAN-STYLE GREENHOUSE

This ornamental Victorian-style greenhouse *is a modern version specially designed to team with a nineteenth-century house. It cannot be hidden away in the kitchen garden as our ancestors would have done. Its decorative structure with different-shaped and curved glazing is underpinned by a brick-and-flint base wall to add a further touch of authenticity. Non-rusting, maintenance-free metals such as aluminium alloys replace the cast-iron framework of the original. Modern conveniences such as double glazing and automated ventilation and heating systems bring this period piece up to date. The double doors are designed to open outwards.*

FURNISHING THE GARDEN

CREATING VISUAL IMPACT WITH
PLANTS, POTS, ORNAMENTS,
LIGHTING, ROCKS, POOLS,
FOUNTAINS, SEATING AND
GAMES AREAS

OPPOSITE *A garden featuring an artificial pool with pebble beaches and lush waterside planting makes a perfect corner for rest and contemplation. Near the sitting area is the soothing sound of water trickling from a waterspout over rocks. Ornamental planted containers bring a sense of order, as do the curved stones bridging the pool.*

A garden's furnishings are any items that supplement its structure, that is, its horizontal or vertical components. These may be so major as to influence the whole layout of the site. A feature like a large pond complete with planted banks, or a swimming pool, or a games area such as a tennis court, must be planned from the outset. This means preparatory landscaping of the site, detailed planning of the services that will supply it and thought given to the handling of its surroundings, for example whether to separate it from or merge it with the rest of the garden.

Other furnishings can be thought of as finishing touches, added after the garden's main structures are complete. Ornaments are in this category. Some of these may be focal points, visible at once, drawing your attention and conveying a message about the garden's character. Others are hidden, surprises to be discovered as you enter another part of the garden. You turn a corner to a new view, and there you may find a sculpture, a seat, a fountain or a sundial. Such objects are not an intrinsic part of the design, but should still be considered part of the overall plan. Although you may have to complete the surrounding structures before you can put these furnishings in place, the staging or background needs to be conceived with them in mind.

Furnishings, whether a large feature or a small ornament, are the tip of a design iceberg: what draws your attention is only the most visible part of the total. When your eye registers the arching spray of a fountain in a formal pool, it sees the result of a long and possibly complex process. The working fountain represents the culmination of many design decisions. The visitor can see that the pool is formal and located on a patch of level ground. The garden designer decided the size of the pool, its materials, the shape and style of the rim, and where exactly to position it. More planning was involved in deciding on the mechanisms needed to make it work. Finally, the ideas had to be implemented, from the initial digging to the switching on of the pump.

Some of the features that catch your eye as you enter a garden may be less obviously 'staged' and entail a more casual approach. They may not even be permanent. A mass of shapely or colourful plants changes with the days and the seasons, and you may move a grouping of terracotta pots around as you please. An arrangement of chairs around a table will sometimes be a focal point in a garden scene even when they are not deliberately positioned,

because the eye picks out shapes and colours that stand out from their background. There may be a subconscious message of invitation: here is where you can come to sit, relax, eat and drink. For this reason, even casual garden furniture conveys an impression of the garden and must 'look right'.

FITTING OBJECTS TO A DESIGN

Your planning will probably have given you a clear idea of the kind of item your garden picture is calling for. Choosing objects to suit a particular setting is partly a question of scale and certainly one of taste. However, making the right decision can be a bit like buying

a pair of shoes when the suit or dress it is intended to complement has been left at home. Some people can buy an item that works perfectly with the rest of an outfit, but not everyone can get it right first time. Most people would prefer to see the two elements together to be sure. Taking photographs of the proposed area of the garden with you to the store or garden centre can help. Some items may be available on a 'return' basis, so that you can check their appropriateness in place.

It is always a challenge to get the size of a garden feature or furnishing just right. If you are trying to decide how big to make a pond, you can mark out the dimensions with stakes or lay a garden hose on the ground to give you a sketch of the size and see how it appears from the garden's various viewpoints and approaches. For an ornament, too, you could improvise a mock-up in position in the garden to help you find the right size and scale for its setting. For example, use boxes to help you choose the height of a plinth and stakes to give the dimensions of any surrounding paving or other framing devices. If you are choosing furniture, barbecues and children's play items, you need to work out the dimensions of the area you have available, allowing space for people to circulate so that the amenity can be used effectively.

CONTRASTS AND FOCAL POINTS

When an object is positioned as a visual focal point it stands out from its setting. You can take this literally – in the sense that a vertical ornament such as an obelisk, a tall tree or the flower-spikes of mulleins and foxgloves physically soar above their ground-level neighbours and so draw the eye first. This also happens when an object is placed so the eye sees it slightly sooner than its background. More often, we use the concept of an object 'standing out' figuratively, meaning that it contrasts with and can be seen clearly against its background. Contrasts of materials, texture, line, form and colour all play their part.

LEFT *The scale and ornamental design of the set of table and chairs, which have been stained to match the painted trelliswork, is perfectly suited to this small paved town garden. A full-length mirror fitted to the back wall inside the trellis archway gives an additional feeling of space to this light and airy design.*

When the background is composed of natural materials and plants almost any man-made artifact makes this contrast. In the garden, light colours enhanced by smooth textures stand out most conspicuously against the mass of foliage. A pearly marble statue or white-painted seat commands immediate attention. If you find this contrast too stark, you could perhaps soften the visual impact by choosing limestone for the statue (lichens would mute the paleness further), painting the seat a pale grey, or using natural wood weathered to a silvery tone. Even if you choose colours and materials that are closer to naturally occurring ones – such as a slate bird bath or a black or deep green bench – the objects will still stand out because of their firm lines.

CREATING PICTURES

Whether formal or informal, the rule is to plan the garden as a collection of individual pictures or theatrical scenes, each of them an 'eye-catcher'. For example, when you have a collection of different-sized individual items such as small terracotta or glazed plant pots, group them so that when first seen they impress the eye as an entity rather than as a distracting collection of scattered objects. Where you have a formal layout, use a pair of urns or specimen plants to add importance to a flight of steps or use equally spaced items to create a regular rhythm.

Use visual tricks such as framing devices to present your garden features. Start with the entrance to the garden. If, when you open the door onto a patio, your eye lights on a plaque on the opposite wall or a central bowl fountain, your framing works. Another device is to isolate a key ornament from its surroundings. Perhaps raise it by setting it on a platform or plinth. To preserve its star status make sure nothing in the periphery competes for attention.

Sometimes the eye is directed by a compelling set of sightlines that centre on the main feature. In large formal gardens perspective is used in this way. Think of looking down the straight sweep of an axial path or an avenue with the horizontal lines on either side converging on a statue or a summerhouse. *Trompe-l'oeil* trelliswork patterns imitate this effect artificially but successfully (see page 115). If your layout is informal you need to guide people's gaze more artfully, contriving curves and using the natural lines of plants to indicate the direction the eye should follow.

ABOVE *Pots and plants of various sizes create a picture in this small town garden. A pair of large pots containing bay trees makes the strongest vertical accents. Smaller pots in front are linked by the massed white marguerites and lace-cap hydrangeas. This colour theme is carried through by the white-edged hostas.*

PLANTS AND CONTAINERS

For planting to amount to a feature rather than just a part of the garden's vertical and horizontal surfaces, it must have strong visual impact or a special quality. This is often simply clever presentation.

Some plants have an outline shape or habit that stands out from the crowd, claiming attention: curvaceous palm trees, columnar evergreens and spiky yuccas are examples. You can exploit these individuals to make eye-catchers or focal points in isolation or as part of a team. Other plants – especially when in flower – are more decorative than sculptural and you can use these like the frosting on a cake. They are a superficial embellishment and are not a visual keynote of the design. The structure of the garden would still exist without them, but with less focus. You can also create an imposing 'chorus-line' effect with plants by the way you organize them in informal compositions or formal patterns. The scale can range from a vast herbaceous border to a few plants arranged in a windowbox, a rich pattern of ground-cover plant colours set in a green frame of edging plants like a traditional parterre or a mass of pansies in a single large container or flowerpot.

As well as being a decorative accessory, a container can make an important design statement in the garden layout. Containers also mean that plants can be grown where it may not otherwise be possible: whole gardens are made in raised planters on patios and rooftops. Raised containers or planters can make gardening a lot easier for elderly people or those with a disability, providing a chief source of leisure and pleasure for the homebound.

PLANTS AS FOCAL POINTS

The scale of your planted feature must be adjusted to the size of the garden picture you have in mind. Suppose you are planning a colour theme with the climax a composition of varying shades and textures of green broken by a blaze of red. In a large garden, your view could encompass a group of trees – perhaps mainly evergreen with a red-leaved maple creating drama in the autumn. In a mid-sized plot, the scale could call for a shrub with red spring or summer flowers, perhaps a rhododendron or a rose. In a patio or on a windowsill, the focal point could be nothing bigger than the red flowers of a geranium.

To hold a starring, eye-catching role, a plant needs qualities that make it suitable to claim the focal point of the scene. Sometimes this is made through sheer size or size enhanced by form or by colour. Where you have a vista terminating in a fine specimen shrub, it is overall shape which most distinguishes it from its neighbours. A seat or ornament at its base will underline its dramatic function.

When you choose a specimen tree to contribute height and act as a focal point in a smaller garden, you can make it seem important

LEFT *A shapely fern in a classical urn backed by an ivy-covered wall makes a spectacular eye-catcher. The colour of the ground-level epimedium harmonizes with the brick path and adds a splash of warmth.*

OUTLINE SHAPES OF TREES AND SHRUBS

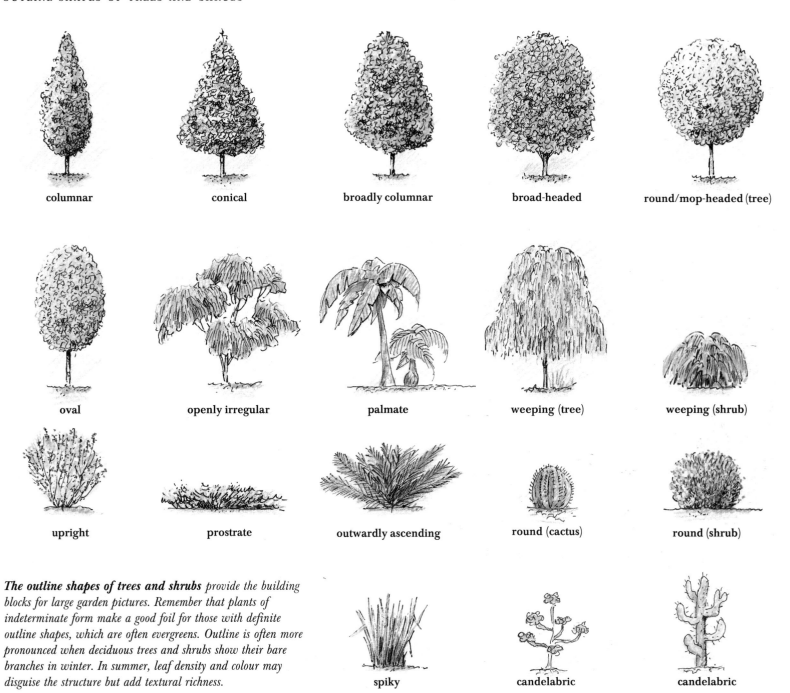

columnar   conical   broadly columnar   broad-headed   round/mop-headed (tree)

oval   openly irregular   palmate   weeping (tree)   weeping (shrub)

upright   prostrate   outwardly ascending   round (cactus)   round (shrub)

spiky   candelabric   candelabric

The outline shapes of trees and shrubs *provide the building blocks for large garden pictures. Remember that plants of indeterminate form make a good foil for those with definite outline shapes, which are often evergreens. Outline is often more pronounced when deciduous trees and shrubs show their bare branches in winter. In summer, leaf density and colour may disguise the structure but add textural richness.*

by isolating it from its neighbours. The mass of the tree is balanced by surrounding space. Flowering trees are often good candidates and when they also colour well in autumn they are particularly rewarding. However, since flower and leaf colours are ephemeral, it is important to choose a tree with a graceful shape or form.

PLANT GROUPS AND PATTERNS

When you are planning a grouping rather than a single specimen plant, relationships between the plants need to work in a different way. The shape of each plant needs to balance with those of its neighbours to build a satisfying picture overall. Study the properties of your plant shapes, the building-blocks of your picture, and balance those with clear strong identities against companions with a vaguer, more diffuse shape. Soaring shapes and lines carry the eye upward. In an informal feature you need curves and diagonals formed by shape and colour weaving across the field of vision to hold your interest and involve you in further visual exploration.

Another idea is to use plants to make patterns rather than pictures. In a formal layout, you seek symmetry to provide balance. You can create horizontal forms such as a traditional parterre – an ornamental patterned garden – using low-growing plants in beds, defined by paths and low hedges. The beds or panels in these patterns can be made of summer and winter bedding plants or more permanent bulbs and perennials. If you punctuate the main points of the design with boxclipped into cone shapes or little upright conifers, the effect becomes more three-dimensional.

Patterns can become completely three-dimensional when you exploit the vertical dimension with other upright plants, such as climbers, to clothe pillars and arches or grow over frames to make weeping or standard shapes. Training plants in this way turns an otherwise shapeless mass into a fine specimen or feature.

A SIMPLE COMPOSITION OF TREES AND SHRUBS

ABOVE *A composition of greens, yellows, purple and white stands out against a background of yew hedges. A tall false acacia* (Robinia pseudoacacia) *forms the apex of a triangle contained by colour and by some dominant verticals. The silvery tones of a pair of globe artichokes* (Cynara scolynus) *are echoed by lower-growing plants in the foreground.*

A simple composition of trees and shrubs *plays with plant forms as a landscape painter does with paint, leading the eye back and forth with sweeping strokes and shapes. The principle of using contrasts and variety to make a harmonious whole applies to smaller-scale planting in an informal style – even to the individual foliage plants and flowers in a tiny courtyard bed.*

CHOOSING CONTAINERS

Choosing a container involves considering both the setting and what you intend to grow. When the combination works well, the container seems right for the garden and the plant seems at home in the container. A showy specimen plant like a standard rose, a small palm or a clipped bay tree could look equally well in a classic Versailles planter, an antique-style stone vase or a large cylinder of smooth synthetic material. You could place them in pairs along a broad path in a formal garden, or one on its own would look good in most gardens. Large or elaborate containers call for large-scale plants: daisies, snowdrops or forget-me-nots would not do justice to the scale and presence of such a grand container.

Look at samples and decide whether you want the bold impact of a single statuesque plant in a shapely container or a more diffuse composition using several pots adding up to more than the sum of the individuals. Take into account whether the plant (or the container) can remain outside in winter and how much maintenance and replanting you are prepared to do. This will help you determine whether to use permanently planted shrubs and perennials or plant ephemeral performers that will change each season.

VERSAILLES PLANTER

The Versailles planter has a restrained elegance that perfectly complements clipped evergreens like this half-standard bay. Its rightful place is in a formal garden, perhaps housing a tender shrub that needs to be moved indoors for the winter. Originally designed in wood, less expensive lightweight versions in plastic and fibreglass are available. These cut down on maintenance but lack solid character.

ABOVE *Simple terracotta pots of pink daisies placed at regular intervals add focus and height to give just the right touch of formality to a flight of squared timber steps. The pattern created by the pots leads the eye up the steps into the unlit area beyond.*

Some containers are portable and so can be used anywhere. Regard these as you do potted plants and cut-flower arrangements around the house: either as constantly changing displays or as semi-permanent fixtures that you groom and tend from time to time. Position them as focal points or accents at the top of some steps or the corner of a path, sometimes raised up to display the contents more clearly, and to allow the branches of a weeping plant to fall gracefully over the container sides. Or group the containers, linking them with some common factor such as a series of pots in the same material or style or a heterogeneous cluster of pots with plant material in a distinct colour scheme.

Plan larger or built-in containers as part of the permanent garden framework. In patio gardens they may be the main planting area. A raised position helps counteract any boxed-in feeling of a small enclosure. Solidly built of masonry or timber, they can double as benches and space dividers.

SELF-WATERING CONTAINERS

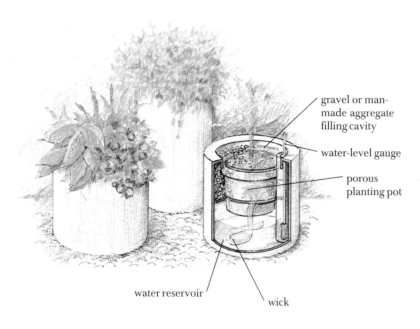

gravel or man-made aggregate filling cavity

water-level gauge

porous planting pot

water reservoir

wick

SAWN WOOD PLANTERS

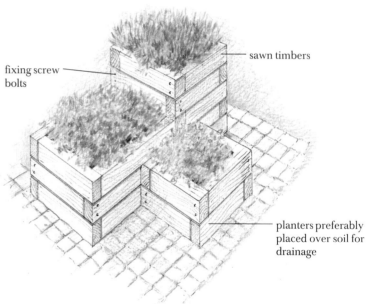

fixing screw bolts

sawn timbers

planters preferably placed over soil for drainage

Self-watering containers *can be bought ready-made or improvised from available pots. The non-porous outer planter is usually made of fibreglass or another rigid plastic. The planted pot is supported above a reservoir of water. The planting medium is linked to the water by a wick that transmits moisture by capillary action. This means that the plant cannot be over-watered, because it takes just what it needs. Instead of daily watering, you check the water level in the reservoir periodically (some proprietary models include a gauge). Gravel or man-made aggregate between the inner and outer containers improves appearance. It can also release water vapour round the plant.*

Sawn wood planters *are solid-looking with sawn sections of planks bolted together to make a series of cubes of varying height. This cluster of modules makes a feature large enough for small trees to be grown in. It would be ideal in a small enclosed courtyard or patio garden where raised beds help the plants gain more light. If possible, position the planters over soil rather than paving to ensure good drainage. You could choose the wood and its finish to suit adjacent decking but any preservative used needs to be harmless to plants. Here, the planting colour scheme explores harmonies of blue, purple and silver, and it tones well with the weathered texture of the containers.*

POTS AND VASES

Ornamental vases and pots are imposing and weighty in all senses. Place them in prominent positions as a foil to stylish plants with lush foliage or extravagant flowers, perhaps with grass or evergreen foliage as a backdrop. Choose nearby horizontal or vertical hard surfaces with care in order to avoid an uncomfortable clash of materials. Natural and synthetic stone, concrete, terracotta and metals such as lead or bronze are among a wide range of materials available. Lightweight containers of fibreglass anchored against the wind are useful for structures that are not built to hold heavy stone or terracotta, and are much easier to move around.

ORNAMENTAL STONE VASE

An ornamental stone vase or high quality imitation in reconstituted stone can come in a great variety of styles. Position it carefully. Stone of a different type or colour or nearby pavers in a style that doesn't match might look awkward.

VICTORIAN CHIMNEYPOT

TERRACOTTA VASE

VERSAILLES VASE

This Victorian chimneypot, like many old earthenware chimneypots, is as ornate and fantastical in design as any ready-made decorative planter. They work just as well on the ground as they did at rooftop level. Group with other pots or place one as a centrepiece in solitary splendour.

Terracotta vases, stylish relatives of the everyday flower pot, gain status by being raised high on pedestals in matching materials. Here, the brick-red warm tones of terracotta are brought alive by the planting. Harmonize with fiery reds, yellows and oranges, or contrast with whites and blues.

The Versailles vase has classical lines that look attractive adorned by a cornucopia of flowers and leaves or left unplanted and used as a simple ornament or finial. It is made of reconstituted stone or a synthetic such as fibreglass, the same material as the solid-looking but restrained pedestal.

PLANTERS FOR WINDOWS, WALLS AND ROOF GARDENS

Some containers such as hanging baskets, wall-mounted planters and windowboxes have special uses in vertical design where they provide welcome visual relief, particularly against a blank wall. Introducing plant interest at waist- or eye-level or even overhead, surrounds you with cool greenery and flower colour. For smaller containers terracotta is useful since it is porous, storing water and remaining cool as water evaporates. Larger planters, especially those for roof gardens, need to be lightweight and must be accessible for frequent watering. Lightness is important anywhere plants have to be moved around. Roof containers need to be wind resistant and have special provision for irrigation and drainage.

WINDOWBOX

strong wall brackets

Windowboxes extend the garden vertically, offering an added visual bonus for people indoors. Fix them securely to the wall or windowsill with strong wall-mounted brackets. Traditional terracotta and wood designs are often imitated in lighter-weight fibreglass and, when seen from a distance, look like the real thing. An internal shell of fibreglass or plastic (or some form of waterproof lining) also helps to extend the life of real wood.

CERAMIC OR METAL HANGING POT

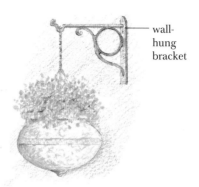

wall-hung bracket

A ceramic or metal hanging pot, attractive in itself as well as for its plant interest, appears to advantage when viewed from below. An enclosed shape without a drainage hole will need careful watering since too much water is as bad for plants as too little. Most metal or ceramic pots can be planted like ordinary hanging baskets, but copper ones should be lacquered or lined with waterproof plastic to prevent harmful copper salts from forming on contact with water and wet foliage.

HANGING BASKET

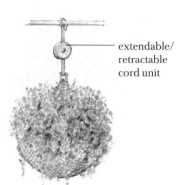

extendable/ retractable cord unit

Hanging baskets are versatile garden accessories. Colour schemes can change to coordinate with nearby paintwork or with each new season's planting. Hanging baskets must be overplanted compared with other containers. As a large quantity of water is taken up by plants or lost through evaporation, water often, especially in summer, by hand or use pulleys or a mechanism (such as that shown) to lower and raise the basket. You can try adding moisture-retaining granules to the compost.

HALF-ROUND WALL POT

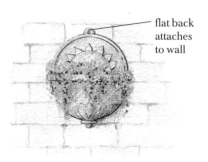

flat back attaches to wall

Half-round wall pots are extremely useful as a means of providing plant interest on an otherwise bare wall. They make good high-level focal points in restricted areas or opposite a window. Many kinds are available, including openwork versions to plant like hanging baskets. This terracotta example has a backing plaque with a rising-sun motif.

RIGHT *With a spectacular aerial view of the New York skyline, this roof-top terrace has a trellis of ironwork to act as a support for climbing plants, provide shelter and screen unwanted features. Matching lower railings ensure safety. Banks of shrubs, a border of flowering plants and small trees in long containers remind the occupants of life at ground level.*

ROOF GARDEN PLANTER

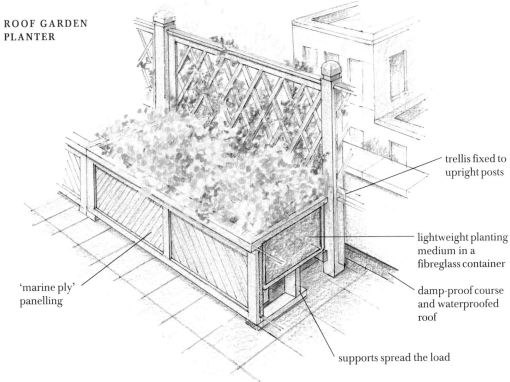

trellis fixed to upright posts

lightweight planting medium in a fibreglass container

damp-proof course and waterproofed roof

'marine ply' panelling

supports spread the load

This roof garden planter *incorporates its own sturdy backing trellis to provide support for plants and shelter for people. The functional fibreglass planters, containing a lightweight planting medium, are raised on a supporting framework that distributes the weight evenly. The planters are pierced underneath to allow rainwater to run away. The façade is panelled with tough water-resistant marine plywood decorated with tongue-and-groove markings. It hides the supporting structure and makes the planters look deeper than they are. The structure could be prefabricated in sections or built in position. It gives an impression of solidity and permanence, furnishing the roof with a luxuriant garden while fully taking into account the restraints of the site.*

FEATURES AND EQUIPMENT FOR SPECIAL NEEDS

If a family member is elderly or has some disability, you will of course want to make the garden accessible and safe for his or her enjoyment. Specially designed raised beds or planters such as those shown enable such a person to join actively in the therapeutic tasks of garden maintenance.

Raised beds provide a visual change of level, and bring plants nearer to the nose and eyes of a seated person or someone in a wheelchair. Many seated gardeners find raised beds easier to cultivate, although you need a certain amount of strength since the weight of long-handled tools used at waist level has to be supported by the arms, whereas at ground level you lean on the tool and the weight is taken by the ground itself.

A layout with no sharp turns and corners is best for wheelchair-users and the partially sighted. Ideally, paths and seating areas should be wide enough for a wheelchair and a walking companion to proceed side by side in comfort. Slopes need to be negotiated by ramps with a maximum gradient of 1 in 20. The design emphasis on horizontal planters and pathways could be offset by using solid banks of trees and shrubs to make vertical accents.

Safety underfoot is a priority for anyone who is unsteady on their feet or cannot see well. Paving should be level and have a non-slip surface. A slight variation in surface texture is easily discernible and acts as a warning of an approaching hazard or difference in level such as steps or a slope, or as an indication that, for example, you have reached a sitting area with a bench. Routes should be direct and well defined. Any steps should be evenly proportioned with the same riser and tread sizes throughout. Handrails will provide additional security.

Scented plants are particularly welcomed, especially by those who are partially sighted – but choose honeysuckles and thornless roses to climb over arches and beside paths. Other appropriate features are those that can be appreciated by touch such as urns, statues and wall-mounted waterspouts. The sound of water also helps partially sighted people with orientation.

USEFUL IMPLEMENTS AND GARDENING ACCESSORIES

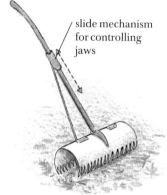

slide mechanism for controlling jaws

lightweight rake and grab tool

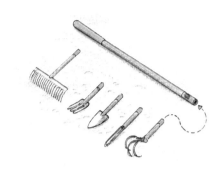

interchangeable hand tools

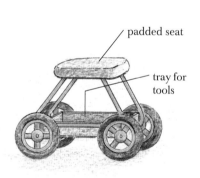

padded seat

tray for tools

mobile stool

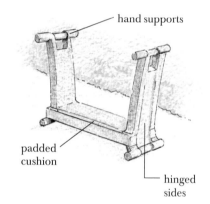

hand supports

padded cushion

hinged sides

kneeler

Useful implements and gardening accessories include hand tools that slot, twist or screw onto a handle of variable length. Brightly coloured tools are less easily misplaced among foliage. The lightweight rake and grab tool is useful for people who are unable to bend down easily. A mobile stool needs a flat firm surface such as paving or a dry lawn – your feet act as brakes. A kneeler makes gardening jobs at ground level easier. The hand supports help you to lower yourself into position and – usually more difficult – raise yourself. Inverted, it provides a seat. Some models are hinged so that they can be folded.

RAISED BED

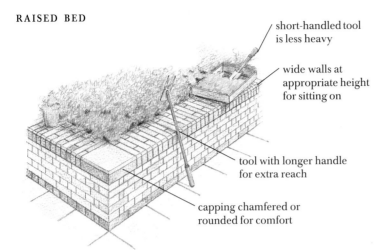

short-handled tool is less heavy

wide walls at appropriate height for sitting on

tool with longer handle for extra reach

capping chamfered or rounded for comfort

Raised beds put plant cultivation within closer reach of people with mobility problems. A low wide wall doubling as a stable seat and long-handled tools can add to the comfort of all gardeners. Compensate for the restricted view of wheelchair-users, who are able to see only the first row of plants, by growing tall plants at the centre of the beds and low ones along the sides.

RAISED BED WITH RAILING

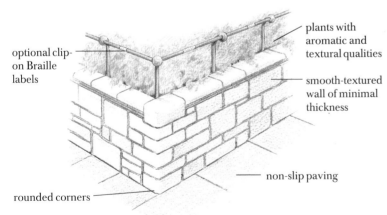

plants with aromatic and textural qualities

optional clip-on Braille labels

smooth-textured wall of minimal thickness

non-slip paving

rounded corners

A raised bed with a railing helps the blind and partially sighted negotiate their way around. The height of the rail allows people to lean forward to appreciate the plants. Emphasis is on subjects with attractive perfumes and textures such as aromatics that release their scents when brushed or crushed. The wall has a smooth texture and rounded corners for safety and comfort.

WHEELCHAIR USERS' PLANTER/WORKBENCH

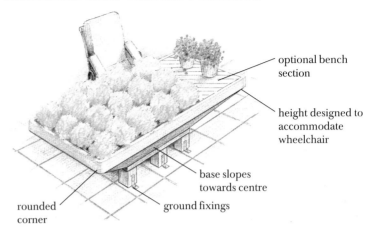

optional bench section

height designed to accommodate wheelchair

base slopes towards centre

rounded corner

ground fixings

This wheelchair users' planter or workbench is made of wood and designed so that you can tuck your knees under the edges and get close enough to do some hands-on gardening. The borders of the planter are shallow, but the increased soil depth at the centre both pleases plants and adds to the stability of the whole unit. As added insurance, the supports are secured to the ground.

PATH AND EDGING TREATMENTS

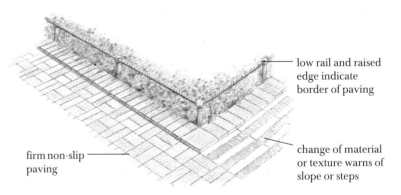

low rail and raised edge indicate border of paving

change of material or texture warns of slope or steps

firm non-slip paving

Path and edging treatments need warning signals such as a change of texture underfoot to tell wheelchair-users and partially sighted people of a change of ground level. The edges of paths and paved areas can be slightly raised to keep wheelchairs on track; an addition, or an alternative, is a low rail such as the barley-twist design shown.

GARDEN ACCESSORIES

This category of garden furnishing includes garden art: statues and plaques, architectural objects such as obelisks and columns, and associated items such as urns. Cost is not necessarily a barrier, even if you want a classical-looking piece because, while originals are rare and expensive, good-quality reproductions are increasingly available. Traditional materials are used as are metals and plastics or you can transform a mass-produced item into something unique with a coat of paint. Choose an appropriate colour that ties in with your garden scheme or a metallic finish such as bronze treated with some of the 'distressing' and antiquing effects that decorators use.

If the nostalgic or historical approach is not appropriate for your garden and you want something modern, abstract or personal, you could call on the work of contemporary sculptors. Alternatively, promote some *objet trouvé* such as a piece of driftwood or a large, shapely, weatherworn rock to sculpture status. The important thing is that it should both please you and enhance the garden composition. You can also make functional objects such as sundials, bird baths or lighting into successful garden ornaments.

ART AND ORNAMENT

Take any base or plinth into account when you are determining the scale of your ornament. It is the way that an object is displayed that determines its importance. If you placed your watering can on a plinth, it would become an object worthy of attention – a piece of art. By contrast, if you placed the Venus de Milo somewhere in a rambling border she would be diminished. Unless you want an element of deliberate surprise, place statues and sculpture to make a bold gesture. Over time, tendrils of ivy may stray and soften outlines, but the visual impact must be from the initial positioning.

WALL PLAQUES

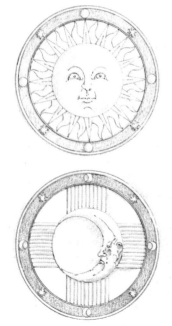

Wall plaques and other two-dimensional bas-reliefs are an asset where space is limited. In some situations a single image will suffice, but where there is a long unadorned expanse of wall, a series of related plaques may be more effective. Singly or as a pair, these Sun and Moon sculptures in anodized and enamelled brass and steel respectively, would add brightness to a courtyard or the end wall of a small town garden.

POLISHED STEEL
SCULPTURE

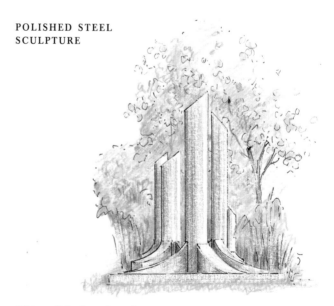

This polished steel sculpture is inspired by the natural forms of tree trunks but is executed dramatically in metal. It makes a particularly effective picture when contrasted against a background of real woodland.

RIGHT *A small piece of sculpture can transform a quiet corner of your garden into a place of mystery and enchantment. Here, a thoroughly modern form imbues a patch of woodland with the charm of a secret awaiting discovery. Its curving spikes echo those of the large-leaved ferns in the foreground.*

OBELISK PLANT SUPPORT

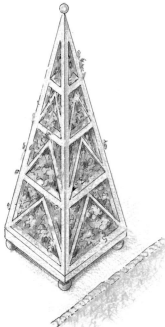

An obelisk plant support *can be used on its own as a single elegant focal point, or in one or more pairs in a formal arrangement. The plant material (here, it is ivy but it could be a rose, for example) is preferably planted directly into the ground, but could be placed in a container if you wished to change the position of the obelisk. To maintain the balanced composition, careful and frequent pruning is needed.*

CLASSICAL URN

A classical urn, *whether a rare original dating from the Renaissance period, a later copy or a modern reproduction in reconstituted stone, has a monumental quality that is underpinned by the solid yet elegant style of the plinth. This example, placed on large flagstones, seems to call for a sober evergreen background of ivy, laurel or yew, and a quiet corner of the garden to suit its contemplative dignity.*

SUNDIALS

Sundials were traditionally used to display family mottoes or remind observers of the fugitive qualities of time and life. A sundial in a modern garden is a piece of unashamed nostalgia. Since it is not needed for its original purpose of telling the time, make sure it plays a significant design role. A sunny position is vital for it is the shadow created by the projection (the gnomon) on the calibrated dial that gives you the time. Research your geographical location when setting up your sundial if you wish for perfect accuracy.

Choose a type of sundial to suit the surroundings. Traditional models may suit older properties, but the subject remains a fertile one for sculptors and designers working with modern materials and new interpretations. As garden accessories, the main choice is between a freestanding ornament or a wall-mounted plaque.

EARLY BIRD SUNDIAL

This early bird sundial is a witty modern version of an old theme, which uses a hapless worm pulled from the ground by a bird as its gnomon. A meandering snail adds decoration to the top rim. The sundial could be raised up by adding a base or a column.

BRONZE SUNDIAL ON FREESTANDING BASE

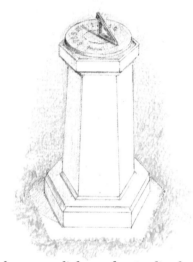

A bronze sundial on a freestanding base makes an attractive centrepiece for an open area such as on a formal lawn or in a courtyard. This dial is in a traditional style and the bronze of the gnomon has become a muted blue with verdigris. The limestone of the hexagonal column echoes that used elsewhere in the garden.

A WALL-MOUNTED BRASS SUNDIAL

A wall-mounted brass sundial makes an elegant focal point high up on a bare wall such as a gable end. It should be directly facing the equator. (For more east- or west-facing positions, the calibration would need to be adjusted.) This dial is cast in brass with raised numerals and rays standing in relief against a painted background.

ARMILLARY SPHERE

Armillary spheres are sophisticated sundials that have graced gardens since the Renaissance. They give information on planetary movements as well as marking the time of day along a calibrated band. This model, topped by a weathervane, stands on a limestone column and base. It could be set in the open or nestle among foliage.

BIRD BOXES, BATHS AND TABLES

Instead of art objects – aimed at appreciation by people only – why not make decorative items focal points that will have a wider appeal? If you haven't room for a water feature to bring wildlife to the garden, perhaps you can find room for a bird box, table or bath to attract birds. Their comings and goings add movement to the garden scene and give you the satisfaction of aiding conservation. For both wild birds and pets kept as a hobby, there are many excellent designs – or try designing your own.

Position the feature out of reach of cats and other predators, but where you can enjoy the birds, such as in view of the house windows. Clean periodically to avoid risk of disease.

TREE-MOUNTED BIRD BOX

*A **tree-mounted bird box** looks best and is most likely to attract customers if made of an unobtrusive wood that more or less blends with the background. This model has a hint of chinoiserie in its scrolled craftsmanship to please the human eye and strike a decorative note.*

WALL-MOUNTED DOVECOTE

*A **wall-mounted dovecote** painted in traditional white makes a striking feature, with its rows of perches, against an ivy-clad brick wall. The copper roof moulds itself to the curving tops of the removeable front panels in a sophisticated design.*

CARVED STONE BIRD BATH

*A **carved stone bird bath** in grey/pink granite makes a handsome focal point set either in a lawn or on paving interspersed with flowering plants. Various reproduction models, many cast in reconstituted stone, offer a curving, less severe outline.*

FREESTANDING RUSTIC BIRD TABLE

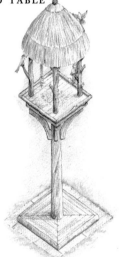

*This **freestanding rustic bird table** draws on natural materials such as the peeled pole and perches as well as old-time crafts such as thatching for the roof. Wood shingles for the roof and square-cut planks would give a more streamlined effect.*

BARREL DOVECOTE

*A **barrel dovecote** is based on a traditional idea where strong, rain-resistant barrels were sometimes constructed especially for this purpose. This example has ventilation under a shingled roof and a turned pole set into concrete.*

LIGHTING

Lighting the garden makes it look attractive when viewed from the house and makes it accessible at night, transforming the site into an outdoor living room. Artificial lighting offers dramatic potential as special features are singled out from the darkness. Shining spotlights upwards into trees or highlighting a statue or fountain can make the night garden positively theatrical. Simple lanterns and flares will enhance romantic evenings and dining out. Some flares incorporate insect-repellents so these have an additional value.

For night-time safety, good illumination for surfaces such as paths and steps is a priority. Use either low-level units, choosing downward-cast beams to avoid dazzle, or taller lamps that diffuse light more widely. Outdoor games call for special-purpose light-ing. Halogen floodlighting means you can continue play after dark. For a swimming pool consider floating or submersible lighting.

As with interior decoration, the light fixtures you choose can be decorative in their own right or functional. During the day, those that are a visible part of the garden need to blend in with their surroundings. A few period reproductions such as lamp posts work well in the gardens of older houses, but discreet contemporary units with a clean neutral style are often preferable.

Most garden lighting is connected via buried cables. Special-purpose fittings include a wide range of ground-level units. Post lights or lamps for paths and drives are neat and inconspicuous. There are brick-shaped lamps that are built unobtrusively into the lower courses of walls and steps, and more decorative lamps which glow prettily as markers in the garden layout. Translucent plastic or hardened glass is best for light covers at a low or ground level. Ground-level directional lights, such as spots, provide a degree of flexibility. However, since the power supply must be implemented as part of the construction process, early planning is vital.

Many modern garden light units are low-voltage and either run off a special low-voltage circuit or incorporate a built-in trans-former. Apart from security lighting, the wattage for garden lamps is usually lower than that indoors. Have your lighting system controlled from a single point so that you can select the precise combination of effects to suit the circumstances. Always use the services of a professional electrician who will install weatherproof units and cables, appropriately insulated according to the statutory safety regulations.

RECESSED LIGHT

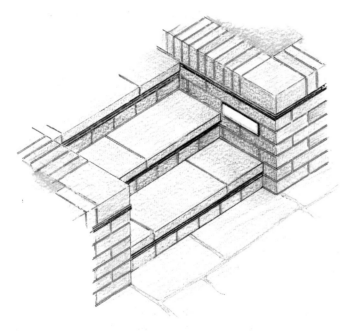

Recessed lights for building into walls come in standard brick and stone sizes. Set into courses a brick or two above ground or step level, they illuminate walkways efficiently without interrupting the streamlined effect of the architecture.

BUILT-IN DIRECTIONAL LIGHT

This built-in directional light is a handsome, low-level unit made of a toughened glass or plastic lens in a circular brass frame. Here, it is contained within a dark marble base, which is softened by ivy. The direction of the beam is easily adjusted by applying hand pressure.

FIBREGLASS BOULDERS

Fibreglass boulders, *which unlit by day blend inconspicuously with their surroundings, glow softly at night. They look pretty by a planted pond edge or in among grasses along a naturalistic path. They are lightweight and easily moveable.*

JAPANESE LANTERN

A Japanese lantern *in real or imitation stone makes an attractive garden ornament during the day. At night, lit by a flickering candle, its effect is magical. You could adapt one of these lanterns to house a low-wattage electric lamp fitting.*

ART NOUVEAU-STYLE FLOWER LIGHT

An art nouveau-style flower light *is made in bronze in the style of a flowering plant with a round bulb as the open 'flower' and a smooth candle bulb as a 'bud'. This light should be displayed to show off its ornamental value.*

CONVEX WALL-MOUNTED LAMP

This convex wall-mounted lamp *is made of coated aluminium with a toughened glass or plastic lens. It is sufficiently good-looking by day and night to fit on the house wall as general illumination for the patio, path or front door.*

COATED-STEEL POST LAMP

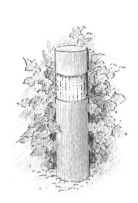

A coated-steel post lamp *has all-round lighting. Alternative versions come in aluminium or hard plastic and may have a lens running only halfway round the circumference of the column, suitable for lighting a path or driveway.*

WOODEN POST LIGHT

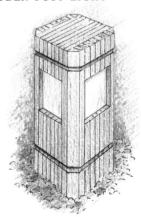

A wooden post light *finished in grooved and jointed cedar with lamps facing in two directions is ideal for a path junction or a corner of an enclosed area of the garden. Other configurations of lamps are available in different styles of finish.*

MOVEABLE SPOTLIGHT

Moveable spotlights *can be placed anywhere within the cable's length for varied lighting effects. Normally finished in black, this spiked version is placed discreetly in the soil, but alternatives with clips or brackets can be affixed to high positions.*

MUSHROOM DOWN-LIGHT

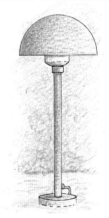

Mushroom down-lights *with the lamp set at about chest height fit into most settings. A row along a driveway gives a neat and soft effect. Available in various designs and finishes, a matte black recedes inconspicuously into the shadows.*

WATER AND ROCK FEATURES

Inspiration for successful water and rock features often comes directly from the natural landscape where they so often coexist. Rocky outcrops, boulders and tumbling streams suggest patterns which can be imitated on a smaller scale when you want to make the most of a change of level in an informal garden setting. On flatter ground, limestone pavements play host to alpine plants and pebble beaches can be used as edging to a water feature.

Nothing brings a garden to life as effectively as water, whether still or moving. Introducing water into the garden artificially has many advantages over gardening around a pre-existing or natural water feature. Not only can you choose the style and scale to suit yourself, but you can control the operation to a far greater extent. Natural pools and streams entirely dependent on local rainfall are subject to variations in water levels which often means unattractive low water levels in dry weather and flooding in heavy rains. With an artificial water supply, the pool level is topped up as necessary and a proper overflow system prevents it from flooding the surrounding garden. You can turn on fountains and other moving water features when you want them – saving both power and water – or install timing devices to work the pumps periodically to filter water and to activate displays.

CHOOSING A WATER FEATURE

When considering installing any type of water feature, research it thoroughly or consult an expert, and check any local regulations. It is not merely a matter of sound construction and proper installation of pipework, pumps, filters and associated electrical supply. You need to plan for a healthy water system designed specifically for the needs of whoever is to enjoy the pool – plants, fish, wildlife or people, or some combination of these parties. (Swimming pools are a special case, and are discussed on page 169.) Your research will help you decide what kind of materials and construction will best suit the special situation of your garden and the scale of feature you want. Your main decision is whether to use a ready-made liner or to construct the water feature from native materials. Professionals will advise on maintenance routines and

explain how soon a new pool can be filled with water and stocked with plants or fish. Although public water supplies sometimes have a high chemical and nutrient content, they are generally more predictable than natural sources, which can be affected by local conditions, including chemicals used in lawn care or by farmers.

Suit your water feature to the scale of the garden. Still water in any form adds interest from the tiniest basin to a boat-sized lake. Moving water gives perhaps even greater pleasure, whether you have space only for a bubble fountain or can accommodate a cascading wall of water. In a level garden, a formal canal or a rivulet of faster-moving shallow water could work better than a natural-looking stream. Any abrupt change of level is an opportunity for a vertical feature such as a waterfall, which is generally informal and naturalistic, or a formal cascade, which is potentially grander.

RIGHT *Rock and stone are used in different ways to provide the main interest in this quiet pool garden. The strongest vertical form is the largest boulder in the background. This is softened and counter-balanced by the sculptural form of the pitcher which harmonizes with the grained horizontal boulders in the foreground. The grey and buff colours of the flat rocks surrounding the pool are picked up by the two-toned gravel.*

LEFT *A trickle fountain with a bamboo spout imitates an outflow from a spring. To help the illusion that this is a real spring, a flat-topped rock has been placed beneath – it would be used for holding a bucket or pitcher to collect water – but here simply makes a pleasing splashing sound. The bamboo cross poles add a touch of artistry. The spout and rock used on their own without a pool would make a safe water feature in a garden where small children are about.*

ORNAMENTAL POOLS

Choose the location of an ornamental pool carefully. Full sunlight promotes the growth of algae so partial shading from nearby walls, garden structures or foliage, or from the leaves of aquatic plants such as water lilies, is desirable. Avoid excessively shady sites, especially beneath trees. A build-up of decaying fallen leaves will alter the acidity or pH value of the water, making it necessary to clean out the pond frequently. The ideal aim is to maintain a balance of plant and animal life that will keep the water clean and clear. Find out which species are likely to thrive in your locality.

The treatment for the pond border is an intrinsic part of planning the whole feature. The advantages and disadvantages of materials and styles echo the formal-versus-informal design debate. It is usually easier to conceal a prefabricated rim or flexible lining material by making a formal hard-edging of natural rock, brick, wood or paving. A slight overlap conceals any lining. A stylized informality can be achieved the same way, but creating an entirely artificial system that looks perfectly natural, especially with planted borders, is more tricky.

A decorative raised rim works well around a formal pool, and this is a good way of maximizing water depth with minimal excavation. Raised pools surrounded by lawn or hard surfacing have a clean geometry and bring the water surface closer to the viewer. You can also set a tank against a vertical backdrop to create a rectangular or semicircular raised pool. You can use this rear wall to introduce moving water in the form of a waterspout or cascade. However, water naturally gravitates to low-lying ground so for a natural look position your informal pond at a level where it appears to occupy the lowest ground. If your garden has a gradient, you may be able to take advantage of this to run a stream or waterfall into the pool. Or you could improvise a slope by building a rock feature next to the water which would also conceal mechanisms such as a pump and reservoir.

LINING WITH A CLAY LAYER

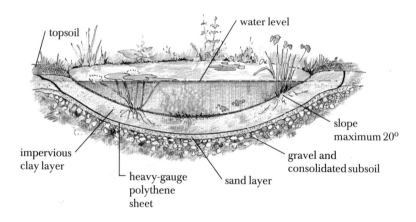

topsoil

water level

impervious clay layer

heavy-gauge polythene sheet

sand layer

slope maximum 20°

gravel and consolidated subsoil

Lining with a clay layer is worth considering where flexible, impervious clay with a low silt content is readily available. A heavy-gauge polythene sheet inhibits plant growth beneath the 300mm(12in) thickness of clay. A gently sloping profile prevents migration of clay particles to the pool bottom. Keep moisture-loving trees and plants with vigorous roots away from the clay layer. An open situation away from trees is advisable.

RIGID PREFORMED LINER

stone edge overlap

matching fibreglass waterfall kit

levelled liner

plant basket on ledge

water level

A rigid preformed liner, readily available from garden centres, offers a quick and economical way to install a small pool. Choose black or dark grey shells of plastic or fibreglass for attractive reflections and a less artificial look. Be sure to excavate an accurate hole for the mould, using sand to level the ground as necessary. Check that the rim is perfectly level. Backfill carefully with sand to support the weight of water when the shell is filled.

CAST CONCRETE

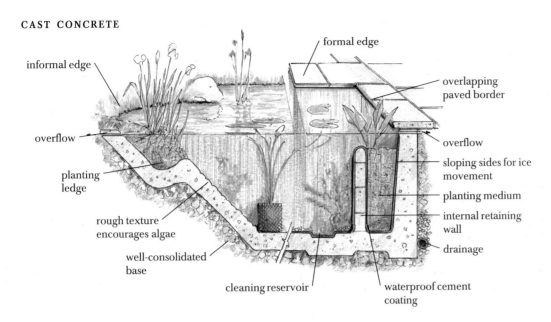

informal edge

formal edge

overlapping paved border

overflow

overflow

planting ledge

sloping sides for ice movement

rough texture encourages algae

planting medium

internal retaining wall

well-consolidated base

drainage

cleaning reservoir

waterproof cement coating

Cast concrete is highly effective for modelling both formal and informal shapes. Special features such as planting ledges or internal planting compartments are easy to incorporate as are services such as overflow channels, pumps and so on. Texture the surface for a natural look or finish with a waterproof coat of cement in a colour of your choice. Well-prepared foundations and technically correct construction, perhaps including steel rod reinforcement, are vital to strengthen the structure against cracking under the weight of water. Where winter freezing is likely, build a slight slope into vertical sides to allow ice to expand upwards harmlessly and avoid cracking the concrete sides.

FLEXIBLE LINER IN AN INFORMAL SETTING

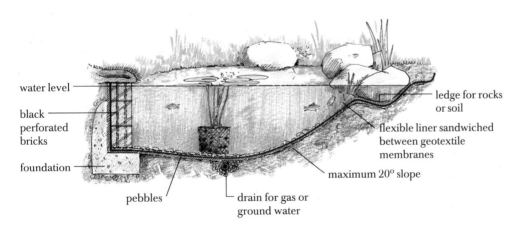

water level

black perforated bricks

foundation

pebbles

drain for gas or ground water

maximum 20° slope

flexible liner sandwiched between geotextile membranes

ledge for rocks or soil

A flexible liner in an informal setting uses natural rocks or
_led turf to conceal its edges. The liner of high-quality butyl
_shioned on both sides to protect it from sharp stones, moulds
_self to the contours of the excavation. For a natural appearance,
_grade sloping sides to no steeper than 20° to allow debris to settle
on the liner and disguise its presence.

A FLEXIBLE LINER IN A FORMAL SETTING

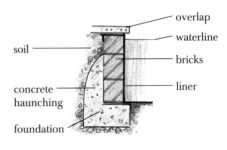

overlap

waterline

soil

bricks

liner

concrete haunching

foundation

A flexible liner in a formal setting needs a firm edge for definition. The sides of the pond are formed from a brick retaining wall set on concrete foundations, and both pond bottom and sides are covered with the liner. The wall supports man-made or natural stone slabs that overhang the surface of the water.

THE WATERSIDE

Formal water features usually have well-defined rims. Because these are soundly built, they act as a structural support when you need access to the water for maintenance, for example. The apparently naturalistic borders of informal pools and bog gardens, on the other hand, need careful planning so that underlying structures remain hidden while still serving their function.

If you want to be able to wade into the water, keep waterfowl or launch a boat, you need to construct a sloping bank or beach for easy access. Functional concrete and pebble beaches are among the options. Planning sound foundations are important and there is the additional need to protect the waterproofing of an artificial pond. Where access is less important, an alternative treatment for the pond edge is to plant it. The happy way plants colonize banks and shallows in nature takes some preparation to imitate where your raw materials consist of liners and piped water supplies. The advantage is that an artificial area of bog planting is often easier to control than a purely natural environment, where water levels fluctuate unpredictably and a few vigorous plants tend to take over. Seek advice on the water depth and moisture preferences of the plants you plan to grow. Bog plants prefer soils low in organic matter and nutrients, and choosing this kind of growing medium keeps any adjacent area of open water healthier. Wherever there is a physical link between the soil in a bog or pond and the surrounding ground, you can expect capillary action to cause some water loss during summer.

Of course, moisture-loving plants can be included in a garden without the presence of open water by adapting pond installation techniques to create a self-contained area of boggy ground.

EXPOSED AGGREGATE CONCRETE BEACH

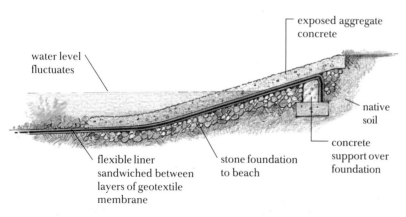

exposed aggregate concrete

water level fluctuates

native soil

flexible liner sandwiched between layers of geotextile membrane

stone foundation to beach

concrete support over foundation

PEBBLE BEACH

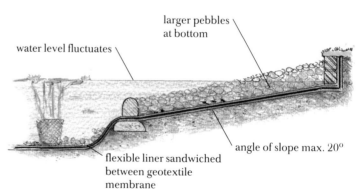

larger pebbles at bottom

water level fluctuates

angle of slope max. 20°

flexible liner sandwiched between geotextile membrane

An exposed aggregate concrete beach is a functional edging for a lined pool. It is laid over well-prepared foundations which need to be calculated to allow for the weight of expected traffic such as a boat and trailer. On laying this surface (and before the pool is finally filled) wash it to expose the aggregate, which both improves its appearance and helps provide grip. If the area of concrete is substantial, you would need to incorporate thermal movement joints (see page 73). The geotextile membranes protect the liner from the edges of stones above and below.

This pebble beach is an entirely artificial construction but will look relatively natural provided that the stone used melds with the surrounding landscape. Water-worn pebbles are the most appropriate choice for a beach though multi-faceted crushed stone would be less likely to migrate downhill when stepped on. A slope of 20° maximum dropping to a kerb below minimum water level keeps the layer of pebbles fairly stable. Grade the stones or pebbles with smaller ones at the top and larger ones at the bottom, with the flattest next to the upper geotextile membrane.

LEFT *An attractive wooden walkway makes a firm footing through boggy ground, winding its way through an area full of varied moisture-loving plants, including large-leaved gunnera and hostas.*

WATERSIDE BOG PLANTING

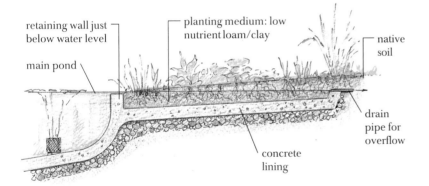

retaining wall just
below water level

planting medium: low
nutrient loam/clay

native
soil

main pond

drain
pipe for
overflow

concrete
lining

Waterside bog planting *that extends from an artificial pond shows that planning is necessary to achieve an apparently natural effect. This pond has a concrete shell but a flexible liner would call for a similar pattern. A retaining wall just below the water surface separates the bog from the deeper open water. The planting medium is an 45cm(18in) depth of low-nutrient loam or clay which slopes upwards from water level until it reaches the level of the surrounding ground. This profile of gradually decreasing water content suits the preferences of a range of plants, from those that thrive in shallow water to bog plants which require a great deal of moisture.*

SELF-CONTAINED BOG GARDEN

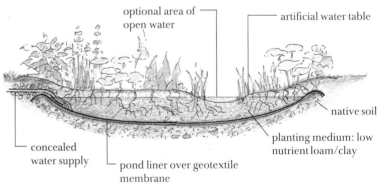

optional area of
open water

artificial water table

native
soil

concealed
water supply

pond liner over geotextile
membrane

planting medium: low
nutrient loam/clay

A self-contained bog garden *is easier to achieve than waterside planting. Choose a low-lying area, perhaps next to a pond, and excavate a saucer shape about 60cm(2ft) deep at the centre. Line this with low-grade pond liner or overlapping sheets of heavy-gauge polythene. A perfect seal is unnecessary and water can be allowed to seep away slowly unless you want to include a permanent area of open water. Fill the depression with low-nutrient loam or clay, 'puddling' or firming it down in the centre and bringing it up to the level of the surrounding soil at the sides. Install a concealed water supply so that the artificial water table can be added to as necessary.*

FORMAL BOG GARDEN

A formal bog garden can be planted in geometrical beds adapted for moisture-loving plants. Raised edgings and paths create the formal pattern within which a variety of lush water plants thrive. Two separate water systems are in operation here. The sunken beds are irrigated by underground pipes while a separate supply circulates through the ornamental fountains that are placed at the centre and at each corner.

RAISED PATIO BOG GARDEN

NATURALISTIC BOG GARDEN

A raised patio bog garden offers a variation on the idea of a raised pool. The wealth of planting and the pleasing movement from the little bell fountain set in the centre brings life to an area enclosed by man-made surfaces. Installing such a feature above ground level obviates the need for extensive excavation although water, power and drainage must be provided. A wide rim not only reinforces the formality of the feature but provides a place to sit and admire the planting in detail.

This naturalistic bog garden has a more traditional approach and creates the illusion of a naturally low-lying, moist area. An option shown here is a bubbling spring head and a small area of open water to attract wildlife. Planting makes an informal composition punctuated by an irregular stepping-stone path for access. The mechanism for the trickling spring is concealed in the realistic-looking rocky outcrop that abuts the moist area, just as it might in nature.

FOUNTAINS

Arching sprays of water droplets lit by the play of sunlight or artificial lighting are among the most lively decorative features for the garden. Wonderfully contrived, tall fountains usually belong in a formal context and there is a wide range of designs from which to seek inspiration. An ornamental fountainhead may be incorporated in the display or, alternatively, the water itself forms the display as it issues from an invisible jet or series of jets. When there is no space for a pool, a simple waterspout offers a welcome focal point. It brings the movement and murmur of water to even the smallest courtyard or alleyway.

It is always a good idea to seek expert opinion in advance when you are contemplating introducing a fountain or any other kind of moving-water feature. Even if you are buying something in kit form, you may need advice on water pressures and pipe diameters and the services of a professional to connect the electrical supply. Pumps are necessary wherever a consistent natural water source is not available, which applies to most gardens. It is against the law almost everywhere to operate fountains, waterfalls and so on

RIGHT *A tiny formal lily pool with a statue and fountain is set off by four clipped conical evergreen shrubs. The simple device of the ornamental fountain jets adds height, delights the eye, and brings movement to the surface of the pool, and also the soothing sound of trickling water.*

wastefully, so you will need to recirculate the water, topping it up as necessary. You will need a holding pool at the bottom level and a header pool or tank at the top. The relative volume of these reservoirs, the rate at which the water circulates, and the technology for controlling the whole system are all matters for experts. The scale and style of a self-contained feature such as a fountain may dictate whether the pump should be submersible or fitted externally. Follow the manufacturer's recommendations.

A sophisticated spray fountain can be costly to run as well as to install and may entail high water consumption. The surrounding basin must be large enough to capture all the droplets and spray, especially on windy days, otherwise the pool could rapidly empty. In warm weather evaporation exacerbates this problem. Fountains that merely trickle rather than being pressurized through a spray consume considerably less water, and offer a soothing rather than a thrilling display that suits many less ostentatious settings.

You can also choose from a range of smaller-scale fountains and waterspouts that don't need a catch basin or pond at the base and in doing so save on both space and water. A basin generally forms part of the design in wall-mounted fountains. In other cases, the liner which collects the water and returns it to the reservoir is invisible, hidden beneath a layer of carefully arranged pebbles.

The display of water in a fountain is controlled by the size of the holes in the fountainhead and the arrangement and number of heads. Tiny holes create a white foaming effect while larger holes produce larger droplets of clear water.

SPOUTING FOUNTAIN

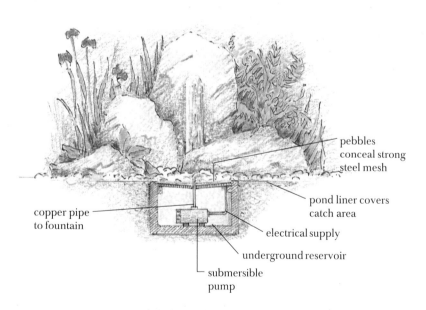

pebbles conceal strong steel mesh

pond liner covers catch area

copper pipe to fountain

electrical supply

underground reservoir

submersible pump

A MILLSTONE FOUNTAIN

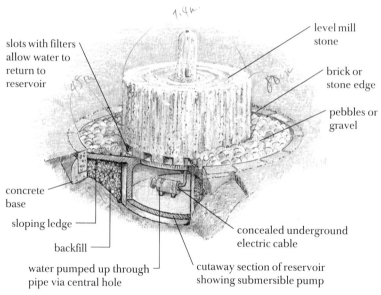

slots with filters allow water to return to reservoir

level mill stone

brick or stone edge

pebbles or gravel

concrete base

sloping ledge

backfill

water pumped up through pipe via central hole

concealed underground electric cable

cutaway section of reservoir showing submersible pump

*A **simple spouting fountain** set in rocks is ideal for a naturalistic setting where a pool is not wanted. The vertical jet provides the right touch of movement and sparkle. The water from the spout collects on a lining sheet of black butyl hidden beneath the pebbles and is fed to the underground reservoir to be recirculated by the submersible pump.*

*A **millstone fountain** is a safe feature for small children since there isn't any standing water. Water emerges from a jet at the centre of the fibreglass reproduction millstone, flows over its surface, and apparently disappears beneath the pebbles. In fact, it collects on a sloping ledge and is returned to a reservoir. A submersible pump is used to circulate the water.*

WALL-MOUNTED WATERSPOUT

A wall-mounted waterspout in a popular mask or 'grotesque' head is available as are floral and abstract designs. Here, the god Pan's head is depicted in glazed green terracotta. A compact submersible pump concealed within the catchment bowl or behind the spout returns water via a pipe to the fountain's mouth. The pipework must fit unobtrusively. Access via the back of the wall is the most convenient means. Some waterspout kits require water to be added to the basin, others have a small reservoir tank.

A BOWL FOUNTAIN

A bowl fountain brings interest to an existing patio where you want to avoid disruptive installations. Choose a frostproof bowl and stop up any drain holes to ensure the interior is waterproof up to the waterline. Drill a small hole at the waterline and through this feed an electric cable to supply a submersible pump and fountain inside the bowl. The hole doubles as an overflow. The hole and cable should be in the least conspicuous position.

FALLEN JAR WATERSPOUT

This fallen jar waterspout plays on the idea that one water-filled jar has just fallen over and is emptying its contents into a pool. The flow, in fact, circulates via a concealed flexible pipe connected between a drainage hole in the jar's base and a submersible pump in the pool. The fallen jar is anchored with a small amount of mortar. The upright jar is purely for effect – it has a greater impact for being left empty. Porous terracotta or stone jars need to be waterproofed before use.

POOL CENTREPIECE WITH FOUNTAIN JETS

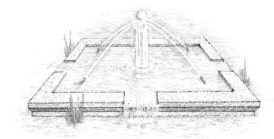

A pool centrepiece with fountain jets echoes the style of a Moorish courtyard garden. Four angled spouts spray water towards the central ball which appears to float on water. In fact, it is firmly set upon the transparent pipe supplying the vertical fountain. The pool rims are textured concrete. Cutaway sections on each side of this centrepiece allow water to cascade into the lower pool and be pumped back through the fountain jets.

CASCADES AND WATERFALLS

What distinguishes features such as cascades and waterfalls from fountains is that they form part of the landscape even if this is clearly an artificial one. The water falling from a higher to a lower level and the vertical surface against which the water flows make an important contribution to the design.

The rockwork for a waterfall can be conveniently built to conceal necessities like the reservoir tank. Sections of waterfall structure can be bought as preformed moulds or you can use flexible pond liners, concrete or even rocks. Organize flanking rocks and the surrounding planting to conceal any synthetic materials and create a natural-looking entity.

A cascade is intrinsically more formal than a waterfall, so it is not necessary to hide the fact that its surroundings are man-made. The most imposing designs are often those that are set in walls of concrete or marble.

WATER SPOUTS SET INTO A GROTTO

Water spouts set in a specially-built grotto with a shell, pebble or flint back wall cascade into a rectangular pool. Shade-loving aquatic plants grow within while an evergreen shrub, groundcover or trailing plant grows in the container above the roof. The walls are tinted and stuccoed concrete blocks.

ROCKSCAPE WATERFALL

A rockscape waterfall looks to nature for its inspiration so that the arrangement of surrounding rocks looks authentic rather than contrived. Place rocks with the grain running parallel to imitate strata. The stream will appear to have found a natural faultline or to have worn its route over the ages. A key challenge is to use natural materials to conceal the artificial parts that are the building blocks of this feature.

FORMAL WALL CASCADE

A formal wall cascade is a simple sheet of water falling over a retaining wall. This soothing cascade is fed by a shallow canal at a higher level. At its foot a square catch tank then feeds a narrower and deeper canal. These components are infinitely variable, and the scale of the adjacent pool/canal and the volume of water can be adjusted to make the most of the available space. Here, planting softens the impact of the hard materials.

STEPPING STONES AND BRIDGES

Bridges and stepping stones are often included for their decorative value across pools that you could just as easily walk around. Paths that cross water features are particularly pleasing in small gardens, where they add variety. They often make it possible to create new routes in the garden tour and provide additional access so that space can be maximized.

Curves add rewarding reflections to the garden composition. The flowing shape of a wood, metal or stone bridge with a semicircular arch and its arc reflected in the water form an appealing circle or ellipse. However, the horizontal sweep of most bridges does interrupt the view over the water. This can sometimes be cleverly exploited by positioning a bridge in such a way that it terminates the view at the far end of a pool, which then appears to continue out of sight.

A bridge, walkway or jetty of staggered parallel planks adds interest to a stream or pond crossing. For a more open vista, consider making your water crossing from stepping stones – as long as the most frequent users are nimble-footed.

Choose materials, forms and a scale that marry with the surroundings. As with all waterside features, safety must underpin style. Structures must be sturdy and stable underfoot with non-slip surfaces. Water exerts a powerful fascination, but gazing at it can induce dizziness. Many people like the added assurance that handrails give on both bridges and jetties.

STEPPING STONES ACROSS A POND

These stepping stones across a pond are set on slightly narrower, darker-coloured supports. It is important to calculate the spacing of stepping stones to provide a comfortable pace across the water. Visually, too, the stones should follow a graceful line. Avoid placing them too close together and consider the effects of viewing them in perspective.

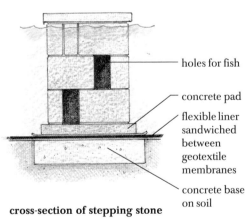

holes for fish

concrete pad

flexible liner sandwiched between geotextile membranes

concrete base on soil

cross-section of stepping stone

This cross-section of stepping stone construction for a pond demonstrates its solidity. Painted black, the blockwork disappears and, viewed across the pond with the water at its correct level, the stepping stones will appear to float on the surface like lily pads. The gaps provide refuges for fish.

WOODEN JETTY

Wooden jetties are useful where pools are large enough for boating. In artificial features where the water level is kept constant, their design can be simple. Supporting posts are set in a concrete footing for stability and rest on concrete foundations. The jetty principle can be adapted to construct decking, bridges or a waterside viewing platform in a country or wildlife garden.

A WOODEN BRIDGE

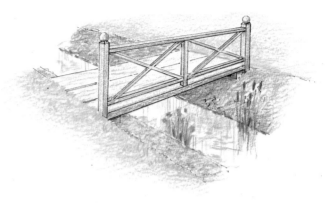

A wooden bridge constructed of planks with a neat handrail structure provides a simple, functional crossing. Treated wood planks or a concrete or stone footing laid at either end support the bridge planks. These must be sturdy enough to avoid any disconcerting spring when people walk across. Rustic poles could be substituted for both bridge and handrail for a less formal look.

STEEL BRIDGE

Steel bridges in both contemporary and period styles and varying dimensions are available from specialist manufacturers. Sound design principles make them relatively light in both weight and appearance. This elegant example spans a wide stream in a graceful arc.

USING NATURAL STONE

The most effective use of stone or rock emphasizes the character of the particular stone. This means placing it in a way that could suggest its original location. Inspiration can also be borrowed from man-made landscapes where terracing or dry stone boundary walls seem an intrinsic part of the scenery.

A rock structure should look as if it has always been there. An exception to this is where you design a self-contained feature such as a Japanese garden of contemplation. But in an informal garden setting local stone gives a better result. A sloping site looks more natural and is easier to deal with than a flat one, though you can, of course, import soil and create your own contours.

The satisfaction of growing beautiful alpines is a good reason for creating a rock feature. These plants relish the combination of gravelly soil (sharp drainage, but moisture for roots) and bright light (enhanced by reflections off the stony surface). Many happily colonize the cracks in paths as well as official niches in raised beds to give the garden a blurred-edged atmosphere.

An idea for a boundary is a hedge wall with a soil top and centre to allow low hedging plants to grow. Use random rubble to create a natural feature or square-cut stones for a more tailored look.

BOULDER ROCK FEATURE

A boulder rock feature should include one or two large rocks which will convey enormous power as elements in a visual composition. Take their great weight into account since you will need a lot of physical strength to move them. Smaller rocks, stones, or an accumulation of gravel at the base of the rocks can incorporate a planting area and helps merge the feature with grass or a horizontal hard surface.

A STRATIFIED ROCKERY

A stratified rockery imitates a fault in an escarpment by aiming to make the stones appear as if strewn by natural forces. Rather than risk a cluttered effect by using numerous small rocks, use larger rocks. Vertical dwarf shrubs and perhaps a prostrate juniper can soften the outline of the flat top of the rock garden.

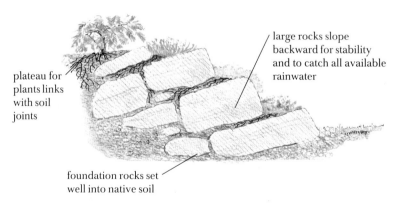

large rocks slope backward for stability and to catch all available rainwater

plateau for plants links with soil joints

foundation rocks set well into native soil

cross-section of a stratified rockery

The cross-section shows the rocks angled backward so that rainwater runs back into the soil joints. Lay the stones with their natural grain on a horizontal plane. Do not tip them on end as this encourages rainwater to penetrate, causing flaking.

PAVEMENT ROCK FEATURE

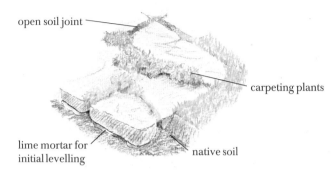

open soil joint

carpeting plants

lime mortar for initial levelling

native soil

*A **pavement rock feature** may have an uneven or smooth surface depending on whether or not it doubles as a path. Select stratified thin-section stones for strength and durability. Large stones will look more pleasing than small ones and are more stable and less quickly overgrown.*

ABOVE *The natural stone of this pavement rockery, which doubles as a broad pathway, makes a perfect foil to a colourful carpet of sun-loving rock roses (Helianthemum). Small areas of gravel could replace some of the stone slabs.*

DRY STONE RETAINING WALL

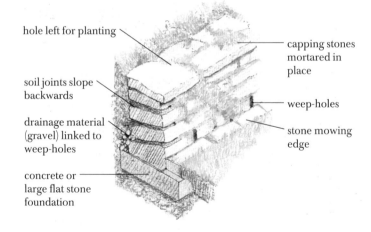

hole left for planting

soil joints slope backwards

drainage material (gravel) linked to weep-holes

concrete or large flat stone foundation

capping stones mortared in place

weep-holes

stone mowing edge

*A **dry stone retaining wall** with a good balance of weep-holes to soil joints can be used to grow a selection of alpines. Plants should be inserted as the wall is built. A layer of drainage material behind the wall links with the weep-holes, allowing excess water to escape. The capping stones, unless they are very heavy, must be secured with mortar. Foundations are not needed for walls less than 45cm(18in) high.*

TRADITIONAL HEDGE WALL

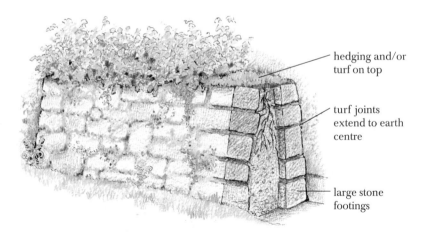

hedging and/or turf on top

turf joints extend to earth centre

large stone footings

*A **traditional hedge wall** built of dry stone uses turf or earth joints which extend to the wall centre, in place of mortar (see page 80). It is set on a single slab of concrete or stone footing as shown here, or on parallel strip foundations with gravel in between for drainage. The earth centre provides space for the roots of hedging material, and creeping flowering plants can be sown or placed in the turf.*

LEISURE AND GARDEN GAMES

For many people, the most important function of their gardens is that they should be places of relaxation and recreation. Here they will eat, sit and entertain; they will use seats, tables, barbecues and other equipment whose design, placing and materials affect the look of the garden. Children will play here – and so may adults; they will have items as varied as play houses, swings, basketball hoops, or mazes marked on patio squares, which take up little space, or those such as tennis courts that need a lot of room. To many garden owners, the swimming pool is the 'jewel in the crown', and there is no doubt that for sheer fun and good exercise, there is nothing to beat it.

Consider what your favourite leisure pursuits are and what equipment you will need for them. All these items and activities and the space they may require need to be thought about in terms of design and how they will fit into the garden plan. A basketball hoop is easy to accommodate but a tennis court may just overwhelm your plot. Harmony of colour and style with the surroundings is the goal whether you are choosing a swimming pool, children's play activities or simply functional furniture for the garden. A table and chairs near the house is one of the first things your eye will light on when you enter the garden, so what you see needs to set the stylistic keynote.

RIGHT *A deck garden partly shaded by shrubs and trees makes an inviting spot for leisurely lunch parties, and provides plenty of space for children to amuse themselves away from the table. The furniture has been carefully chosen. The handsome white umbrella makes a design feature of the white table, benches and chairs that it shades. The varied alignment of the sections of timber decking enhances the feeling of spaciousness.*

SEATING

Your lifestyle will dictate the part played by furniture in your garden design. If you regularly use the garden as an outdoor living or dining room, an area with paved flooring is advisable. A sturdy surface is also necessary beneath most permanent garden seats, both for your comfort and the furniture's well-being. If a flexible arrangement is a priority, choose tables and seats that can easily be moved into new configurations.

The wide range of materials – particularly wood, stone, metals and plastics – offers every combination of the practical and the ornamental. It is easy to find something to suit both the tastes of the family and the demands of the climate. The spectrum ranges from lightweight items that you can reposition to follow the sun (or the shade) across the garden to permanently built-in features. You could combine a seat with a planter to make a low space-divider between a patio and the main garden, or to provide a self-contained planting area backing onto a boundary fence. Maintenance considerations range from easy-care items requiring no more than wiping down to more vulnerable woods and metals that need preservative or paint treatment from time to time. A wide range of upholstery is available in weatherproof fabrics.

BRICK AND TIMBER SEAT IN A RETAINING WALL

A FREESTANDING BRICK PLANTER AND SEAT

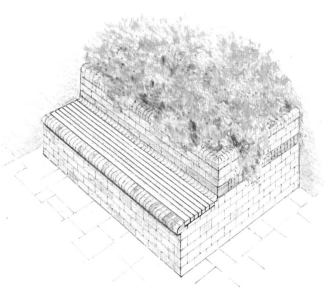

A brick and timber seat built into a retaining wall can be an integral part of the garden design. This painted wood seat is simply set into the rear and sides of a brick wall which retains a raised bed for herbs or low-growing shrubs. The site is pleasantly sheltered by the walls and the planting, and the rear wall slopes back gently to make sitting more comfortable.

A freestanding brick planter and seat is here virtually a raised bed with built-in seating and storage. The seat, of individual slatted wood planks to speed drying after rain, lifts up to allow access to a handy space where garden equipment can be stowed. The seat back slopes gently and bull-nosed bricks form a comfortable curved edge. Scented plants would be ideal in the bed.

A TRADITIONAL TREE SEAT

A traditional tree seat enhances the tree around which it is built, while offering a shady place to sit and enjoy garden views in any direction. Since such seats are often made of metal sections, or metal and wood combined, they can easily be made polygonal rather than circular.

A 'GOTHIC' COVERED SEAT

A 'Gothic' covered seat offers the privacy and shelter of an arbour. This 18th-century design is built in wood with chamfered (angled) posts and tongue-and-groove panelling. Traditionally, it would be painted in a dull muted colour. The curving roof would be covered in copper.

A SERPENT BENCH

This serpent bench displays the design versatility of metal supports. These can be fancifully shaped in cast iron in a variety of organic forms, or more functionally bent and moulded in straight-section steel. Wooden slats for the seat and back have an intrinsic warmth.

FORMAL WOODEN SEAT

A formal wooden seat in a popular early 20th-century design is particularly suitable for a formal setting. It looks best in a pale colour such as cream or in light natural wood. Left permanently in an outdoor location, it needs a dry footing of bricks or blocks sunk to ground level to be inconspicuous.

ELEGANT WROUGHT-IRON 'GOTHIC'

Elegant wrought-iron 'Gothic' designs of this kind were originally popular in the late 18th and early 19th centuries. Painted in traditional muted hues of blue or green, this seat is decorative enough to serve as a garden's focal point. Wrought iron needs regular painting and maintenance.

EDWARDIAN-STYLE SEAT

This Edwardian-style seat with its detailed carving is sturdy and imposing. Made of an untreated hardwood such as teak or redwood, it needs minimal maintenance.

PATIO DINING TABLE

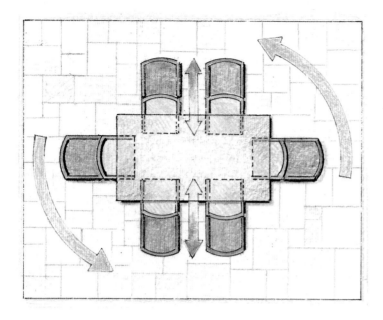

A patio dining table for six calls for a surprisingly large area to allow guests comfortable access to and from their seats, plus circulation space around them for serving food and drinks. This plan demonstrates how a 90×180cm(3×6ft) table could command a total space measuring some 3.65×4.65m(12×15ft). Each chair occupies an 45cm(18in) square area. Obviously, smaller tables and more casual styles of entertaining need less room, but make sure people can move around the table freely.

ENAMELLED STEEL FURNITURE

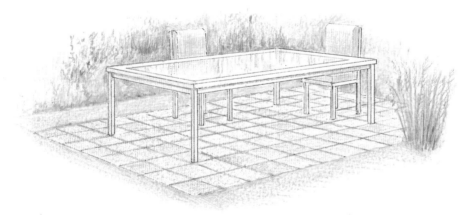

Enamelled steel furniture has clean lines that look elegant in a contemporary setting. This table-top is toughened glass and the seats have removable upholstered covers. Some styles come in plastic-coated steel. Choose fabric for the soft furnishings that can be left outdoors, although prolonged exposure to strong sunlight or bad weather will eventually cause fading and deterioration.

AN ALL-IN-ONE PICNIC TABLE

An all-in-one picnic table fits into most settings except the very formal. This circular version with satellite seats acts as a fulcrum for family activities. The wood may be unpainted but stained or coated with a preservative. The table remains permanently outdoors, but you can reposition it with little effort in different parts of the garden.

BARBECUES

Barbecues come high on the list of garden items for many adults. The barbecue provides a forum for relaxation and recreation, the grown-up equivalent of play. There are dozens of mobile and portable models, often gas-fuelled for convenience, but serious fresh-air cooks often like to make a permanent barbecue as part of the outdoor living space. Building a barbecue to suit yourself can be as therapeutic as cooking on it. The choice of harmonizing bricks or tiles turns it into an attractive feature – it could even be a focal point (remember that 'focus' has its origins in the Latin word for hearth – the centre of the household). Consider positioning the barbecue so that the principal chef can face the company seated at the table while doing the cooking.

RIGHT *A barbecue for the outdoor-cooking enthusiast has plenty of work or serving space at each side. It becomes a garden feature in its own right, flanked with pots of flowers when it is not in use.*

BASIC BRICK BARBECUE

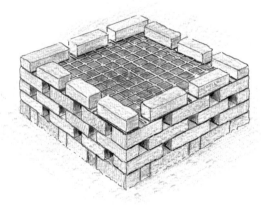

PERMANENT BRICK-BUILT BARBECUE

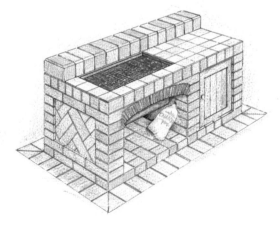

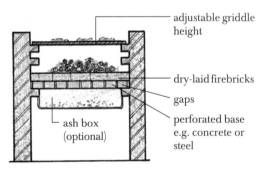

adjustable griddle height

dry-laid firebricks

gaps

perforated base e.g. concrete or steel

ash box (optional)

cross-section of the permanent barbecue

A basic brick barbecue can be easily dismantled. The bricks are dry-laid (without mortar) but their weight lends stability. Spaces between the bricks above the solid foundation course allow up-drafts of air to achieve good fuel combustion. The grill of builder's steel mesh, set in place when the fire is hot, is held firm by the top row of bricks.

A permanent brick-built barbecue has the grandeur of a kitchen range. Build it to the height of an indoor stove top to provide adjacent work surfaces in an easily cleaned, weather-resistant material such as quarry tiles. The useful storage space for fuel or utensils below the work surface could also incorporate a small refrigerator.

This cross-section of the permanent charcoal-fired barbecue shows how none of the surfaces close to the fire is fixed. Gaps are built in to allow for heat expansion. If you use concrete for the base, lay firebricks over it to prevent direct contact with burning fuel. The height of this barbecue is approximately 90cm (3ft).

CHILDREN'S PLAY

High on many families' lists of priorities are places for children to play. Their siting depends primarily on convenience and safety, but also partly on how good-looking they are. You can make some children's features into positive eye-catchers or build them into the garden's structure. Sandpits, for example, belong to open spaces in the horizontal plane, and can be designed to look attractive to adult eyes. Swings and play houses belong to the vertical framework and can be as ornamental as you wish. You can tuck some children's areas away in separate garden compartments. Their exact positioning will depend on the age of the children and the size of the garden. Play areas for very young children need to be supervised, so designing them entails planning adjacent space for adults' comfort, or at least positioning them near the house.

Flexibility in the short or long term is a consideration. Some children's areas and features may have to double up for grown-up recreation, too. Children's interests and priorities change as they grow older and your garden design will have to adapt.

Take play areas into account when planning planting schemes. Where ball games or other boisterous activities infringe on other parts of the garden, grow tough resistant plants as a buffer zone rather than precious fragile ones. Avoid growing prickly or poisonous plants where children might come into contact with them. And if a child actually wants to garden, try to allot a small space where the soil and sun are potentially good enough to produce rewarding results, rather than relegating it to some corner where you can't grow anything anyway. Early success with easy subjects like annuals or quick-growing herbs and other edibles may inspire a lifetime's enthusiasm for gardening.

MODULAR PLAY SYSTEMS

Modular play systems *include a wide spectrum of items such as slides, ladders and playrooms to assemble in any number of permutations. Some are made in wood, others in plastic, steel or a combination of materials. Make sure they are situated on a safe play surface (see page 41) Most systems are designed with safety in mind, though adults need to supervise very young children.*

PLAY HOUSE

Play houses *provide children with their own private space. They are safer than tree houses and useful where you don't have a suitable tree. Many are handsome enough to play a role as a special feature in the garden tour, but their miniature status makes them suitable for sites too small for the scale of a grown-up summerhouse.*

HOOP-LA

pegs or targets with score values

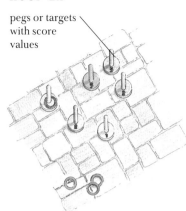

Hoop-la *is a very old game. Players take turns throwing three same-colour hoops over pegs marked with different values – the highest being the hardest to reach. These pegs have bases so they can stand on hard surfaces, but lawn versions simply have pointed ends. You could make and paint the pegs and hoops yourself, and since the deployment of the pegs is flexible, you can move them about and space them in different ways to increase or decrease the difficulty of the game.*

SEESAW

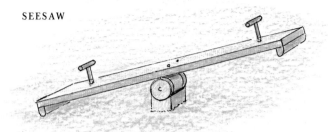

Seesaws *are among the simplest (and possibly oldest) of play items. For years children were content with a simple plank and log construction, but this example is a little more sophisticated. A well-designed seesaw in wood or steel placed within a woodland clearing or on a far lawn could assume the status of a focal point.*

AN ARCHWAY SWING

An archway swing *is an original idea, both ornamental and useful for a garden in which space is limited. The frame for the swing doubles as a decorative archway and a support for climbing plants. The swing can be hooked to the side or detached when not in use. It calls for substantial permanent supports, which may be bought ready-made.*

SANDPIT AND PADDLING POOL

Sandpits and paddling pools *are children's favourites, and this example shows them neatly placed side by side. Both are best constructed like a shallow pond using a concrete or rigid synthetic liner. Both require drainage, such as a layer of crushed gravel beneath. A paddling pool can be emptied periodically by means of a sink basin plug unit. Use clean coarse sand for the sandpit, change it regularly, and remember to cover it when not in use to prevent contamination, especially from animals. The best place for siting these features would be near the main patio or sitting area where adults are close by.*

INFORMAL GAMES

Most games and activities need space and a specially designated area even if it is only a little-used courtyard or enclosure at the back of the garage where you can rig up a basketball practice net or a space to put up a trampoline. A smooth lawn is needed in some cases, for example, in games such as croquet, or there are fabric mats than can be unrolled to provide the play surface. For games needing a fixed area defined on the ground, install unobtrusive markers and embed post sockets so that outlines can be marked and the equipment set up in a relatively short time. If there is enough space, adjust the positioning periodically to prevent wear on heavily used areas of the lawn.

There are also ways of incorporating into the garden's ground plan decorative features that can be used for play, such as chequerboard patterns and mazes. These satisfy both active participants and more passive garden enthusiasts. Mazes and laby-rinths have long been favourite garden devices. Some traditional garden mazes are delineated with hedges and take both time and space to achieve, but alternative versions using contrasts of colour or texture in horizontal surfacing need less room and make pleasing ground-patterns. You can pleasantly fill winter evenings working out the intricacies of the patterning on a scale plan.

A maze or chequerboard pattern can be worked into an area of paving. The contrast can be low-key – distinct enough for a player to follow, but not so arresting that it dazzles the eye when people are relaxing nearby. Simple lawn mazes are another possibility. The route can be via grass paths marked by narrow bands of some material such as brick or tiles, marking a primarily green surface with sinuous patterning. Or the route can follow narrow paths of brick, paving or gravel through grass, making a stronger visual impact. Either make the grass strips the width of your mower or use an edging that you can mow over, otherwise maintenance will involve edge-trimming.

BASKETBALL HOOP AND BACKBOARD

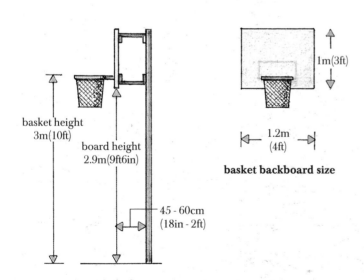

A basketball hoop and backboard can be freestanding or attached to the side of a garage or a suitable stretch of house wall and provides plenty of practice and fun. Single practice shots, games of one-on-one, or pick-up games can be played.

PATIO MAZE

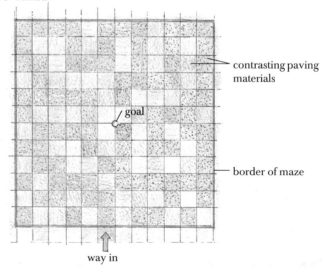

This patio maze is marked out in two different colours of the same paving material. The rules are that you must follow the dark squares, making only right-angle turns and not stepping over any lighter-colour slabs. Here, the goal at the centre is marked by an ornamental crystal ball, but you can have fun choosing a device to represent the culmination of your quest.

SPECIAL GAMES AREAS

Most families improvise an informal practice area for their favour-ite sport, whether it consists of a badminton or volleyball net strung between two specimen trees on the lawn, or a small putting green. But if a family member has included serious sports activities such as a tennis court on the garden plan, it implies that your site is large enough to fit in an area designated for specific games. However, unless you want to be a spectator on the terraces of a sports ground, you need to allow not only for the dimensions of the court itself, but also for a zone of planting around the games area. Chain-link fencing is entirely alien to most people's concept of a garden.

The first step is to work out where, or whether, an appropriate space can be found in your garden. A good method is to cut out a piece of paper representing the outline of the game space drawn to the same scale as your garden plan. By moving the card about on the plan, you can judge where to place the game. Courts for games such as tennis or badminton should ideally be orientated with the net running from east to west for even sunshine. Almost all games call for level ground, so check the contour lines or datum marks on your plan. If the site needs levelling bear in mind any side-effects such as the need for retaining walls and drainage provision.

Protective netting such as chain-link fencing is visible from a great distance unless disguised. Portable nets erected on lawns for the duration of the season are less uncompromising than perma-nent wire netting and its supporting posts (trees in full leaf can help to mask them), but their presence is none the less conspicuous.

Both practically and aesthetically, the best disguise is planting. Ideally, set special games areas in a garden section ringed with evergreen hedges. If the area is sunken, the perimeter fencing can afford to be lower. With foliage the borders can be turned into a decorative screen which not only hides the functional surfaces but also muffles the voices of the players. Yew makes a fine background to other planting in its own right, or it could provide the cue for a colonnade in Italianate garden style, with classical statuary or ornaments set at intervals along its length.

RIGHT *Decorative planting around this tennis court distracts the eye from the functional chain-link fencing surrounding it. Pencil junipers are positioned at regular intervals, and clematis, roses and Russian vine scramble up the fence.*

TENNIS

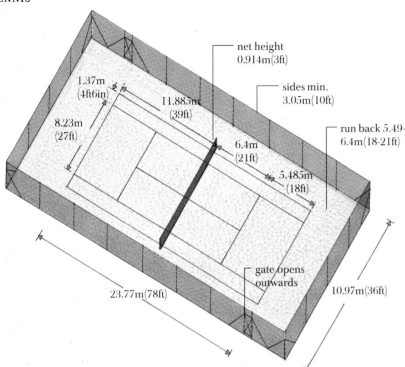

net height
0.914m(3ft)

sides min.
3.05m(10ft)

1.37m
(4ft6in)

8.23m
(27ft)

11.885m
(39ft)

run back 5.49-
6.4m(18-21ft)

6.4m
(21ft)

5.485m
(18ft)

gate opens
outwards

23.77m(78ft)

10.97m(36ft)

A tennis court needs a lot of space, as these dimensions show.
Having the surface in a colour that blends into the surroundings
and a dark green or black finish to the chain-link fencing around
the perimeter can partly disguise the severe rectangular lines of
such a large feature.

BADMINTON

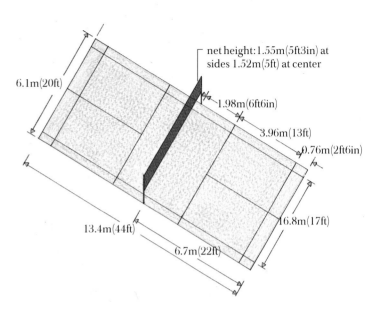

net height:1.55m(5ft3in) at
sides 1.52m(5ft) at center

6.1m(20ft)

1.98m(6ft6in)

3.96m(13ft)

0.76m(2ft6in)

13.4m(44ft)

6.7m(22ft)

5.18m(17ft)

Badminton needs less space than tennis. It is played with rackets
and a feather shuttlecock which is light and doesn't travel far so
it doesn't need a court surround, but it means a calm day is
necessary. It is a good active game for the garden as it doesn't
damage nearby plants. For two to four players, it can be enjoyed
on any level lawn or even in a courtyard.

TENNIS COURT SCREEN

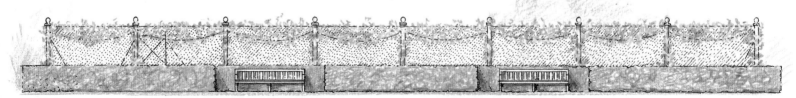

This tennis court screen makes a fine ornamental feature. Each
wooden post is positioned in front of an upright that supports the
chain-link fencing. Two lines of rope pass through the posts near
the top, the upper one fairly taut and the lower one looped in
swags. Climbing roses can be trained along the ropes. An evergreen
hedge at the base of the fencing hides the court's surface from view.

SWIMMING POOLS

Installing a pool is obviously a task for professionals, but you can go a long way towards choosing the shape and design that pleases you, and the way this integrates with the rest of the garden. The construction engineer will then check that your proposed siting is feasible – not too near building foundations or trees, for example – and will help you decide on the most appropriate materials for construction. The professional should also advise on practicalities such as covers, on safety, and regulations such as fencing. You may even require the permission of a local planning authority or water company to install a pool, so check this at an early stage.

Many garden swimming pools can play a dual role. When they are not in use for bathing, they should make pleasing shapes in the garden's ground-plan and can even double as ornamental pools. For this reason, geometric pools look best in formal settings. Free-form shapes will look more at home in an informal layout. Slope the pool borders outwards to a concealed drain to conduct splashes, rainwater and debris away from the pool itself. Well-designed borders based on harmonizing natural materials and an organized display of plants help to create an integrated look. Link the style of buildings serving as changing rooms with that of the pool and its surroundings. Keep the style of related structures intended to house filtration and heating units in the same spirit.

RIGHT *An irregular red brick pool surround on two levels has angled and curving edges that soften the impact of this swimming pool positioned close to the house. The colour of the bricks is carefully chosen to reduce glare. The same material is used for the low retaining wall, and the terracotta plant pots continue the colour theme. The bed near the side of the pool containing a small tree and flowers provides interest and welcome light shade.*

The colour of the interior also helps to make a pool seem to belong in its setting. Light-coloured interiors – blue, grey, turquoise – permit inviting views of the sides through the water and belong best in sunny latitudes, where bodies of water reflecting blue skies naturally look this way. (Light refraction makes the colour of pool interiors appear several shades lighter, and makes the water seem shallower than it really is.) In temperate climates, black or a very dark blue are better choices for a pool's interior. These have the effect of turning the water's surface into a mirror which, when seen at an angle, reflects the sky, neighbouring trees and so on.

The cross-sections of pools here show typical examples of depth variation according to different family needs. Actual distances and slopes will, of course, be determined by the length allowed for the pool. It is easier (and safer) to accommodate deep water in a long pool than in a short one, where slopes may have to be made steeper to achieve the desired depth.

POOL FOR GENERAL PLAY AND RECREATION

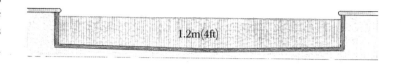

The pool for general play and recreation *is a single-depth pool deep enough for swimming, but with a water depth of only 0.9-1.2m(3-4ft). The base should still slope either towards the centre or to one side to ensure that debris migrates towards the filters rather than collecting on the bottom.*

POOL FOR FAMILY PLAY

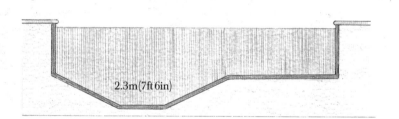

This pool for family play *has a shallow area in water about waist deep, then grades down to a depth of about 2.3m(7ft 6in) to permit jumping in and shallow diving from the pool edge. Even the flatter areas should have a gentle slope to encourage debris to migrate to the filter inlet, which is usually situated at the pool's lowest point.*

POOL FOR THE DIVING ENTHUSIAST

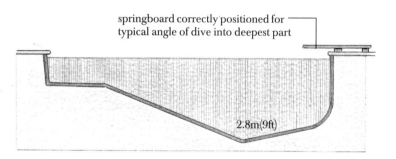

A pool for the diving enthusiast, *though small, has a depth of 2.45-2.8m(8-9ft), allowing scope for underwater swimming and the use of a springboard. The springboard is correctly positioned to take account of the typical angle of dive relative to the water depth. A high diving board needs much deeper water.*

RIGHT *This beautiful swimming pool was designed by the eminent landscape architect Thomas Church. The geometric lines are softened by the sinuous figure at the pool edge, while two large rounded shrubs frame the fountain and abstract sculpture.*

OASIS-STYLE POOL

A KIDNEY-SHAPED POOL

An oasis-style pool and border is designed as a complete landscape feature. At the deep end, the natural stone used for the paving (and diving board) appears in its uncut state in the guise of a rocky outcrop, complete with a tumbling cascade using recirculated water. A tunnel beneath the outcrop leads to the housing for the filtration and heating units. Plants grow close to the pool at some points. Hidden containers protect their roots from possible contamination by chemicals in the pool water.

A kidney-shaped pool with a natural stone border set into random edging blends well into an informal garden layout. A black or dark blue lining helps to imitate the light-reflecting qualities of a natural pool when the surface is still, further reducing the artificiality of the feature. This pool could be made with either an almost level or a more sloping base. A cover would have to be specially made to the pool's shape in a suspended or floating design rather than a fully automated system.

A ROMAN-ENDED POOL

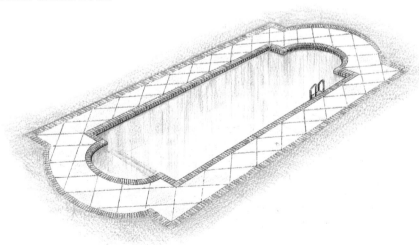

A Roman-ended pool gives a rectangular shape a more decorative impact while maintaining its formality. This example repeats the semicircular feature at both ends with steps descending at the shallow end only. A ladder allows access at the deep end. Warm-coloured bricks frame the main paving, which is laid with buff-toned exposed-aggregate concrete or precast units. Canted or angled bricks soften the edging of the pool rim.

RECTANGULAR POOL

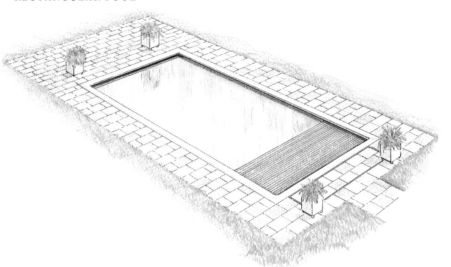

A rectangular pool is the best shape for fitting with a fully automatic pool cover (shown here partly extended). The cover mechanism is contained within a recessed area in the paving (between the planters in the foreground). The rectangular shape also provides the maximum regular swimming area and is likely to be the least expensive to construct. Here, the deck border is of blue-grey non-slip paving with matching continuous copings along the pool sides. The four planters underpin the cool formality of the design.

L-SHAPED POOL

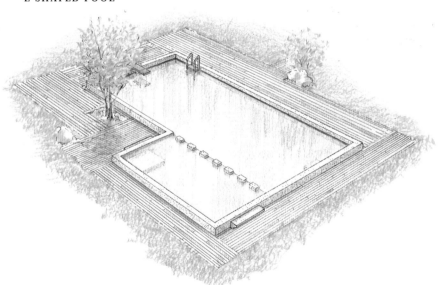

PLASTIC POOL

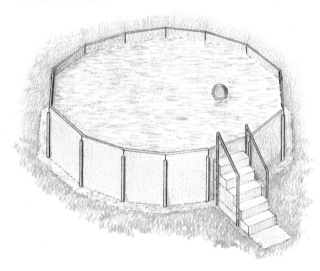

This plastic pool is made of tough PVC formed and held in place by an aluminium alloy or steel frame. Typical water depth is 90cm(3ft). The impact of an above-ground pool can only be lessened by careful positioning and screening, but not from the view of watchful adults when younger swimmers are about.

An L-shaped pool designed for family use gains considerably in character from its handsome decking border. The pool has a raised rim of exposed aggregate or hammered concrete with the sharp edges rounded off. The shallow and barely sloping children's area is separated from the conventional deepening pool for swimmers by an underwater safety wall. The castellated top of the wall appears above the surface and serves as seating.

GARDEN PLANS

SAMPLE DESIGNS FOR A RANGE
OF GARDEN STYLES

OPPOSITE *Balance, harmony and visual interest are
evident in this well-planned garden. An archway
overgrown with roses echoes the flower-laden porch.
The open area of lawn is bisected by a brick path
leading to the arch framing an enticing view.*

The plans featured on the following pages illustrate design solutions to typical garden situations. Of course, gardens vary widely in shape, size and their position in relation to the house. But for easier orientation, these samples are all rectangular in shape and, with the exception of the Xeriscape garden plan on page 198, show the house at the bottom of the page.

Each plan is a carefully constructed and coordinated scheme, but you may use or adapt those individual elements that appeal to you. That is why you should study even those garden plans that might not seem to apply to your situation. You may live many miles inland, but you could still be interested in the texture of the paving or the shape of the water feature in the Seaside garden on page 186. And even if you don't live in a city, you might introduce one of the City garden's intimate paved areas from page 196 into your suburban or country garden. Another possibility is to reinterpret a design with a different kind of planting: you could, for example, implement many of the layouts with the colour scheme of your choice, or concentrate on your favourite native plants, or species attractive to butterflies.

But always remember that garden designs evolve from several starting points. Pure inspiration is one of them, but the nature of the site itself and the needs of the people who use the garden are paramount. Many ideas or themes are feasible whatever the nature of the site. If you want a low-maintenance garden or one for a wide variety of family activities, the main constraint is usually simply one of size and cost. Given careful planning, good use of man-made structures and surfaces, and hard-wearing, undemanding plant materials, you can have a garden that is practical and attractive.

If the starting point is a style of planting or a planting theme, you either have to choose your site carefully or be prepared to mould your ideas to suit it. For example, roses will grow in all sorts of sites and climates, but for the full glory of a rose garden, a sunny, not-too-windy site is necessary. A planting for cottage-style profusion might suit a town-centre site with adequate soil, but would not suit a coastal site where battering winds and salt spray would damage many of the plants that give such a garden its true character.

So then, use the plans on the following pages both for practical help and for inspiration. But remember that every garden is individual, and stamping your own preferences and personality on a design is the key to creating a garden that is truly your own.

FAMILY GARDENS

Gardens that are to be used by a family often have to accommodate various activities to meet the requirements of the different generations. This large rectangular garden site has been designed with an asymmetrically formal layout creating separate areas for the changing needs of an active, growing family. The result is a variety of practical features that can be incorporated without sacrificing aesthetic considerations. The bold use of handsome, well-proportioned structures, like the pergola of octagonal columns (3) and the trellis screen (9) supported by matching columns (8), sets a stylistic keynote for the whole garden. Materials such as terracotta and gravel are repeated in different features so that the separate ingredients come together as a whole.

The virtue of creating different compartments with their own use and identity is evident in this garden plan. Open areas (6 and 7) contrast with enclosed ones (5 and 14). The enclosed areas are linked by narrow paths, while frequent glimpses of hidden spaces encourage exploration. Carefully planned views lend an air of elegant formality, but there is also plenty of space for children to play and grown-ups to sit and relax.

This family's checklist of priorities included somewhere to grow vegetables and herbs. The adults are avid gardeners whose idea of recreation is to spend time tending their plot. They do not see regular tasks, such as mowing, as onerous chores. Garden owners without such enthusiasm might prefer to build a swimming pool or tennis court in the enclosure (13) beside the container garden (14). Others might allocate a smaller area to ornamental lawn and increase the proportion of low-maintenance planting in the wild area of the garden (7).

Children's play activities are high on the agenda for this garden. The wild garden or informal shrubbery, complete with tree house (12), becomes a secret world for imaginative play. The lawn bordered with sturdy plants provides plenty of space for energetic games and a soft surface for toddlers' play. While the children are very young, wise parents will either barricade access to the pool (5) with fencing or gates (making these attractive features in their own right), or convert it into a sandpit in the short term.

House

A COMPARTMENTED
FAMILY GARDEN

*The terrace (**1a** and **1b**) is in two sections, its overall outline echoed in the shape of the lawn. It is large enough to use for outdoor play when the ground is wet as well as for entertaining and al fresco meals. A barbecue (**2**) stands permanently ready. Two small trees at the corners of the larger terraced area (**1a**) frame the view from the house. This view runs along the garden's major axis, passes beneath a pergola (**3**) and terminates at a bronze statue on a terracotta base (**4**).*

The view towards the statue (4)

*The smaller section of the terrace (**1b**) has an oblique view of the pond (**5**). The surrounding lawn (**6**) is kept closely mown, both for a play surface and for its smooth visual effect.*

*The pergola, made with octagonal terracotta columns, provides a passageway between the main lawn and the wild garden (**7**) beyond. Matching columns (**8**) are used to support the panels of trellis (**9**) at the far end of the garden, making a dividing screen.*

*To the left of the pergola is an ornamental greenhouse or summerhouse (**10**) surrounded by a herb garden (**11**). The wild garden (**7**) is the children's secret play area. Here, the grass is longer, shrubs create hiding places, and a tree house (**12**) is built in the branches of a large tree at one end. Play equipment such as slides and swings could also be located here. Once the children have grown up, their parents may use this area for their own interests – perhaps for fruit trees and beehives.*

*A vegetable garden (**13**) in ornamental style is aligned on the cross-axis of the pergola. It is divided into four symmetrical sections and the vegetables grown in the well-groomed beds are chosen for their attractiveness as well as their culinary use. A small, gravelled container garden (**14**) with a built-in seat leads from the vegetable garden and provides an area for rest and contemplation.*

*The formal pool and fountain (**5**), visible from the lawn and terrace, are approached along an angled gravel path (**15**). The trees around the pool complement its angular form and a weeping tree (**16**) makes a beautiful backdrop.*

ABOVE *The vegetable plot in this family garden is protected from the sweeping areas of lawn by a low hedge. Vistas have been created using existing mature trees and by planting shrub and herbaceous island beds.*

WATER GARDENS

Water is always an attraction in a garden. It can be introduced as an incidental feature, for example as a small fountain, or it can be a major theme. In the garden plan here it is both ornamental and, in the form of a swimming pool, functional. Ingenious planning accommodates four distinct types of water feature: a still pool for plants and wildlife, a formal fishpond, a stream of moving water and a pool for bathing. All are integrated in a design that is asymmetrically formal near the house, giving way to informal curves the further from the house you go. Two separately powered pumping systems are used, each with its own water supply, filters and disposal system. Thanks to modern technology and artifice, water gardens are feasible in almost any situation.

The natural-looking informal pool (4) ringed with water-loving plants feeds a stream (3), which takes advantage of a slight slope in the site to flow into the fishpond (2) beside the terrace (1). This water is filtered as it travels to suit fish and plants. For the swimming pool (6), a different and more rigorous set of criteria must be applied to govern the quality of the water. The swimming pool is the highlight of this garden, working efficiently but looking more ornamental than utilitarian. Designed to appear continuous with the adjacent informal pool, there is in fact a wall hidden beneath a line of stepping stones (7) to separate the two bodies of water. The dark-coloured lining of the swimming pool has been chosen to reflect light in just the same way as the water in the neighbouring informal pool (4), reinforcing the sense of this being one expanse of water. Both pools are held together by a smoothly curving outline and by similar background planting.

The choice of exposed aggregate concrete for all paths and hard surfaces unifies the complex layout of this garden. This neutral material is uniquely suited to both rectangular and curved forms. It plays a dual role as a surfacing material for the paths and as the necessary non-slip surfaces around the pools.

LEFT *A Jacuzzi and swimming pool have been so carefully integrated into this terraced hillside that they seem to be part of the natural landscape. The free-form shape of the pool, the use of a dark-coloured lining, and the way in which the planting has been encouraged to grow to the water's edge, all create an effect that is attractive and natural-looking.*

A VERSATILE WATER GARDEN

The shape of the concrete terrace (1) echoes the rectangular lines of the house, while the L-shaped fishpond (2) continues the formal theme. A narrow stream (3) enclosed by geometric paved edging adds the sparkle of moving water and connects the fishpond with the informal pool (4).

The informal pool (4)

The pool's shallow edges grading into marshy soil provide a habitat for lush aquatic and marsh plants. The water from the informal pool discharges into the L-shaped pond from beneath the textured concrete path (5). The swimming pool (6) with its curved outline and dark-coloured lining looks like a continuation of the informal pool, but has a separate chemically controlled environment. The stepping stones (7) add to the illusion of a continuous body of water, but in fact disguise the underground barrier between the water of the informal pool and that of the swimming pool. An area of decking (8) at the shallow end of the swimming pool leads to a pool house (9). The lawn (10) acts as a neutral foil – a pool of space – to offset the areas of high interest that surround it.

The water discharges into the fishpond (5)

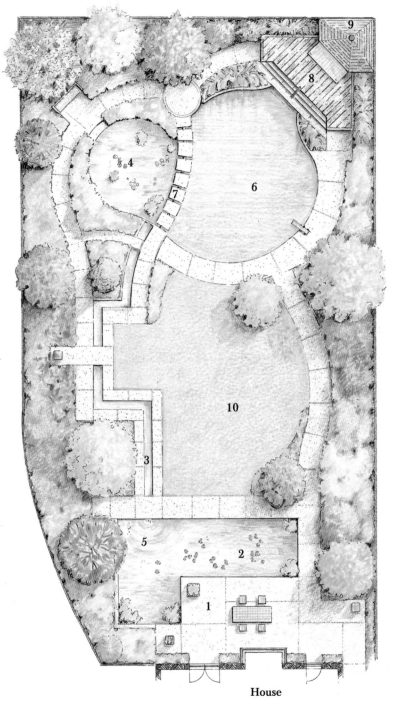

House

ROSE GARDENS

Scent, colour and blossom forms come first to mind when choosing roses for a new garden. However, in terms of garden design, it is most useful to consider the growth habit of different types of rose.

The rose repertoire includes many shrub and bush forms with compact, sprawling or arching habit to feature in beds and mixed borders, or to grow as hedges. For vertical accents, grow climbers and ramblers along walls, or train them over arches and pergolas. There are compact or low-growing roses for ground cover, and vigorous scramblers to use as cover-ups on banks and over unsightly sheds or tree-stumps. For eye-catching touches of formality, bush and weeping roses grown as standards make effective centrepieces. Using different colours and heights, these also set up pleasing rhythms when planted in groups or rows.

The owners of the broad rectangular plot shown here have a passion for roses and wanted their favourite flower to shape the design. Their rose garden is no humdrum bed of Hybrid Teas (now properly known as large-flowered bush roses), glorious for a period in summer and ungainly during the rest of the year. They have used roses of different types and habit, for example climbers, shrubs, ground-covering patio roses, as design tools to create a highly sophisticated layout in which the wonderful blooms are a decorative bonus in season. Carefully chosen trees, shrubs and hedges provide both structure to complement the roses and year-round visual interest. Some beds include bulbs for spring colour and ground-cover planting chosen to complement the roses. Restful lawns and gravel paths act as a low-key foil to the planting interest.

A rose garden on this scale calls for the right conditions – shelter, plenty of sun, sufficient moisture and a fertile, well-drained soil. It also demands commitment on the part of its owners and some expertise to train and prune the rose plants. Even if you do not pursue the rose theme so exclusively, you may find many welcome ideas here for your own garden.

LEFT *At the height of summer, pink and white roses complemented by delphiniums in pastel shades fill the garden with gentle colour and delicious fragrance. The clipped box hedges that edge the circular, maze-like arrangement of beds give a firm structure to the scheme. Together with the decorative shapes of the pretty gazebo, the urns and the patterned porch railings, they ensure year-round visual interest.*

House

A PATTERNED ROSE GARDEN

*The broad terrace (**1**) paved with natural stone and brick makes a visual foundation for the house. Climbers and ramblers (**2**) decorate the house walls, trained on unobtrusive horizontal wires spaced 45cm(18in) apart. You could choose one or more varieties to suit the architecture and colour tones of your own façade.*

*The lawn and beds near the house (**3**) have a formal layout. Six matching round-headed trees punctuate the corners (**4**): Crataegus prunifolia– a hawthorn, which is a member of the rose family – would be an appropriate choice. These trees are underplanted with low patio roses, while the bed to the left (**5**) combines roses with other shrubs and bulbs selected for winter interest. The main axis from the terrace focuses on a terracotta ornament (**6**), behind which is glimpsed the opening to the maze of rose hedging (**7**).*

*The maze is composed of robust large- or cluster-flowered bushes (Hybrid Teas or floribundas). These grow just high enough to conceal, from the viewpoint of someone standing, the configuration of the gravel path (**8**). The maze works not just as an effective intellectual puzzle, but also on an aesthetic level with the colours of its planting corresponding as closely to the colour wheel as the palette of rose flowers allows. The surrounding neat evergreen hedge (**9**) has only two openings.*

*An informal area of longer grass beyond the maze (**10**) is planted with large lax species shrub roses, most of which have interesting foliage and attractive hips in the autumn. A mown path (**11**) leads from the summerhouse or gazebo (**12**) to a focal point (**13**), perhaps a statue, in the opposite corner.*

*A rose-clad T-shaped pergola (**14**) draws attention to the gravel path (**15**) that leads back to the house via an ornamental pool (**16**). The short arm of the pergola extends to shelter a seat (**17**) aligned with one of the entrances to the maze. In this area small lawns are framed by low hedges and white-flowered roses (**18**).*

*The circular sunken pool with paved edge forms the centrepiece of a semi-formal area separated from the main lawn by a hedge of rosemary (**19**). In one corner a seat (**20**) is set among shrub roses chosen for their colour and scent. The border opposite (**21**), backed by the evergreen boundary hedge (**22**), features more roses and Rubus species. A weeping cherry tree (**23**) adds height to the whole composition.*

ROCK GARDENS

Rockeries first became popular in Europe in the nineteenth century. These artificial rocky outcrops built with pieces of natural stone were used by people as showcases for their alpine plant collections. There was little or no attempt to make them harmonize with the garden as a whole – a design oversight that is, unfortunately, still prevalent today.

For a rock garden to work on an aesthetic level, it must appear that nature has had a hand in it. To give the impression that the rocks occur naturally, try to place several more in well-chosen positions in parts of the garden other than the rockery. Features such as steps and terraces can be constructed in matching stone to ensure they blend unobtrusively into the scene.

Where space is limited, or where a rockery seems inappropriate (in a very formal setting, for instance), natural stone walls can be used as the ideal hosts for many rock-garden and alpine plants.

In the plan for the hillside rock garden shown here, visual continuity is assured by the repeated use of similar stones in several places. Everything works to lead the eye to the main feature – a rocky hillside with a romantic grotto from which water cascades into the lower pools.

LEFT *The natural look of this rock garden is enhanced by the stream winding gently through it. The backdrop of trees gives the rockery the appearance of a woody hillside. The contrasting forms of the planting – the spiky phormiums, feathery ferns, leathery leaves of variegated hostas, and the flat flower heads and fleshy leaves of stonecrop – make a satisfying picture.*

A HILLSIDE ROCK GARDEN

A sheltered extended terrace off the house (1) is the main sitting area. The stone of the paving, the screen walls (2) and the retaining walls (3), is the same grey as the large boulders in the garden. The alpine plants in pots (4) provide a visual link with the alpines elsewhere in the garden.

A pavement rock garden (5), raised slightly above the sitting area, provides an attractive foreground to the bed of dwarf conifers (6) set among boulders immediately beyond it. The small pool in the corner (7) is fed by underground pipes from water on the higher ground.

The main lawn (8) on the next level is reached by broad stone steps (9). Instead of closely mowed grass, this could be a grassy meadow, cut a couple of times a year and studded with bulbs in spring and colourful annuals in late summer.

The tall evergreen hedge (10) bordering the lawn serves as a backdrop and protects the conifers, shrubs and large border plants in the undulating beds at its foot. A garden seat (11) is positioned to look across to a specimen tree (12) and to give a broad view up and down the garden.

The stone steps (13) by the main ornamental pool (14) are made of regular natural stone. The same natural stone is also used for the path (15) that crosses the rocky slopes and forms a bridge over the water cascading from the grotto (16) set in the hillside. The

The stone steps (13)

smooth slabs of the steps (13) contrast with the shapes of the nearby boulders, yet the material preserves the unity of the whole design. The bridge leading from the steps eventually joins a mowed path (17) to the summerhouse (18).

The grotto is the main feature of the garden and completes the impression that it is set on a rocky hillside. Behind, small mountain trees (19) and the open summerhouse heighten the effect of a wild, natural landscape with rocks, plants, a sequence of pools and running water.

The grotto (16)

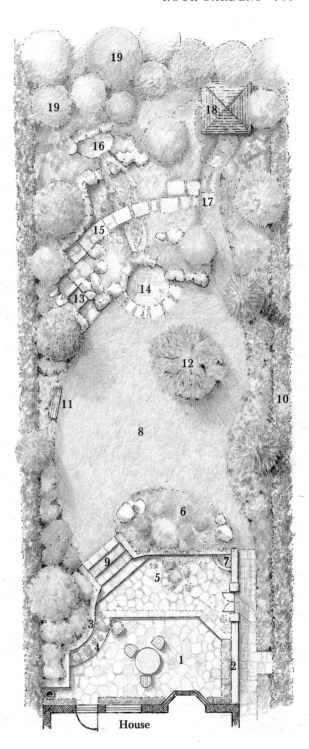

House

GRASS GARDENS

The grasses, including bamboos, offer a great range of effects from feathery edging to robust fencing (see page 93), and can work in every conceivable climate and habitat. Green, as well as greyish-green or blue, yellow and variegated foliage is available, and many grasses turn attractive buff tones in winter. Rustled by the wind, grasses add movement and sound to a garden. Neat mounds, stiff tufts, soaring curves – grass plants have abstract qualities that are superb in modern designs and can look soft and elegantly curva-ceous juxtaposed with man-made straight lines. Some kinds, such as pampas grass and miscanthus, have spectacular flower heads.

The owners of the plot on the right wanted a garden to comple-ment the modern architecture of a new house. Viewing plants more in terms of shapes and textures than flowers and colour, they decided on a predominantly green garden with the emphasis on plants of the grass family. Structure and height is provided by ornamental trees with attractive bark and winter berries.

The treatment for this garden is on a bold scale, but the approach could be scaled down to work very well in a small garden. Near the house, the ground plan is characterized by swirling shapes (1a,1b, 3 and 4). The smooth green lawn (3) is framed by banks of medium-tall grasses and other plants. The height of the planting increases towards the perimeter to form a leafy screen against the border fences (14 and 15). Along the left-hand side of the garden this becomes a jungle-like thicket through which a narrow gravel path (4) meanders. A slight depression in the ground on the opposite side of the garden has been made into a bog garden (6) with moisture-loving grasses, including sedges and rushes, chosen to contrast with other perennial plants. Trees, such as swamp cypress and alder, provide vertical accents in this boggy habitat.

Walking around the garden you glimpse a secluded hedged area (8), accessible only in two places. One is through a square arch in the hedge reached by a narrow pebble path that curves off the main lawn (16), and the other is through the pavilion (12) at the far end of the garden. This area proves to be a rectangular room reminis-cent of a cloister set on slightly raised ground. This meditation garden is striking in its austere formality, contrasting dramatically with the naturalistic forms of the surrounding planting of grasses and providing a highly original heart to the garden.

LEFT *Grasses are particularly effective when planted in natural-looking drifts. Here, the tall background planting of* Calamagrostis *'Karl Foerster' and the paler feathery plumes of pennisetum make a dramatic picture, the grasses contrasting well with the round fleshy forms of the stonecrop,* Sedum telephium, *in the foreground.*

A GREEN GARDEN OF GRASSES

The split-level terrace (1a and 1b) that nestles beside the house and conservatory (2) is made of concrete decorated with flat pebbles. Its texture and curved shape give it an abstract quality.

The main lawn (3) beside the terrace has a bold swirling shape. This expanse of green carpet presents a brilliant foil for the taller surrounding plant forms. It is cut regularly, but not closely cropped. A medium-coarse textured grass (or a hot-climate substitute, such as lilyturf) is good in this situation. A perfectly smooth surface of the finer grass species could look too manicured.

A gravel path (4) runs down the left-hand side of the garden, beneath a circular pergola (5) and around the back border. It curves between a jungle of ornamental shrubs and trees mixed with rustling bamboos and other grasses (14). This dense planting is similar to that screening the opposite fence (15).

A boggy low-lying area (6) along the right boundary is home to moisture-loving grass species and lush large-leaved plants. The pathway (7) is made of long slabs of exposed-aggregate concrete laid in a herringbone pattern. Its zigzag route gives plenty of opportunity to concentrate on the strong plant interest of the area.

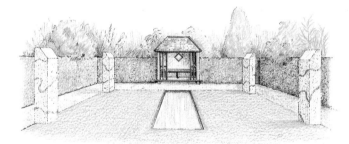

The meditation garden (8)

The meditation garden (8) provides a peaceful retreat amid the dense planting surrounding it. The mown grass lawn is surrounded by a gravel path (9) and a clipped hedge (10) and is flanked by a series of stone monoliths (11). A pavilion (12) presides over the space, facing a rectangular pool (13) with its ever-changing reflections. It is a contemporary interpretation of one of the classical elements of great country-house gardens. An inner room, its ingredients of grass, water, stone ornament and resting place, offer a calming oasis in a busy world.

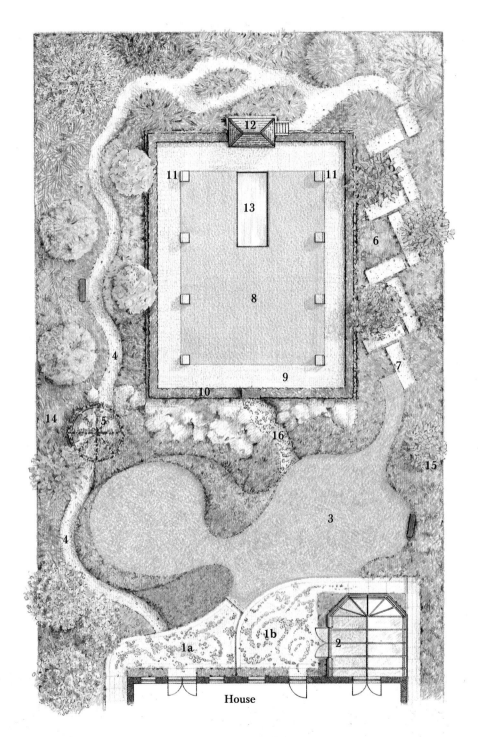

House

SEASIDE GARDENS

A coastal environment brings particular challenges to the gardener. Countering the advantages of a splendid setting, perhaps with stunning views, are the constraints of a maritime climate – principally salt-laden winds. People and plants may both require extra shelter for comfort. The garden design needs to use appropriate vertical barriers to filter the winds and materials that will withstand bleaching by the sun and corrosion by salt. In exposed sites, plant sturdy windbreaks of bushy maritime species perhaps supplemented by well-anchored brushwood fences. All the plants you choose must tolerate salt spray; foliage in gardens even some distance inland can be scorched by persistent onshore winds.

On the plus side, seaside gardens are more hospitable than inland ones to certain very desirable plants. Another advantage is that extremes of temperature are generally moderated by proximity to the sea, making severe frosts rare in temperate regions. The stronger ultraviolet light on the coast is favourable to some slightly tender shrubby plants that would not survive inland at the same latitude. With a seaside garden, it is especially important to find out what grows well in neighbouring gardens before you introduce a new plant in your own plot.

The garden design on the right overlooks the sea. It is planned for a minimum of maintenance by owners who use it principally for weekends and holidays, preferring to get on with the serious business of relaxation rather than spending time on gardening. An octagonal swimming pool (3) is the garden's main feature, and nearby is a small paddling pool (6) for younger family members.

In this periodically unused garden, a sophisticated automatically timed watering system is built in. A contracted maintenance service is an alternative option for absentee gardeners.

Most of the horizontal surface is paved with local stones that are easy to sweep clean and plants grow between pebbles and boulders in the beds, minimizing the area where weeds could colonize. These hard materials echo the pebble beach nearby and link this garden with the surrounding coastal landscape.

LEFT *A break in the trees and shrubs that shelter this seaside garden is the setting for a pretty wooden terrace overlooking a bay. A 'Kiftsgate' rambler rose encloses one end, while the white agapanthus, or African lily, lights the foreground. Smaller plants in moveable pots furnish most of the plant colour during milder weather.*

A WEEKEND GARDEN BY THE SEA

An area of decking beside the house (1) serves as a terrace. Its texture is echoed in the decking (2) that surrounds the swimming pool (3). Hardwood (from renewable sources), left to weather naturally, is easily maintained.

Low-maintenance paving (4) consists of flat local stones set in a random pattern, the spaces between the stones colonized by sun-loving creeping plants. Adjacent areas (5) feature pebbles and boulders with dramatic sculptural plants growing among them.

The children's paddling pool (6)

The children's paddling pool (6) opposite the swimming pool (3) is flanked by low seats (7) finished with a terracotta capping and off-white cement that match the garden walls. The swimming pool is fed by a fountain (8) set as the focal point in one of the high sheltering walls. Along this side of the pool the decking (9) bridges the water flowing from the fountain.

A tented arbour (10), its hexagonal design echoing the shape of the main pool, provides a vertical accent at one corner of the garden. It shades a table, chairs and barbecue (11).

A view of the sea provides an added attraction in the far corner. Seats (12) and a screen of toughened glass (13) make it possible to enjoy the view in comfort. A telescope (14) adds the final detail for ship – or star – gazing. Strategically placed lights (15) allow the garden to be apreciated at night.

House

PLANT-LOVERS' GARDENS

There are many kinds of plantspeople: what they share is a desire to grow particular plants as well as possible. Their preferences may be wide-ranging or they may target on a particular plant genus (dahlias, for instance), or a certain class of plants (alpines, perhaps).

One pitfall for this type of plant enthusiast is a failure to envisage the garden as a whole. The desire to grow all sorts of intriguing specimens tempts them to acquire plants piecemeal and to grow them in conditions where the plants themselves may thrive, but do not contribute to the broader garden picture. To avoid this, the plant-lover needs to spend some time creating an overall layout that will contain the individual types of plants, yet create a series of satisfying displays. This careful preparation makes the best use of variations in the site – such as areas of sun or shade – and a coherent design allows interesting plants to become more than the sum of their individual parts.

The garden plan here has been designed to provide a variety of habitats and situations for growing plants both formally and informally, as well as areas for relaxing. Each separate garden area has a distinct form, created by structural trees and shrubs in the vertical plane complementing a firm outline on the ground plan. Massed plants are balanced by areas of space.

The skeleton of this layout is a set of three vistas radiating from the patio (1). A short view across the width of the garden ends in a circular decorative pool (6) set in the lawn. This intimate formal garden makes the perfect environment for a few choice plants. A diagonal view from the house leads across the lawn, between herbaceous borders, to an inviting seat (3) that is positioned to be invisible from the rival focal point of the pool. The third vista follows the gravel path (8) down the length of the garden, terminating at the greenhouse (12). The space between the vistas is divided by curved lines and points of emphasis, such as weeping or mop-headed trees, to create areas of different character – herbaceous borders, shrubby screens and beds of flowers for cutting.

The corner furthest from the house has a more informal feel, with rougher grass and a naturalistic pool (14). The vegetable garden (11) is enclosed in a separate area, which includes the all-important greenhouse (12) and potting shed (13) that all keen plantspeople require for propagation and general plant care.

LEFT *Beautifully tended hostas are the showpiece of this stream garden with its fine collection of plants. In a relatively sheltered setting, shrub roses, astilbe,* Rheum palmatum *and hardy cranesbill geraniums make a dramatic display of leaf forms with highlights of flower colour.*

A VERSATILE PLANT-LOVER'S GARDEN

The patio (1), with low bordering walls, is for relaxation but can be used as a home for container-grown plants. Steps lead to a paved path (2) lying flush with the lawn. The angled corner of the patio opens a diagonal view into the garden with a seat (3) at its focus. The doors on the long side of the patio (4) look straight between a pair of round-shaped trees (5) – box (Buxus) or strawberry trees (Arbutus) would be attractive choices – to a small round formal pool (6) with a central fountain.

The pool is set in a circular lawn edged with brick and ringed with aromatic plants such as lavender or catmint. A weeping tree makes a delightful backdrop in the corner (7).

A gravel path (8) down the right side of the garden borders a wide flower bed backed by three mop-headed trees (9). The path continues under an arch (10) and on into the hedge-enclosed vegetable garden (11). Between the greenhouse (12) and potting shed (13) are beds for flowers grown especially for exhibition or propagation purposes.

The informal pool garden (14) and its surroundings provide a range of habitats. Water lilies float on the surface of the deeper water and marginal plants such as primulas colonize the edges. The surrounding grass is studded with fritillaries and field orchids. Mowing is timed to allow these wildflowers to set seed.

A simple timber bridge (15) crosses the central narrow neck of the informal pool.

The simple timber bridge (15)

House

COTTAGE GARDENS

The traditional idea of a cottage or country-style garden conjures up a happy mixture of bright flowers, herbs and vegetables packed into a relatively small area without considering colour coordination or arrangement. But underpinning this initial impression of charming artlessness, true cottage gardens have strong elements of formality. Often set in small rectangular plots, they have direct, functional paths, sturdy hedges or fences to keep out straying chickens and livestock, and vegetables grown in neat rows.

A synthesis of the two ideas – the romantic impression of abundant flowers versus the reality of practical order – can in fact make a successful design solution for today's small plots, even those in urban settings. As in the garden design shown here, ebullient planting is teamed with simple, low-key structures made in natural-looking materials with traditional finishes. Moss softens the lines between areas of mellow brick and flagstones; plain or rustic styles are chosen for fencing and arbours. Pots, ornaments and furniture are in keeping with the country feel.

Cottage-style plantings can be authentic, using old-fashioned annuals and perennials, or updated with carefully chosen slower-growing shrubs, climbers and ground-cover planting. Modern roses, for example, have longer flowering periods and lack the cultivation problems of some older varieties. Fruit trees can double as specimens and the planting principle of fitting in as much as possible is adapted to create potager-style pockets of vegetables and herbs in small spaces. The aim is a sense of intimacy, enclosure and pleasant nostalgia, with plants and artificial structures working in harmony, as in this plan, with its well-integrated conservatory (13) and sitting area (11).

LEFT *A gravel path edged with brick separates flower beds that overflow with plants, their informal exuberance perfectly suiting the rustic cottage garden setting. In the foreground, pink lupins tower over delicate mauve cranesbills. A few stray buttercups invade the borders and, with the yellow tones of the low-growing euphorbia, echo the sunny plumes of golden rod on the far side of the garden. Bright sprinklings of shasta daisies place white accents throughout the garden, while honeysuckle climbing around the doorway adds the final touch.*

A CONTEMPORARY COTTAGE GARDEN

The front garden entrance (1)

The front garden entrance (1), a double-leaf gate and simple picket fence adorned by climbing roses, sets the cottage style. It opens onto a central path of warm-toned rustic brick that widens to a circle featuring a sundial (2). On either side, colourful massed planting (3) is retained by hedges of dwarf box (4).

The driveway (5) to the garage is surfaced with local pebbles laid in concrete. Brick edging visually links it with the brick paths.

A service path (6), patterned with old bricks and paving slabs, provides wheelbarrow access down the length of the garden. A narrow border of shade-loving plants runs along the right. A statue (7) is set in this border opposite the ironwork gate (8), linking the path to the terrace (11) behind the house. The perimeter path curves past the specimen pear tree (9) and runs alongside a border of shrubs and old roses and, in the far left corner, leads to the vegetable garden (10).

A brick-paved terrace (11) displays a variety of flowers and herbs in containers. A raised triangular rockery (12) contains more herbs, alpines and other compact plants, and a small greenhouse/conservatory (13) connects the garden and house.

The lawn (14) is a pool of space shaded by an attractive apple tree (15) with an old birdbath beneath. This area behind the house is sheltered by a privet or euonymus hedge (16).

A sculpture (17) is the focal point of the vegetable garden, while the toolshed (18) and compost container (19) are unobtrusive.

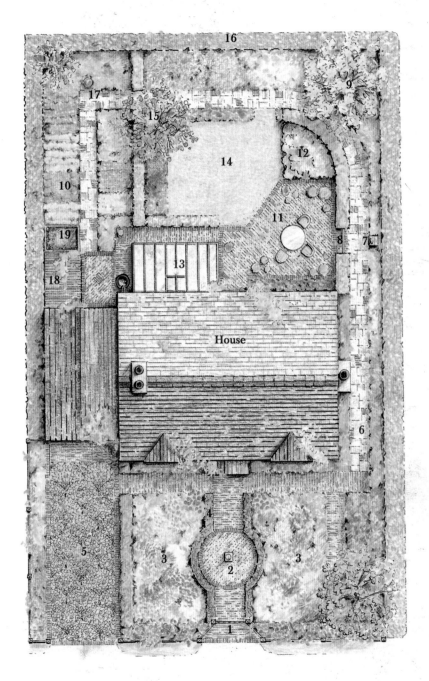

WILDLIFE GARDENS

If you want to attract wildlife to a garden in the country, the suburbs and even some city locations, the best strategy is to imitate nature closely. This means creating a natural-looking ground plan and choosing trees, shrubs and other plants that offer food and shelter to birds and animals. Many plants preferred by wildlife are native species that are often categorized as weeds and are very vigorous growers. If you give them space, be prepared to spend time and energy controlling their spread.

As with other informal designs, a wildlife or conservationist's garden involves a surprising amount of active management. Flower meadows, for example, need to be prepared and tended carefully so that desirable species are not crowded out by other grasses and weeds. Some flowers, such as poppies, germinate only if the ground is hoed annually (some of the most effective wildflower meadows are actually planted anew each year). Keeping paths passable, shaping wayward shrubs so that they look natural, guiding climbers in the direction you want them to go – these are the jobs that make the vital difference between a garden and a jungle. Plenty of space is a definite advantage when creating a wildlife garden in order to have enough room for a wide range of attractions for both people and animals.

In the design on the right for a large plot at the side of a house, thick belts of trees and shrubs around the boundaries provide shelter for garden inmates and exclude evidence of the outside world. The central area has grass for a ground cover. The panel of mown lawn near the house (2) gives way to an area of longer grass (5), which is cut only after the flowers growing in it have re-seeded. Here, the shaggy grass offers a transitional zone between the manicured look nearer the house and the more natural-looking planting further away. There is room for a substantial pool (7), flanked by marshy areas (11) where moisture-loving plants create key habitats for wildlife.

This wildlife garden is planned for enjoyment and relaxation, with seats (12) and a shelter (10) that look attractive as well as being vantage points. Access from the lawn has been made via an inviting mowed path (3) which disappears deep into the garden. Gravel paths (4) branching from the stone-paved terrace (1) offer alternative all-weather routes. All the functional surfaces, including the wood used in the bridge, benches and garden building, are chosen to blend in with the natural ambience.

LEFT *This naturally planted garden with a stream trickling through one corner makes a good habitat for wildlife. Rocks and boulders of local stone look attractive and offer refuge for small mammals and amphibians. Grass has been left long on the high bank, and woodland and moisture-loving plants such as the striking foxgloves and primulas* (P. florindae) *thrive. Fallen tree trunks are part of the natural cycle and provide habitats for insects that birds and other creatures feed on.*

A NATURAL WILDLIFE GARDEN

The terrace (1) is paved with random natural stone. Grass or moss growing in the joints softens its appearance and links it to the lawn (2) and mowed grass path (3) heading into the trees. Gravel paths (4) lead into the shrubs of the perimeter planting.

The wildflower meadow (5) is cut only twice a year. This informal area of longer grass studded with flowers makes a graceful transition between the lawn and the wilder treatment of the main garden. In shorter grass to the right, are the beehives (6) for the bees that pollinate the flowers.

The informal pool (7), which could be existing or artificially created, has been contoured to offer both deep water and shallows. Its banks include beaches, marshy areas (11) and steep banks, all suiting different plant types and encouraging a range of wildlife. A plank bridge (8) crosses at the narrowest point, and a small jetty (9) is built of the same material.

The rustic garden building (10)

A rustic garden building (10) deep in the undergrowth serves as an observation site and summerhouse. It has fine black net shades fitted to the windows instead of glass. When pulled down, these prevent the viewer from disturbing wildlife creatures.

Thick planting (13) surrounds the plot, affording shelter and seclusion for wild creatures, while seats (12) are provided for the human visitors. Shrubs and trees merge into the mixed hedge (14) to create a natural-looking perimeter. There is a mixture of native species as well as a few more exotic ornamentals.

House

ABOVE *The crisp geometric lines of the timber decking give a modern feel to this city garden. The pale weathered hardwood provides a perfect setting for a sculptural arrangement of large white pebbles and planted terracotta pots.*

DECK GARDENS

For a family seeking to use their garden as a multifaceted outdoor living space, hardwood decking provides a handsome, versatile and low-maintenance framework. It can be used for many different types of surface such as paths, terraces, steps, bridges and jetties, and ties together a garden design, however complex. Timber decking provides a sympathetic background for plants and combines particularly well with water.

The use of a natural material – timber– in a highly formal design suits this plot surrounded by high, staggered walls. It could be in an urban or rural setting. The decking widens into platforms for recreation, and narrows into paths. The diagonal alignment of the planking sets up a vigorous, dynamic feel, and the use of slopes and different levels brings an added dimension to the layout.

From the large platform near the house two wooden paths (4 and 5) lead off into the garden, one leading upwards to a shaded sitting area beneath a tent (3). To the left of the sloping walk, a slightly raised deck path (6) crosses a shallow pool (10) and leads eventually to a summerhouse (8). From here you can make a circuit back via some stepping stones (11) and a smaller decking path (7). Strategically placed lighting makes the garden accessible at night.

The design offers an intriguing interplay of hard-edged formality and natural elements. The use of wood for both horizontal surfaces such as the decking, and vertical structures such as the fences and walls, unifies their appearance, and the crisp geometry of the decking provides the ideal foil for dramatic foliage plants. At ground level, cover is provided by permanent low planting set among pebbles and sculptural boulders (12). A large decorative informal pool (10) creates lively reflections. Although the mood of this water feature is predominantly naturalistic, its obvious origin in a fountain set in the far wall is thoroughly artificial.

This garden is designed for a warm climate so there is a shady tented area and the lush growth of the subtropical palms and tender ferns. However, decking is a style that suits a wide range of latitudes. Similar planting effects can be achieved in temperate zones by choosing specimens with luxuriant foliage that are appropriate to the site: rheums, bamboos and other grasses, phormiums and yuccas; or evergreen shrubs with shapely leaves such as fatsia or mahonia.

A LOW-MAINTENANCE DECK GARDEN

*The large platform near the house is made of two split-level sections (**1a** and **1b**), allowing plenty of space for entertaining, sunbathing, and other recreations. Flowerpots and containers provide visual interest and the barbecue (**2**) is nearby.*

The tented pavilion (3)

*A tented pavilion (**3**), set on a raised deck, is one of the focal points of the garden. It is reached from the house by a wooden ramp (**4**) edged with handrails. The upward slope of the ramp steadily entices you towards this pool of restful shade which is surrounded by rustling foliage. Beneath the ramp, exciting deep shadows make an excellent habitat for ferns, all of which require little or no maintenance. In a cooler climate, where shelter from the elements may be required, a more enclosed garden building such as a summerhouse could substitute for this pavilion.*

*The main decking walkway through the garden (**5**) is slightly raised above ground level and becomes a bridge (**6**), which crosses the shallow pool (**10**). A narrower walkway (**7**) branches off near the pavilion.*

*The structure in the far left-hand corner (**8**) is a summerhouse but could be a garden shed or a sauna, depending on the owners' preference. Whatever its use, its vertical lines make an excellent counterpoint to the predominantly horizontal plane of the rest of the garden.*

*A wall fountain (**9**) terminates a vista stretching from the main deck beside the house to the far wall. This view follows the line of the informal shallow pool (**10**) which stretches almost the length of the garden. Near the fountain the gap between the decking paths is closed by a series of stepping stones (**11**). These repeat the theme of pebbles and boulders in the sculptural groups in and around the pool (**12**).*

House

CITY GARDENS

Many plots in urban areas are rectangular and often long and narrow, their boundaries clearly defined. High fences and walls are obtrusive and can cut out the light. Sometimes tall neighbouring buildings make it necessary to position trees or create sheltering structures for privacy, while these same buildings and sheltering structures can deepen the shade.

The main design challenge is to create interest within a limited shape and space. The plan here solves the problem by alternating narrow passage-like areas (7 and 15) with wider spaces extended almost to maximum width (1, 12 and 16). Together with planting that softens and disguises the perimeter, this layout successfully masks the corridor-like feel of the basic shape. A selection of interesting small trees, plant-draped overhead structures (2 and 15), raised beds (10) and container planting, establish interest at all levels and allow the occupants to indulge in some easy gardening or to relax in comfortable, shaded sitting areas. The use of well-positioned lighting permits the garden to be enjoyed after dark.

This is a fairly sunny site where a good variety of plants grows well. Given a different orientation, the owners would have chosen shade-lovers for the darkest corners. Tending plants has been given priority over more routine tasks such as mowing by opting for attractive and easy-to-maintain paved surfaces rather than grass. Lawns are seldom satisfactory in cramped sites that are in shade for a good part of the day, and sweeping the surfaces is far less time-consuming than mowing. Here, the directional bias of the paving patterns underpins the design layout, directing the eye alternately along a pathway and outward towards the corners.

The different areas flow gracefully and logically from one to another in a series of separate spaces. These are, however, carefully organized to provide a vista from the courtyard window all the way to the far end of the garden along an axis that is just to left of centre.

LEFT *With the help of a mirrored archway, a long thin space next to the side wall of a house has been transformed into an arcaded vista, reflected in the narrow pool. The lush green plants in fine cream pots along the pale green walls lend an air of cool tranquillity. In the tradition of the courtyard garden, it is a complete contrast to the hot, dusty city street outside — a world enclosed yet open to the sky.*

A PAVED CITY GARDEN

The small courtyard (1) immediately outside the back door is sheltered by an arbour (2). This creates dappled shade and screens the area from the neighbouring upstairs windows. There are potted plants (3) in the courtyard and a small fountain or sculpture can be seen on the boundary wall (4).

The angled steps (11)

Angled steps (11) lead upwards from the first section of path to an intermediate sitting area (12) with a permanent bench (13), table, and a small raised ornamental pool (14). Here, the paving runs diagonally, visually contradicting the linear, corridor-like feel of this long narrow plot. Small trees at opposite corners contribute height, while containers bring interest at ground level.

A pergola walk (15) narrows the vista with parallel paving patterns hastening the pace through this passageway between shrubby plants. Details of this pergola's construction echo the construction of the arbour in the courtyard.

The open area for family use or children's play (16) uses bias patterns underfoot to draw attention from the enclosing right angles. The built-in barbecue (17) is framed by grid-like flagstones that become narrow pathways among the planting. Subdued blue tones in the planting along this far boundary increase the sense of distance when this area is viewed from the house.

The sunken sitting area (5)

The sunken sitting area (5) lies to the left of the courtyard. A tree (6) chosen for its spring blossoms softens the impact of the hard surfaces and offers seclusion. The drainage of this low-lying area of the garden has been specially planned to ensure that rainwater does not collect.

A broad path of grey-blue stone paving (7) passes between low edgings of scented lavender. A narrow bed of climbers on the right (8) furnishes the fence with flower and foliage interest. On the left is a patch of low-growing herbs and flowers (9) backed by a raised bed of permanent planting (10).

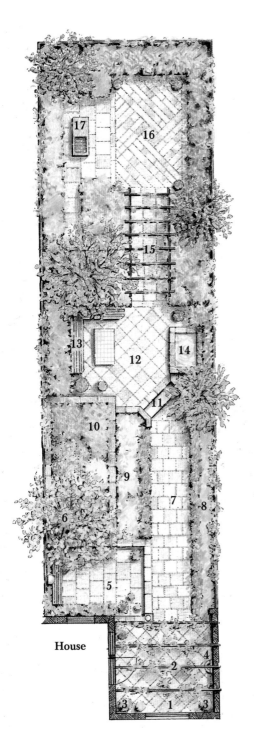

House

DRY OR XERISCAPE GARDENS

Naturally dry landscapes – xeriscapes – are essentially desert or low-rainfall areas inhabited by plants that have adapted themselves to survive with very little water. With some careful thought even such inhospitable areas can be host to an interesting range of plants, while hard surfaces can provide the structural backbone of a garden. In addition to the cactuses and other succulents, there are many attractive garden subjects that can survive with little water. They include plants with leathery, cordlike or spiny leaves which are often aromatic. Shrubby plants of the sage family, lavender, rock roses, and other sun-loving herbs such as rosemary, are among garden classics, but the spectrum ranges from ground-covering grass substitutes to soaring palms. Furnishing your garden with appropriate drought-tolerant plants is a commonsense conservationist policy in an area where water is in short supply.

The garden design featured here is in just such an area. It has an interesting, individualistic layout around a somewhat unusual, off-centre focus, but elements of this design could easily be adapted to more traditional house and garden layouts. The house consists of two parallel blocks separated by an elongated patio. This is enclosed at either end by ornamental iron gates (19) that provide security without cutting off the view. The main garden – an L-shape behind and to the right of the house – accommodates a satisfying blend of formal and informal features, readily accessible by paths. Paths are an important theme of this garden, conveying a great sense of controlled movement and providing logical transitions between the different areas.

Plants have been chosen that are well suited to low-rainfall conditions so they largely look after themselves. Gravel is used as the main form of ground cover. In a dry setting, this approach of going with rather than against nature is surprisingly rewarding. Paradoxically, water features are a key element in the design, but their bold, abstract shapes hold the eye as sculptures when left empty of water. Like a well-planned oasis, they spring into life at the flick of a switch whenever the occupants please.

LEFT *In this charming courtyard, plants that enjoy dry conditions have been planted directly into gravel and around rock features, while smaller alpine plants and succulents grow in pots and stone troughs. Red rock roses and yellow poppies and wallflowers bring colour, and their soft round shapes contrast well with spiky iris leaves.*

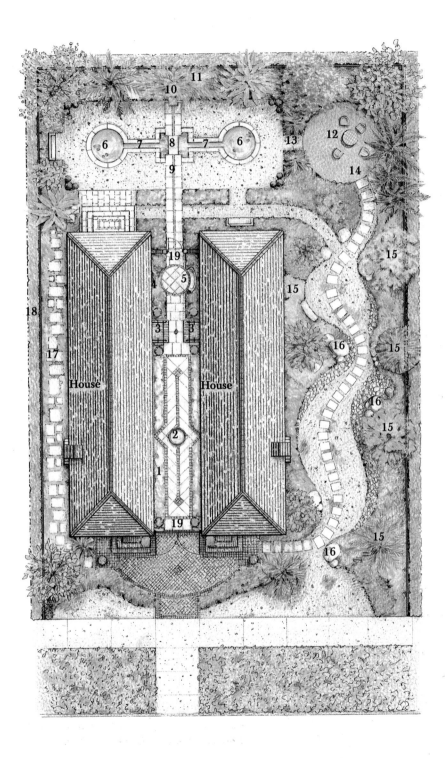

A XERISCAPED PATH GARDEN

*The planting around the main patio (**1**) is yellow and white. The central focal point, a bowl fountain (**2**), is easily emptied when the house is unoccupied. Beyond the paired steps leading up into the house (**3**), blue and mauve flowers frame a circular area where a wall sculpture (**4**) can be studied from a seat (**5**).*

*The formal pool garden echoes the paired geometry of the house. Two shallow circular pools (**6**) with bowl fountains are linked by a narrow canal (**7**). At its midpoint, the canal widens to form a square sunken iris bed, which is dramatically bridged by a stone slab (**8**). This is part of the main axis from the patio, marked by a split path with creeping plants growing between parallel paving stones (**9**), and terminating in a sculpture (**10**). Architectural plants form a backdrop (**11**).*

*An intimate sitting area (**12**) occupies the shady far right corner. Set in a framing circle of interesting foliage plants, its two entrances offer a glimpses of the formal pool area on one side (**13**), and a view along the winding stepping-stone path (**14**) down the length of the garden on the other. This path meanders around buttresses of planting (**15**) and outcrops of massed stones and boulders (**16**).*

The view of the stepping-stone path (14)

*The flagstone walk (**17**) along the left perimeter is a shady corridor sandwiched between the boundary hedge (**18**) and one block of the house. Small shade-tolerant plants grow in the narrow beds and colonize the spaces between the stones.*

*The entrance gates (**19**) offer a dramatic view along the main axis.*

ADVICE ON MAINTENANCE

Every garden needs some maintenance, so try and estimate how much your garden will need. This will ensure that your plan doesn't over-commit you when the garden is realised. Research your chosen plants, for example. Will they need regular clipping, staking or dividing? Will your wooden structures need regular repainting? Also consider your resources. Mowing a large expanse of lawn is time-consuming. However this is a job that you may easily delegate. It will also take more or less time depending on the equipment you have.

Unless you have unlimited time and help you will want to keep maintenance within reasonable bounds. Below are some tips that I have found useful for keeping maintenance to a minimum.

PLANTED BEDS AND BORDERS

1 Plan beds and borders to be permanently rather than annually planted. This saves time year-round. Try to group together plants that have similar growing and siting requirements. As well as their natural affinity, maintenance of these plants will then be simpler.
2 The edges of beds and borders will be easier to maintain if they are simply shaped, especially next to a lawn. Trimming complicated grass edges can take longer than mowing the main lawn.
3 Make sure that the soil level in beds is not too high. If it is, soil can migrate into surrounding paved or lawn areas. A hard edging can help, although this tends to make the beds look more formal.
4 Mulching is excellent for soil enrichment, moisture retention, weed control, and even moderating soil temperature. This means applying a layer, a minimum of 75mm(3in) thick, of composted organic material from time to time. To conserve moisture and inhibit weed growth, one application of an inorganic material such as gravel or even polythene (if it can be hidden from view under pebbles or bark) can be effective.
5 Sufficient drainage and water retention is essential for the well-being of plants. This may mean incorporating gravel and/or sand into wet soil, often with coarse organic material. To help water retention in dry soil, add fine organic material and/or polymer granules, buried so as not to harm birds.

6 Weed control is a large part of bed and border maintenance, which is why mulching and growing ground-covering plants (see below) are so important. To prevent the growth of weeds already present as seed or root you need to prepare beds thoroughly before planting; this is always labour-saving in the long run. For established beds, light hoeing is better than deep digging as roots are less likely to be disturbed or damaged. It also avoids opening up the soil to receive more weed seed.

TREE PLANTING

1 To ensure survival and minimum upkeep, trees are best planted when small. They grow more readily when introduced to a new environment, often outgrowing those planted at much larger sizes.
2 Planting maturer trees will have better results if the tree is properly supported by staking, and then regularly checked for wind rock, particularly at the base of the trunk, and chaffing from ties. Adjustable or flexible ties are best. Remove stakes and ties as soon as the tree is established, usually after a couple of years.
3 To assist in establishing trees of all sizes, an organic, gravel, polythene or fibre felt mulch at the base is advisable.
4 Protect trunks to prevent damage by mowers, trimmers or animals. There are commercial systems – tree spirals or guards, or metal frames – which are all very effective.
5 To help irrigation on slopes or in dry places, place a large flower pot sunk into the ground on the higher side of the root area. Directing the hose or irrigation system into the pot ensures that water goes into the soil instead of running off. A ball of chicken wire put in the pot prevents small creatures from being trapped inside.
6 Compost and fertilizer, particularly slow release kinds, will also help the tree to become established.

PLANTED GROUND COVER

Ground cover refers to desirable low-growing plants that spread themselves quickly and widely. Planted ground cover comes into its own when soil beneath tall plants or small trees would become weed infested or would otherwise be bare, perhaps because of dry or shady conditions. When choosing ground cover it is a good idea to seek out plants indigenous to your area that naturally tolerate these circumstances. These are often the most effective in blotting out other contenders, so long as they themselves are not too invasive and will respond to control.

LAWNS

1 Although a lawn will always need a fairly high degree of maintenance, it will be reduced if you make sure that the grass species you choose suits your climate, the soil and the proposed use of the lawn. There are species that are, for example, tough and hard-wearing or more suitable for dry conditions

2 Where a lawn abuts paths, walls or plantings, a hard edge (for instance, to keep gravel away from grass) may be necessary. A mowing edge of brick or stone next to the planting or against a wall, set down fractionally from the level of the grass, prevents damage to the plants, wall or machinery.

3 Plants grown over lawn edges may cause deterioration of the lawn, and even take over, increasing the bed size. A restraining border need not be obstrusive, and in formal gardens some hard edging may be necessary to preserve the lawn's precise shape.

PAVED SURFACES AND STEPS

1 Correctly installed, these will require little maintenance beyond being kept clean and, in moist shady situations, moss free – unless you like a mossy look. In cold climates frost may cause some dislodging of pointing which will need attention.

2 Gravel paths need to be raked, and gravel in a clay-like matrix may need attention such as filling potholes, levelling or rolling, especially following hard winters.

VERTICAL STRUCTURES

1 Treat softwood structures with long-life preservative at the outset. Otherwise they will need treating again regularly.

2 Try to avoid painting outdoor stuctures. Once embarked upon, it is a lifetime's work as the paint surface needs constant attention.

3 Hardwoods should always be left unpainted since the paint does not penetrate to the same extent as on softwoods and is more liable to flake. For appearance sake, they can be stained.

GARDEN PONDS

1 Remove leaves and wind-blown grass clippings promptly from the pond's surface as these may create an accelerated build-up of detritus or alter the pH value of the water or the level of micro-organisms and increase carbon dioxide and other gases.

2 Care should be taken in using herbicide or fertilizer applications to plants and lawns close to ponds. These can have disastrous effects if they contaminate the water.

SWIMMING POOLS

1 Well-defined maintenance regimes should be set out by the installers to meet the owners' particular requirements and to maintain the health of both bathers and pool water.

2 Maintenance planning should include simple measures such as ensuring that the pool surrounds slope away from the pool edge so that dust, dirt or rainwater are not washed in. Similarly the pool should be located away from trees – pine needles are particularly effective at blocking filtration units.

3 A footbath at the shallow where children are likely to play reduces the amount of dirt entering the pool, especially if grass, sand or soil are close by.

MACHINERY AND GARDEN AIDS

1 Always make sure that sufficient access for mechanical equipment is allowed for at the planning stage.

2 If you intend to use powered equipment in maintaining your garden, this should be considered and costed in at the planning stage. If the equipment is too costly, the design or planting may have to be altered to make manual upkeep easier.

3 Always ask for a free demonstration of any equipment to ensure it is exactly what you need for your garden.

4 An irrigation system is a great time saver and reduces watering to a minimum. The system is usually maintained by the installers.

INDEX

ACKNOWLEDGMENTS

AUTHOR'S ACKNOWLEDGMENTS

I must express my grateful thanks to every member of the team at Frances Lincoln involved in the production of this book. They are always helpful, entirely professional and a real pleasure to work with. I would also like to thank Kate Besley for typing the manuscript.

PUBLISHERS' ACKNOWLEDGMENTS

Frances Lincoln Limited would like to thank Mr and Mrs Stanley Silver for allowing us to photograph their garden, and Coleen O'Shea and Susanne Mitchell for their input and advice.

Art Editor	Louise Tucker
Project Editor	Sarah Mitchell
Picture Editor	Anne Fraser
Contributing Editor	Penny David
Editors	Alison Freegard
	Hilary Hockman
Assistants	Helen Cleary
	Auriol Miller
	Annabel Morgan
Designers	Sally Cracknell
	John Laing
Page checker	Patti Taylor
Production	Adela Cory
	Annemarieke Kroon
Index	Pamela Brown
Horticultural Consultant	John Elsley
Editorial Director	Erica Hunningher
Art Director	Caroline Hillier
Production Director	Nicky Bowden

PHOTOGRAPHIC ACKNOWLEDGMENTS

Neil Campbell-Sharp 167
Garden Picture Library/Gary Rogers 9, 21 (d: Henk Weijers); John Miller 18, 122; C. Pemberton-Piggott 72; Ron Sutherland 1 (d: Edna Walling), 86, 93 (d: Paul Fleming), 102, 106 (d: Edna Walling), 116 (d: Duane Paul Design Team); Henk Dijkman 88; Brigitte Thomas 5 top left, 92, 96; Zara McCalmont 118; Michele Lamontagne 159 (d: Erwan Tymen); John Glover 5 top right and 194 (d: John Duane); Steven Wooster 198
Jerry Harpur 2 (d: Ian Teh, London) 4 (d: Rick Mosbaugh, Los Angeles), 5 below (Japanese Stroll Garden, New York), 7 (d: Helen Yemm, London), 11 (d: Christopher Masson, London), 14 (d: Roy Strong, Ross-on-Wye, Hereford and Worcester), 16 (d: Patrick Presto, San Francisco), 19 (d: Jane Fearnley-Whittingstall, Wotton-under-Edge, Gloucestershire), 20 (d: Claus Scheinert, Alpes-Maritimies), 35 (d: Simon Fraser, London), 36 (d: Mark Laurence), 37 (Felicity Mullen, Johannesburg), 38 (Terry Moller, Johannesburg), 40 (Shepherd House, Inveresk, Lothian), 44 (d: Oehme and van Sweden Associates, Washington D.C.), 50 (d: Jim Matsuo, Los Angeles), 52 (d: Cyrille Schiff, Los Angeles), 54 (d: Mel Light, Los Angeles), 58 (La Mamounia Hotel, Marrakech), 59 (d: Rick Mosbaugh, Los Angeles), 61 (d: Tom Stuart-Smith, Bedmond, Hertfordshire), 63 (d: Edwina von Gal, New York), 71 (d: Paul Miles, Woodbridge, Suffolk), 74 (d: Geoff and Faith Whiten, London), 77 (d: Phillip Watson, Fredericksburg, VA), 78 (Fudlers Hall, Mashbury, Essex), 84 (d: Alan Izard, Ohoka, North Canterbury), 94 (d: Edwina von Gal, New York), 105 (Broughton Castle, Oxfordshire), 110 (d: Bruce Kelly, New York), 113 (d: Gail Jenkins, Melbourne), 120 (d: Chris Rosmini, Los Angeles), 121 (Tyninghame House, Dunbar, Lothian), 127 (d: Simon Fraser, London), 128 (Cruden Farm, Victoria), 130 (Manor House, Birlingham, Hereford and Worcester), 135 (d: Edwina von Gal, New York), 139 (Bishops House, Perth, WA), 144 (Japanese Stroll Garden, New York), 145 (d: Isabelle C. Greene, Santa Barbara, CA), 151 (Lower Hall, Worfield, Shropshire), 169 (d: Jim Matsuo, Los Angeles), 171 (d: Thomas Church), 175 (d: Michael Bates, Sonoma, CA), 178 (d: Randon Garver, Los Angeles), 182 (d: Berry's Garden Co., London), 184 (d: Oehme and van Sweden Associates, Washington D.C.), 188 (Lower Hall, Worfield, Shropshire), 190 (Mill Cottage, Higham, Suffolk), 192 ("Dolwen", Powys), 196 (d: Raymond Hudson, Johannesburg), Front cover (d: David Stevens)
Courtesy of **Leaky Pipe Systems Ltd.,** Frith Farm, Dean Street, East Farleigh, Maidstone, Kent ME5 OPR (tel: 01622 746495) 32
Clive Nichols 10 (Redenham Park, Hampshire), 42 ©FLL (d: Robin Williams), 46 ©FLL (d: Robin Williams), 49 ©FLL (d: Robin Williams), 57 (Redenham Park, Hampshire), 66 (Wollerton Old Hall, Shropshire), 81 (Bennington Lordship, Hertfordshire), 98 Barnsley House, Gloucestershire), 108 (Pyrford Court, Surrey), 126 (d: Jill Billington), 131 (d: Lucy Gent), 163 ©FLL (d: Robin Williams), 177 (Ivy Cottage, Dorset)
Elizabeth Whiting and Associates/Jerry Harpur 158
Steven Wooster 13 ©FLL, 28 (Jan and Brian Oldham, Garden Creations, Auckland), 69 ©FLL, 125(d: Anthony Paul, London), 149 (Gordon Collier, Titoki Point, Taihape), 180 (Bruce and Jetta Cornish, N.Z.), 186 (Liz Morrow, Auckland)